Amy, Jimi and Janis
A Unique Perspective

ANDREA J MILES

GREEN MAGIC

Amy, Jimi and Janis © 2025 by Andrea J Miles.
All rights reserved. No part of this book may be used
or reproduced in any form without written permission
of the Author, except in the case of quotations in
articles and reviews.

Green Magic
53 Brooks Road
Street
Somerset
BA16 0PP
England
www.greenmagicpublishing.com

Front cover images of Amy Winehouse, Jimi Hendrix and Janis Joplin,
licensed by Bridgeman Images

Designed and typeset by Carrigboy, Wells, UK
www.carrigboy.co.uk

ISBN 978 1 915580 32 0

GREEN MAGIC

Contents

CHAPTER ONE • AMY WINEHOUSE

Part 1. The Story of Amy Winehouse — 7
Part 2. What Amy Winehouse's Natal Chart Reveals and the Astrology in Action — 24

CHAPTER TWO • JIMI HENDRIX

Part 1. The Story of Jimi Hendrix — 65
Part 2. What Jimi Hendrix's Natal Chart Reveals and the Astrology in Action — 99

CHAPTER THREE • JANIS JOPLIN

Part 1. The Story of Janis Joplin — 135
Part 2. What Janis Joplin's Natal Chart Reveals and the Astrology in Action — 166

APPENDICES

Appendix 1. Saturn's Return — 201
Appendix 2. Glossary of Terms — 203
Appendix 3. The Natural Zodiac — 206
Appendix 4. The Meaning of the Houses — 207
Appendix 5. Identical Astrological Data in Their Natal Charts — 208

Acknowledgments & Sources — 209

THANKS TO

Family & friends.
A big shout-out especially to Valerie Daines, Sarah Dowding, Kevin Rowan-Drewitt, Krista Everington, Mark Hetherington, Diane Hollingworth, Andrew Jenkins, Paula Mallotides, Kathy Rowan, Carlton Thomas, and Billy & Lucy Miles.

Thanks also to Alamy UK, Bridgeman Images, Astrodienst, Frank Clifford and Green Magic Publishing.

FOR

Pete Gotto

and

in memory of

Amy Winehouse, Jimi Hendrix and Janis Joplin.

CHAPTER ONE

Amy Winehouse

Amy Winehouse, MTV Movie Awards, 2007. (Byline David Longendyke, Credit: Dave Longendyke/ZUMAWire/Bridgeman Images).

PART 1

THE STORY OF AMY WINEHOUSE

Singer, Guitarist & Song-writer
(1983–2011)

"Amy Winehouse was so great for me because she made me feel like what I did mattered."

– Ronnie Spector.

Heritage

Amy Winehouse was born Amy Jade Winehouse on Wednesday, 14th September 1983, at 22.25pm in North London at Chase Farm Hospital near Enfield. She was of Jewish heritage, both her parents being from large Jewish families with Eastern European origins.

She was born to Janis and Mitchell Winehouse, and when their daughter was born, they lived at Osidge Lane, Southgate (Winehouse, 2014, 18). When Amy was approximately eight years old, the family moved to a larger house which was a short distance away from the former address (Winehouse, 2014, 50).

They also had a son, Alex, who was born approximately four years earlier to Amy on the 19th October, 1979 (https://amywinehouse.fandom.com/) in University College Hospital in Central London (Winehouse, 2014, 20). Janis and Mitchell became Mr and Mrs Winehouse in 1976 and remained so until they divorced in 1993; both of them later remarried.

Mitchell (also known as 'Mitch') Winehouse was born on the 4th December 1950 in Stoke Newington, North London. He is a jazz singer and also director at the Amy Winehouse Foundation, which he established with his family after Amy's death. His other jobs have included taxi driver and working in the double-glazing industry.

The Amy Winehouse Foundation was set up in 2011 to assist children and young adults who face adversity and complex difficulties. The organisation provides support through the following schemes: music therapy for children, recovery housing for young women (called *Amy's Place*), resilience work with young people, as well as recovery pathways programmes and music projects outside of the UK. The organisation has now become one of the UK's leading charities that work with young people (https://amywinehousefoundation.org/).

Mitchell Winehouse was born to Alec Winehouse and Cynthia (née Gordon); they also had a daughter called Melody. Alec was born in December 1923 in Bethnal Green, East London. His parents were Benjamin Weinhauss/Winehouse and Fanny Grandish, who lived in a flat in Commercial Street, East London, above his business, which was called *Ben the Barber* (Winehouse, 2013, 6).

His parents both worked in his grandfather's shop; his father was a barber and his mother a ladies' hairdresser. Alec died in Enfield on

28th February 1967 (https://www.ancestry.co.uk) when Mitchell was seventeen years old. His mother was also a jazz singer, and before she married Alec Winehouse, she was romantically involved with Ronnie Scott, the co-founder of the jazz club *Ronnie Scott's*.

Cynthia Gordon was born on 21st October 1927 in the City of London and died on 5th May 2006 in Barnet, Greater London, aged 78 (https://www.findagrave.com/). After Alec died in 1967, Cynthia married Larry Lawrence Montague Levy, who was born in 1933 and died in 1996 aged 63 (https://www.geni.com/people). Cynthia was born to Max Gordon and Celia Gordon (née Berger), and Cynthia's siblings included her brother Nat and sister Lorna.

Cynthia's father was born in 1892 in the then Russian Federation and died in 1930 aged approximately 37–38 (https://www.geni.com/people). Celia Gordon was born in Whitechapel, London, in 1892 and died in Haringey, London, in 1976.

Janis Holly Winehouse (née Seaton) was born on 10th January, 1954, in New York City, New York (https://amywinehouse.fandom.com/). Her father was Eddy Seaton (née Steinberg), who worked as a ladies' garment tailor. As a child he was brought up after the death of his father with his two brothers in a Norwood Jewish orphanage. Janis's mother was Esther Seaton (née Richman), who was born in Newcastle, England (Winehouse, 2014, 24). There were jazz musicians as well as a singer in Janis's family (Winehouse, 2014, 38), which inspired some of her own love for jazz.

Her maternal grandmother was called Deborah and was an Eastern European Jewish immigrant. She came to London from Newcastle with her three daughters, having left her husband, and Esther was the youngest of the children (Winehouse, 2014, 23/24). Her maternal grandfather died when Esther was thirteen years old (Winehouse, 2014, 25).

Whilst raising her family, Janis also developed her education by firstly undertaking a part-time Open University course in general science between 1984 and 1989. She later went on to study at the London School of Pharmacy between 1996 and 1999, where she qualified and gained a degree as a Bachelor of Pharmacy (BPharm) (https://uk.linkedin.com/). Previously to that, when she was nineteen years old, Janis successfully completed her apprenticeship and eventually became a Pharmacy Technician (Winehouse, 2014, 35). Her jobs briefly included being a playgroup leader, later a laboratory technician, and then a pharmacy technician in full- and part-time roles (Winehouse, 2014, 48), now she is retired.

Education

As a toddler, Amy first attended a Hebrew Sunday school (www.huffingtonpost.com) Yavneh which was attached to Southgate Synagogue. After that she attended pre-school at Hamden Way nursery (Winehouse, 2014, 29/30), then attended Osidge Primary School, followed by Ashmole Secondary School.

By the time she was seven years old, Amy had started weekly three-hour lessons on a Saturday morning at a theatre class in Southgate called *Stagecoach* (Winehouse, 2014, 40). In 1991, she started to attend the Susi Earnshaw Theatre School in Barnet, which again was three hours of acting, singing and dancing; she continued at the theatre school for four years.

When she was twelve years old, she changed school, having gained a scholarship to become a full-time student at the Sylvia Young Theatre School (https://www.sylviayoungtheatreschool.co.uk), and she stayed there for three years (Winehouse, 2013, 23). When she became a teenager, she gained employment through the Theatre School; for example, she appeared in a sketch in BBC2's *The Fast Show* and also appeared in a play about Mormons which was performed at the Hampstead Theatre in Northwest London (Winehouse, 2013, 25).

However, her academic achievement at the school was poor, largely because she was bored and weary with the educational side of study. Her mother was advised by an academic head teacher that if Amy remained at Sylvia Young, it was probable that Amy would fail her GCSE exams (Winehouse, 2013, 26). Previously, the school had supported her by moving her up by one year in the hope that it would challenge her; she was an intelligent student but found it difficult to comply and focus.

Eventually, her parents decided to move her to a girl's school in Mill Hill, North London, called The Mount, concerned that their daughter would not pass her exams at Sylvia Young School. Amy disliked the single-sex school; however, she left there with five GCSEs. After she left Sylvia Young Theatre School aged sixteen, Sylvia Young herself helped to initiate Amy in becoming a member of the NYJO (National Youth Jazz

Amy Winehouse.
(Credit: Picture Alliance/Photoshot/Bridgeman Images).

Orchestra). They released a CD, and Amy was one of the singers on the album; she sang *The Nearness of You* (Winehouse, 2013, 28/29).

Formal education did not suit Amy, and she persuaded her parents to send her to another performing arts school. Her parents granted her wish, and when Amy was sixteen, she started attending the BRIT School for Performing Arts and Technology in Croydon. She was there for less than a year, where she studied musical theatre and was able to fully express herself creatively, and she flourished academically (Winehouse, 2013, 27).

Music Genres & Working Relationships

Amy became a legendary international singer and songwriter; her unique contralto vocals (the lowest female voice type) were instantly recognisable, as were her graphic, streetwise, dramatic and witty lyrics. Her cover versions of tracks such as *Monkey Man*, *Valerie*, *Moon River* and *Will You Still Love Me Tomorrow* all showed her irreplaceable and unmistakable style. Her diverse mix of musical genres included jazz, rhythm & blues, soul, and reggae. Her brother, father and paternal grandmother were influential in Amy's love for jazz through their own passion for artists such as Tony Bennett, Ella Fitzgerald, Billie Holiday, Thelonious Monk, Frank Sinatra, Sarah Vaughan and Dinah Washington. Amy was also brought up hearing her mother play records which were sung and written by Carole King and James Taylor.

In her youth, she adored hip-hop duo *Salt-N-Pepper*, and her favourite song of theirs was *Whatta Man*. She formed a band with her friend Juliette Ashby called *Sweet n Sour* – Amy was *Sour* and Juliette *Sweet* (https://www.amywinehouseforum.co.uk/); however, there was never a performance from the duo.

Amy was self-taught in guitar playing, and she bought her first guitar when she was approximately thirteen years old. The guitar she learnt to play on was a Fender Stratocaster acoustic guitar; she also played a custom Gibson Melody Maker, as well as a Daphne Blue Fender Stratocaster (The Winehouse Estate/HarperCollins, 2023, 29). As well as being an adept guitar player, Amy could also play the piano (https://www.youtube.com) and drums. She cited Jimi Hendrix as being influential to her and said, "There is room in everyone's life for Jimi Hendrix" (https://www.musicradar.com).

She worked with numerous CEOs, A&R representatives, dancers, managers, producers, musicians, singers and management companies. These included the following: Guy Moot (head of EMI Publishing) and Nick Shymansky, a talent scout at Simon Fuller's *Brilliant 19* (a subsidiary of *19 Managements*). Her first manager was Nick Godwyn (head of Island Records), and her last manager was Raye Cosbert of Metropolis Music. She also worked with A&R representative Darcus Beese for Island Records. Her producers included Commissioner Gordon (aka Gordon Williams) and Salaam Remi, who produced her debut album, *Frank*, in 2003, which was largely jazz influenced.

Three years later, Mark Ronson produced the album *Back To Black*, which was steeped with harmonies and style similar to those of the 1960s girl groups such as *The Crystals, The Ronettes* and *The Shirelles* – the jazz had been abandoned. Her guitarists included musicians, producers and songwriters such as the distinguished Ian Barter and Mitch Hiller. Her pianist was Sam Beste, and the musical arranger and director was Dale Davis. Amy said of the latter, "My favourite person to go anywhere with" (https://www.daledavisbass.co.uk/).

Whilst Amy was in New York working with Ronson, she hired Sharon Jones and the Dap-Kings to help back her up in the studio and while she was touring. They were a band who helped to revive the mid-1960s to mid-1970s style of funk and soul music from 2002. Better known to Amy's fans were her backup dancers and singers, Ade Omotayo and brothers Heshima and Zalon Thompson.

She also collaborated with a range of singers of different musical genres, who included Tony Bennett with *Body & Soul*, first recorded by Libby Holman; The Rolling Stones with *Ain't Too Proud To Beg* by The Temptations; and Paul Weller with *I Heard It Through The Grapevine*, the original recording by Gladys Knight & The Pips (https://faroutmagazine.co.uk/).

Distinctions

Her debut album, *Frank*, earned her an Ivor Novello Award; from the British Academy of Songwriters she was awarded Best Contemporary Song for *Stronger Than Me*; she was also nominated for a Brit Award for Best British Female Solo Artist.

Her second studio album, *Back To Black*, generated many nominations. These included two Brit Awards, which were for Best British Album, and won her Best British Female Solo Artist. She was also nominated for six Grammy Awards, four Ivor Novello Awards, four MTV Europe Music Awards, and three MTV Video Music Awards. The album was also nominated for the Mercury Prize Album of the Year and a MOBO award for Best UK Female Artist. *Back To Black* was also named as the eighth best album of all time by Apple Music (https://www.amywinehouse.com).

A third album, *Lioness: Hidden Treasures*, was released posthumously and compiled by producers Salaam Remi and Mark Ronson. The album is a collection of recordings made prior to the release of *Frank* (Winehouse, 2013, 294).

In 2013, an exhibition curated by Amy's brother and his wife entitled *Amy Winehouse: A Family Portrait* was displayed at The Jewish Museum in London. Two years later, in 2015, the exhibition was shown at the Contemporary Jewish Museum of San Francisco (https://en.wikipedia.org/wiki).

Several documentaries and films have been released posthumously about Amy Winehouse; probably the most well-known ones to date are *Amy, The Girl Behind The Name*, released in 2015, directed by Asif Kapadia; *Reclaiming Amy*, which aired on BBC2 television in 2023 and was directed by Marina Parker; and *Back To Black*, released in 2024 and directed by Sam Taylor-Johnson.

Enterprises

In 2009, Amy formed the *Lioness Records* label. She was motivated by both Berry Gordy's *Motown* record label and The Specials' *Two Tone Records* to create her own label. She named her record label *Lioness* in honour of her late grandmother Cynthia's strength of character. Artists that have recorded albums for *Lioness Records* include Dionne Bromfield in 2009 and Liam Bailey in 2010 (https://en.wikipedia.org/wiki).

Also in 2009, the Winehouse family was the subject of a documentary called *Saving Amy*, made by Daphne Barak. The film was not released, but in 2010, a paperback book with the same title was published. In 2009, Amy collaborated with EMI and launched a range of gift cards and wrapping paper with her song lyrics from the *Back To Black* album, and the merchandise lines were successful (https://www.digitalspy.com).

Another business venture included a partnership with *Fred Perry* on a seventeen-piece fashion collection with the *Fred Perry* label. Twenty per cent of the net revenue received by *Fred Perry* for the Amy Winehouse collection goes to the Amy Winehouse Foundation. Throughout the duration of the collaboration, over two million pounds have been donated by *Fred Perry* to the foundation (https://www.fredperry.com).

It is believed at one point Amy had an estimated ten million pound fortune, which in 2008 tied her to tenth place in *The Sunday Times'* wealth list of musicians under the age of 30. However, in 2009, that sum was estimated to have fallen to five million pounds (https://en.wikipedia.org/wiki).

Philanthropy

Amy was generous and dedicated her money, time and music to several charities and was particularly interested in organisations that supported children. Charities that she supported included 21st Century Leaders, BID 2 BEAT AIDS, LIFEbeat, Save the Music Foundation, V-Day, and Whatever It Takes (https://www.looktothestars.org).

In 2008, she appeared naked along with singer Sade and actor Helena Bonham Carter in the *Easy Living* magazine. This was part of a campaign that was raising awareness about breast cancer in young women. Then, in 2009, she appeared on a CD called *Classics* alongside bands such as The Rolling Stones and The Killers as well as many Cuban musicians; this was done to help raise awareness of climate change.

Also in 2009, when she was in Saint Lucia, she befriended a local, Julian Jean-Baptiste. She learnt that he was in need of urgent medical treatment, but he did not earn enough money to pay for it. He was desperately in pain and she gave him £4000 so that he could pay to undergo hernia treatment. He said that her generosity saved his life (https://web.archive.org/web/://www.contactmusic.com).

In 2011, Amy donated over £20,000 worth of designer clothes to a charity shop in North London. The donation included Alexander McQueen dresses and designs by Luella Bartley (www.webarchive/www.looktothestars.org).

Significant Relationships

Before the album *Frank* was released in 2003, Chris Taylor and Amy were in an on-off relationship. She described him as being "my first proper long-term boyfriend" (Barak, 2010, 41). The heartbreak behind their separation inspired her to write much of the material on her debut album, *Frank*. The song *Stronger Than Me* is about her experience of their relationship (https://www.last.fmi) and how she perceived him to be lacking in emotional strength (https://www.mojo4music.com/).

Apparently, in approximately 2005, she met Blake Fielder-Civil (a former video production assistant) in The Old Blue Last pub in Shoreditch in East London; he was a regular there, and Amy started to frequent the pub, knowing he'd be there. Apparently, she would "stare at him salivating and was in awe of him" (James, 2021, 64). However, others believe that she first met him at the Good Mixer pub in Camden.

The two began a relationship which was tumultuous and also was not helped by him being a substance user, of which he also became an addict. When they first met, he already had a girlfriend, and at one point he went back to her; this was much of the inspiration behind the album and track *Back To Black*.

Come 2006, Amy was in a relationship and briefly lived with Alex Clare, whom she met at The Hawley Arms pub in Camden, North London (https://www.thejc.com). At that time, he was a budding musician, and since then has achieved great success. Interestingly, he shared the same birthday as Amy, the 14th September, although he was born two years later than her in 1985. The two became a couple whilst Amy was on a break from her then on-off boyfriend, Blake Fielder-Civil. However, in 2007 the couple had reunited and were married in Miami Beach, Florida, in May of 2007.

Between 21st July 2008 and 25th February 2009, Fielder-Civil was imprisoned as a result of being found guilty on charges of grievous bodily harm with intent (https://en.wikipedia.org/wiki). One evening in 2006, the victim, James King, who was then landlord of the Macbeth pub in Hoxton, East London (Winehouse, 2013, 113), was brutally attacked by Fielder-Civil and his friend Michael Brown. The latter sought revenge on King, as earlier one evening he had thrown Brown out from the premises.

Fielder-Civil assisted Brown, who had knocked King to the ground; the former repeatedly stamped on King and kicked the victim in the head and body. Such was the ferocity of the attack that King needed twelve hours of surgery, with bolts and metal plates to reconstruct his face (ibid.). Brown and Fielder-Civil were arrested and charged with GBH (grievous bodily harm) with intent – i.e., the attack was malicious and premeditated. Both men pleaded not guilty, and the case was transferred to Crown Court and scheduled to be heard at a later date; the pair eventually faced their charges in November 2007 (Winehouse, 2013, 114).

The police arrested and cautioned Fielder-Civil, the charge this time being on suspicion of perverting the course of justice (Winehouse, 2013, 117). He was worried that he would be found guilty of the charges that he was accused of. This was because he and Brown had tried to bribe King into not testifying and to withdraw his complaint. The two friends enlisted the help of two other friends to act as middlemen and pay King £200,000 to ensure that he did not testify in court. The police had reason to believe that King had been prepared to accept the bribe and not testify in court.

However, Fielder-Civil was denied bail and sent to Pentonville Prison in North London on remand (Winehouse, 2013, 117). Whilst the press wrongly speculated that such a vast sum of money must have come from Amy, there was no evidence whatsoever to suggest that Amy had been involved in the alleged plot. Little did the press and general public know that her father was managing her financial affairs and would have known about such an immense amount of money (Winehouse, 2013, 118).

In 2009, Amy was romancing rugby player and actor Josh Bowman whilst she was holidaying in Saint Lucia with some of her friends. Fielder-Civil got to hear about her romancing, and his solicitor issued papers to Winehouse for divorce proceedings on a claim of adultery. An uncontested divorce was granted in July 2009 and became absolute in August 2009; Fielder-Civil received no money from the divorce settlement (http://www.sfgate.com).

The following year, she was in a relationship with film producer Reg Traviss, and remained so until her death in 2011. Apparently, they were happy together, and the couple planned to marry and have children (Winehouse, 2013, 248/256).

Health & Ill-health

Amy was addicted to crack cocaine and heroin for approximately a year. Fielder-Civil told a tabloid newspaper that he introduced Amy to crack and heroin (https://people.com). Aged eighteen, Amy was questioned by her mother about whether cannabis was the only drug that she had ever taken. Amy's reply was, "I've smoked heroin, Mum, but it was nothing ... Yeah but I just tried it, Mum. It's not for me." At that point, Janis Winehouse was uncertain as to whether her daughter was being truthful or not. At that time in her life, Amy was apparently anti-Class A drugs, and her mantra was "Class A drugs are for mugs" (Winehouse, 2014, 101). When it became apparent that Amy had a substance addiction, Janis commented that her daughter would get angry and frustrated about her performances and that she would get high in order to cope with the anxiety (Winehouse, 2014, 170).

Eventually, and with persistent support from her family, Amy sought treatment, albeit reluctantly, by participating in various treatment programmes in rehabilitation; finally, she remained in recovery. Medications which Amy was treated with to help with the drug withdrawal process and to help relax her included methadone and Subutex (Winehouse, 2014, 187), as well as Valium (Winehouse, 2014, 179). Her song *Rehab* from the *Back To Black* album was autobiographical and narrates how her former management company wanted her to go into rehabilitation. She was fervently against it, claiming that she was not an addict, and at that time in her life her father agreed to it, although later on in her life it was evident to both her parents that she would benefit from doing so.

There is a high prevalence of substance use disorders with mental health conditions such as generalised anxiety disorder (GAD), depression, attention-deficit hyperactivity disorder (ADHD), psychotic illness and borderline personality (now referred to as emotionally unstable personality disorder) (https://nida.nih.gov). Several times, her parents had considered whether Amy should be assessed by the appropriate experts for being sectioned under the Mental Health Act 1983.

Before a person can be lawfully sectioned, a team of health professionals must be sent out to assess the individual, and this could happen at home, in a place of safety or in hospital. The panel would consist of a person who is an Approved Mental Health Professional (AMPH), a registered medical practitioner who knows the person, such as a GP, as well as a Section 12 approved doctor, who is usually a psychiatrist (https://www.mind.org.uk).

One instance of what led to this thinking can be seen where her father described her behaviour as a psychotic episode, which was devastating for him to see. It happened when Fielder-Civil was still in custody and Amy had an almighty argument with him over the telephone. Afterwards, she "went on a two-day drink and drugs binge, and she had flipped out completely." She had cuts on her arms and face and had stubbed out a cigarette on her cheek. Her hand was severely cut from punching a mirror, and she was crying hysterically (Winehouse, 2014, 190).

Her father stated that "… her behaviour was not extreme enough for her to be considered a danger to herself or to other people." He added that by the time medical help arrived, Amy's episodes had subsided and she was calmer (ibid.), she never was sectioned.

Her mother recalled that when Amy was living in Camden Square, she could hardly remember meeting the same Amy once; by that, she is referring to the different personas that Amy adopted. On some days, she behaved like a small child. She would sit on her mother's knee, speak in a baby voice and suck her thumb. At other times, she'd be aggressive and butch. Her mother believed that these characters were used as coping mechanisms to help her manage anxious and stressful situations (Winehouse, 2014, 246).

While it is treatable, substance addiction withdrawal is challenging and unpleasant for the patient to overcome. In Amy's case, during the withdrawal process from substance addiction, she experienced physical conditions such as diarrhoea, flu, severe stomach cramps and sickness (Winehouse, 2014, 182). She also contracted the highly contagious bacterial condition impetigo, which was palpable with blisters across her cheeks.

Aged fourteen, she was prescribed an antidepressant (Kapadia, *Amy: The Girl Behind the Name*, 2015), Seroxat. This was a brand name for paroxetine, a drug which was used to treat the following: generalised anxiety disorder, major depression disorder, OCD (obsessive compulsive disorder), panic disorder, social anxiety disorder, PTSD (post traumatic stress disorder), and premenstrual dysphoric disorder (https://en.wikipedia.org/wiki/paroxetine). Her friend and flatmate who lived with her at Jeffrey's Place in Camden, Catriona Gourlay, commented on how Amy kept her nail varnishes in their fridge, and they were all organised by colour (Parry, 2021, page un-numbered).

Her lifelong friend since the Sylvia Young stage school days, Tyler James observed and commented that after her success with the *Frank* album and pre-success with *Back To Black*, "Amy started to lose the plot. She wasn't happy. She was **really** bored. She'd been a clean freak, and now she was seriously OCD. Then she became nocturnal" (James, 2021, 61).

By the time Amy was 21, Seroxat was banned for under eighteens. Evidence was provided to the MHRA (Medicine and Health Regulatory Agency) where trials showed that the drug could cause young people to experience mood changes and/or self-harm and potentially become suicidal (https://www.theguardian.com). Upon reflection, and speaking of depression and Seroxat, Amy commented that at age fourteen she didn't really know what depression was. She said that she knew she felt funny sometimes and that she was different. Seroxat made her loopy and really scatty (Kapadia, *Amy: The Girl Behind the Name*, 2015). By her early to mid-teens, she was smoking cigarettes and cannabis as well as drinking alcohol.

She also was diagnosed with the eating disorder bulimia nervosa (Kapadia, *Amy: The Girl Behind the Name*, 2015), which exacerbated after she became famous. In addition, she had an irregular heartbeat and lung damage. Such was the harm done to her lungs that medical professionals concluded that by continuing to smoke, not only would it ruin her voice, it could also lead to early-stage emphysema (https://web.archive.org/).

Although she recovered from substance dependency, she remained addicted to alcohol. She took Librium, a withdrawal medication, to help prevent the onset of alcohol-induced seizures, which she experienced many times before she was prescribed Librium. It was her friend Tyler James' responsibility to administer and ensure that she took her medication (James, 2021, 302).

Her battle with alcohol and substance addiction was also aggravated by the bulimia nervosa. Her weight plummeted; she was physically weak and malnourished. The constant purging and making herself sick, coupled with the immense pressure put on her internal organs, would have weakened her tremendously (Winehouse, 2014, 247).

Janis Winehouse said, "Amy was naturally petite, but suddenly I felt how painfully thin her frame had become. I could feel her ribs as she hugged me and the bones in her elbows" (Winehouse, 2014, 163). Amy's

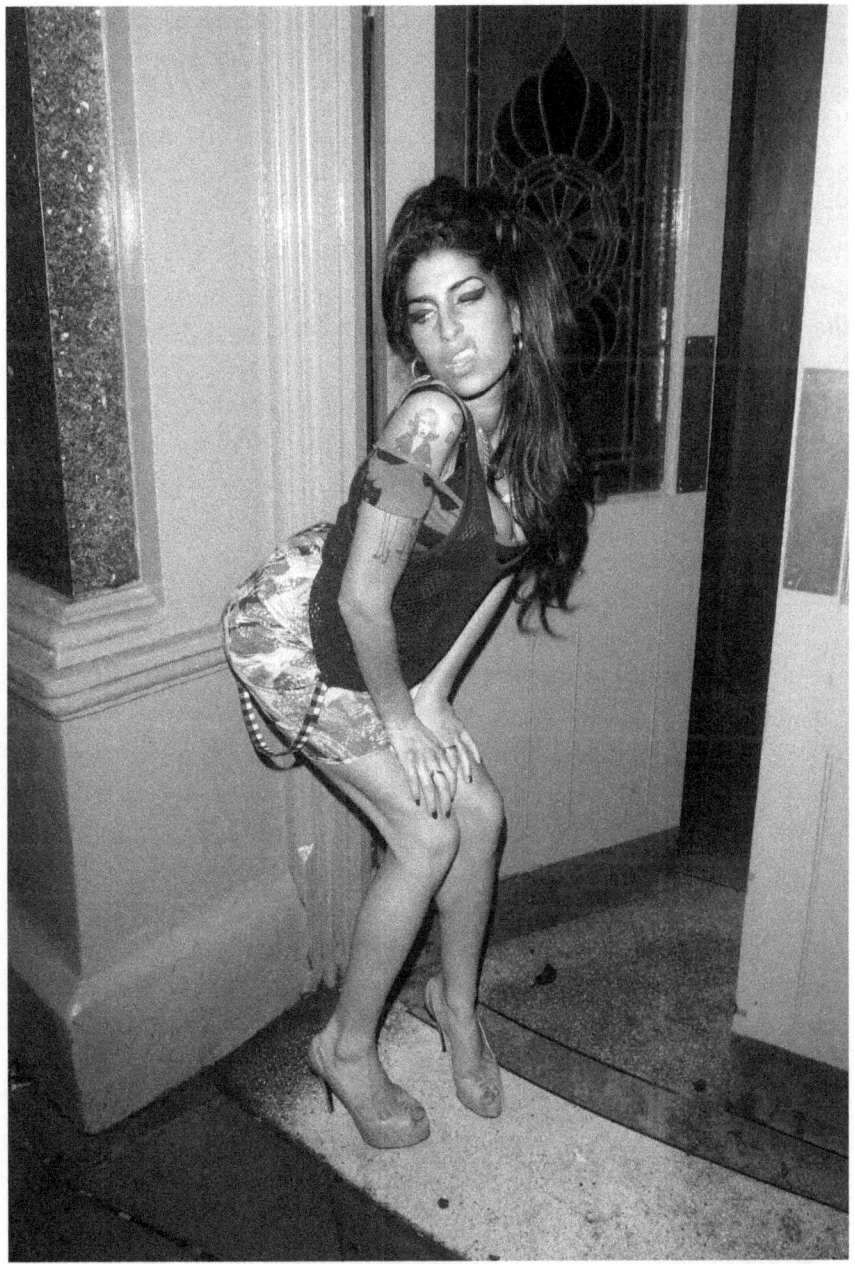

Amy Winehouse.
(Credit: Picture Alliance/Photoshot/Bridgeman Images).

step-brother, Michael Collins, commented that he found hugging her uncomfortable because he could almost feel her body disintegrating in his embrace (Winehouse, 2014, 249).

Her mother also described how Amy became obsessed with her health, virtually to the point of hypochondria; however, it did not stop her from abusing her body (Winehouse, 2014, 186). There were times when she took the initiative to improve both her physical and spiritual health. For a while, she practiced yoga and had an instructor visit her at the flat in Camden Square; furnished in the basement of her home was her gym equipment and music studio.

In February 2011, monitoring blood tests revealed that Amy was consuming approximately 30 times more than was the safe limit of alcohol each week (ibid.). In March 2011, her medical problems were highlighted in no uncertain terms by her doctor. Her thyroid gland was severely underactive, which indicated that her body was producing insufficient hormones.

The deficiency meant that it would contribute to Amy's depression, tiredness and high blood pressure, as well as affect her fertility (potentially making her infertile) and heart function in the long term. Amazingly, the tests did not identify any liver damage (ibid.). However, at one point, the skin around her liver was yellow and jaundiced (Winehouse, 2014, 249). She was warned by her doctor that if she continued with the same level of alcohol intake that she had, then inevitably she would die.

Her mother warned her that she needed to reduce her drinking gradually, as irregular periods of abstinence could be dangerous. Amy ignored this advice and experienced periods of sobriety, followed by bouts of binge drinking.

Tragically, she died on 23rd July 2011, of alcohol poisoning, aged 27; the coroner recorded a verdict of misadventure from a sudden and unexpected death. Toxicology tests showed that there were no illegal substances in her system when she died. However, the inquest heard that she was more than five times over the drink-drive limit. The pathologist who conducted the post-mortem said that the amount of alcohol found in her system was considered a fatal level and could have stopped her breathing and put her into a coma (https://www.bbc.co.uk/).

Her bodyguard, Andrew Morris, who lived with her at her residence, observed that three days before she died, she had been drinking moderately; on the day that she died, he found her body. She was not breathing and had no pulse. He called the emergency services, and Amy was pronounced dead at the scene by the paramedics; the police confirmed her death. When forensic investigators arrived at the scene, they found three bottles of vodka in her room – one small bottle and two large ones.

Later in a press interview, Morris told a *Daily Mirror* spokesman that on the day Amy died, she was in good spirits and had been "laughing, listening to music and watching TV" (https://www.express.co.uk/), right up until the early hours of the morning. During their conversation at that time, Morris recalled that Amy said to him, "If I could, I would give it all back just to walk down the street with no hassle" (ibid.).

Family and close friends attended a private funeral in July of 2011 at Edgewarbury Lane Cemetery in North London; she was later cremated at Golders Green Crematorium. The following year, Amy's ashes were buried alongside her paternal grandmother, Cynthia Levy, at Edgewarbury Lane Cemetery.

PART 2
WHAT AMY WINEHOUSE'S NATAL CHART REVEALS AND THE ASTROLOGY IN ACTION

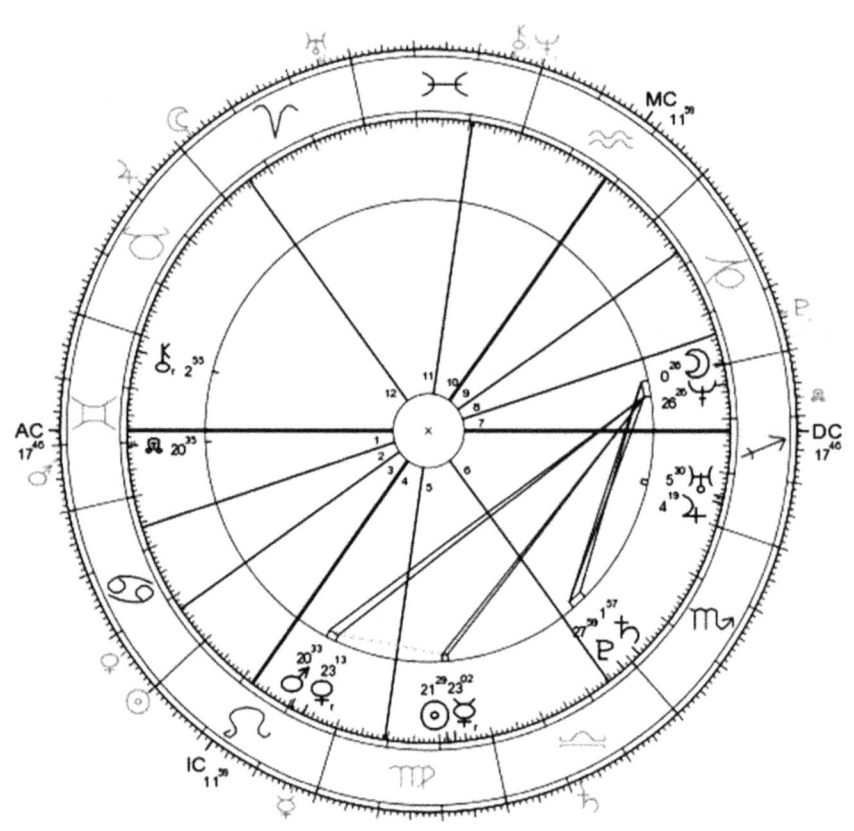

ASTROLOGY DETAILS

Amy Winehouse's natal and transits chart via www.astro.com (Astrodienst).
Co-ordinates of Amy Winehouse's natal chart: 0w05, 51n40.
Rodden Rating: A.

Amy Winehouse's Natal Chart and the Transits to it on the Day She Died, 23rd July 2011

Amy Jade Winehouse was born on Wednesday, 14th September 1983, at 10.25pm in Enfield, Middlesex, England. In her natal chart, the shaping of the planets is defined as being a Bowl. This is because there are planets in one half of the chart, and they span from the fourth to the seventh house (*see glossary*).

The Bowl is a stimulating pattern which indicates that Amy could be highly motivated, although at times she may have felt perturbed by a feeling that something was missing in her life. By taking action, she could fill that void with self-reliance. Once, in an interview, she was asked to describe herself in five words; her reply was, "Driven, motivated, easygoing, maternal, alcoholic" (Newkey-Burden, 208, 207).

The ruler of her natal chart is Mercury – the planet which rules Gemini, the ascendant sign. Mercury rules both Gemini and Virgo (her Sun sign). Mercury's symbol is a simplified pictograph of the caduceus. This is a symbol of the healing arts, and it is pertinent to Amy, given what we know about her challenges with her physical and mental health. The symbol is still used today as an emblem of the medical profession. Amy was born on a Wednesday, which is ruled by the planet Mercury.

Mercury & Virgo

In mythology, Mercury is the god of all types of communication: reading, commerce, speaking, teaching, and writing. He is known as a messenger, a humorous but also cunning trickster and, as previously noted, is also the God of the Healing Arts. In medical astrology, Virgo is associated with the small intestine; its task is to facilitate absorption and transportation of the food we eat by breaking down foodstuffs into small molecules.

It has been observed by many astrologers that, of the twelve astrology signs, Virgos particularly are prone to suffer from anxiety and worry about their health and also their family's health. Sufficient exercise, a healthy diet and a reliable method for helping to reduce stress are essential to help manage anxiety and sleep-health.

Being able to relax and slow down may have been challenging for Amy, given that Mercury's energies include restlessness and needing stimulation from a variety of sources; this was confirmed by her parents. In approximately 2008/2009, whilst Amy and her mother, Janis, were in St. Lucia in the Caribbean, her mother reflected, "I noticed a deeper restlessness about her. She needed to be doing different things all the time, as if her brain was constantly on overload." Janis continued, "She'd always been a nervous ball of energy, even at school, but now it was more pronounced" (Winehouse, 2014, 216). Her mother also described her as having "never-ending unrest, which had always been part of her personality" (Winehouse, 2014, 229). She also observed that her daughter was a perfectionist and meticulous about detail but also needed to be in perpetual motion (Winehouse, 2014, 111).

Her father, Mitchell, commented that from the age of eleven, Amy wouldn't go to bed. She sat up all night in her bedroom busying herself with activities, such as listening to music, doing puzzles, reading, and watching television. She did not want to go to sleep, which, as a consequence, made getting her up for school in the morning near impossible because she was so tired (Winehouse, 2014, 20). Amy's lifelong anxiety and tension must have been exhausting both to herself and to those closest to her.

Amy practiced yoga for a while and also had a fitness bike installed in her last flat in Camden Square. For a while, it seemed that Amy was practicing self-care; she signed up for a six-month course with a yoga guru. A friend recalled how Amy loved the yoga, which was practiced to music. "The idea is it gives you a natural high and takes away the desire to do drugs" (Newkey-Burden, 2008, 189).

Virgos are associated with minutiae and detail-orientated work, and the theme of smallness is carried through by this sign having an affinity with domestic pets. As a child, Amy had a cat called Katy and a hamster called Penfold (Winehouse Estate, 2023, 85). When she was an adult, for a short time she had a dog called Freddie until it ran away, never to be found.

Amy also had a canary called Ava, who was named after the actress Ava Gardner. When the bird died, Amy was heartbroken. She wrote and dedicated a song to Ava called *October Song (In Loving Memory)*, which was included on the album *Frank* (presumably, the bird died in October). Some of the lyrics reveal how Amy used to sing a lullaby to Ava each night; Amy said, "I loved that bird. It was a sad time. But I got a good song out of it" (www.facebook.com). She also had a tattoo of a bird on her arm with the wording 'Don't clip my wings'.

She also took in stray cats, and at one point she had thirteen cats. Her friend Juliette Ashby remembers Amy wanted to save cats and open a cat sanctuary (*Amy Winehouse: Back to Black*, 2018, DVD). Clearly Amy loved having pets throughout adulthood and childhood.

At the time of Amy's birth, the Sun was in Virgo, the Moon in Capricorn, and the ascendant sign was Gemini. This suggests (among other things) that she was intelligent, practical and quick-witted. The Sun in Virgo shows that Amy was analytical, intelligent, modest, self-critical, observant, and humorous. She was also kind and thoughtful – qualities that her family and friends experienced and observed.

Amy's friend and make-up artist, Talia Sparrow, said of her relationship with Amy, "Over the years of working with Amy, I experienced so many loving and funny moments; she was definitively a carer, not a taker" (Parry, 2021, page un-numbered). Virgos are also associated with abilities for craft, technique, and skill – areas which were certainly borne out in her abilities as a songwriter, musician and singer, and self-make-up artist. She told Talia Sparrow when they first met that "she didn't like people touching her face or doing her make-up," and preferred to do her own (ibid.).

The exacting nature of Virgos lends itself to perfection and self-improvement. One example of this can be seen whereby Amy candidly admitted, "I'm my own worst critic, and if I don't pull off what I think I wanted to do in my head, then I won't be a happy girl" (Winehouse Estate, 2023, 239). She also disclosed, "I'm quite a self-destructive person, so it's always giving me material" (Winehouse Estate, 2023, 226).

Amy also recalled how when she was at the Sylvia Young stage school, she had a stage school voice, and although she could do loud things with her voice when she sang, for her it was about the "magic in sensitivity and subtlety. You can do so much more with a quiet voice than with a belter" (Winehouse Estate, 2023, 100/101).

Another example of enhancement and perfection can be seen in Amy having breast implants. Even after her surgery, she was still dissatisfied with her look and took to wearing gel-filled push-up bras to help create an illusion of even bigger breasts (Winehouse, 2014, 232). Just weeks after that operation, she considered having plastic surgery to enlarge her nose. However, the procedure never happened, much to her mother's relief.

Janis Winehouse commented that Amy thought "her nose was overly small, and she (Amy) didn't like looking at it" (Winehouse, 2014, 233). This shows how Amy had grown increasingly dissatisfied with her own body and fostered a perfectionist attitude about her physical shape. It is not unusual for Virgos to be concerned about their body, and for some it can border on hypochondria, something not lost on her mother.

She commented that at one point Amy had "become obsessed with her health, almost to the level of hypochondria. She constantly complained of a sore throat or a cold or a stomach bug – but it never stopped her abusing her body" (Winehouse, 2014, 186). Amy's mother further commented that Amy was "turning the perfectionist attitude with which she approached everything else in on herself" (Winehouse, 2014, 233).

Mercury is also positioned in Virgo in Amy's natal chart and is conjunct (*see glossary*) the Sun. This suggests that Amy was bright and quick-thinking. In comedy, Mercury is associated with comic gestures and swift one-liners. Various people who knew Amy commented on her being funny, witty, a good laugh and a mimic.

Two such people were her producers Salaam Remi and Mark Ronson, who said, respectively, that she was "very comedic" and "had a razor-sharp wit" (Amy Winehouse, *Back to Black*, 2018, DVD); Remi also remembered Amy's "big giant laugh" (Amy, 2015, DVD). Her friend and flatmate, Catriona Gourlay, knew Amy when she was a teenager (they became friends in approximately 2002). She remembers Amy as having "rapier-sharp humour" and being "searingly intelligent to boot" (Parry, 2021, pages un-numbered).

Faculties associated with Mercury are hearing, memory, sight and adaptability, speech and powers of observation. Her mother described her daughter as being "a natural observer ... an obsessive documenter" (Winehouse Estate, 2023, 16). Amy was something of a wordsmith and gravitated towards learning, reading and writing. Apart from her song-writing, she also wrote poetry and kept diaries, journals and detailed lists.

As a child, she would work in her bedroom until the early hours of the morning. She filled one notebook after another "with lists and drawings, maps and plans, which she would constantly revise and update" (ibid.). Even her lists were given titles; e.g., 'Fame Ambitions' and 'Better Stuff for My Room' (Winehouse Estate, 2023, 164/165). She also wrote endless notes and made homemade cards for her family, often with love hearts drawn on them and telling the family member that she loved them and why she loved them.

Her mother recalled how Amy made countless lists of items that she wanted her parents and grandparents to buy for her. She would list the item, the shop where it could be bought from and its cost, all neatly totalled up at the end, which would be followed by plans of where those items would go in her room.

In 2000, after she left school, she worked for an internet news agency, WENN (a celebrity and entertainment news agency), as a show business journalist, earning approximately £150 a week, writing articles for the organisation (Barak, 2010, 38). Working as a show business journalist was an ambition that she had written about in one of her early journals (Winehouse Estate, 2023, 178). She secured the job through her friend Juliette Ashby's father.

It was while she was working at WENN that she met her boyfriend Chris Taylor, whom she had an on-and-off relationship with and who was the subject of the song *Stronger Than Me*.

Such a busy and active mind like Amy's would benefit from being productive and occupied with mentally demanding and exciting work, if not for the dilemma that it could lead to distraction, nervousness and/or disruption. As a child, her mother recalled how her daughter would often be in her bedroom, her sanctuary, busy working on something such as drawings, making cards, or writing. Amy was always keeping occupied, being creative and productive.

Music was her first love, and she revealed, "Music is the thing that means the most to me. I love everyone in my life, but you don't get any shit with music. It's pure beauty, and there's no small stuff attached. It's an immense thing" (Winehouse Estate, 2023, 223). However, when it came to performing, she disclosed, "I'm not a natural-born performer" (Winehouse Estate, 2023, 39).

Her father confirmed this when discussing her stage fright. Whilst outwardly confident, inwardly Amy harboured a fear of being onstage; this worsened over time, and the fright never left her, but she was a master at concealing her stage fright (Winehouse, 2013, 50). There were also small telltale signs of her insecurity and nervousness when she performed, such as twiddling with a piece of material at the edge of her dress, skirt or shorts, and also one of her feet would often be turned inwards.

At times, she may have felt overwhelmed, almost as though she was lost in a sea of ideas. A creative writer, especially one in the public eye, needs a vehicle for their imagination where thoughts and fantasies can find a valid channel.

The Sun conjunct Mercury suggests that not only did she have a lively and quick mind, but also a level of self-knowledge where she could express herself with confidence, hold strong opinions and was capable of independent thinking. Amy's debut album, *Frank*, was called so because it alluded to the candid nature of her lyrics, as well as paying homage to Frank Sinatra, one of her idols.

Whilst being interviewed and speaking on film, she was implicitly honest. Her work and health were often the subjects which dominated conversation. These areas are pertinent, given that they are subjects important to Virgos. Certainly, they are significant to what we know about Amy's short life and how her ill-health was the focus of the media.

Creativity, Drama & Love

The Sun and Mercury are positioned in the fifth house, the area associated with creativity, hobbies, romance, and children (including our inner child). The Sun in the fifth house suggests that Amy had a great talent and was unafraid to let it shine for the world to see. Amy felt good when she was the centre of attention and needed to feel that others were revolving around her, especially when her family was her audience.

She said of them, "I'm happiest with my family around me" (Winehouse Estate, 2023, 48). Another time she said, "While I love music, I'd really love to have a family, and that's the most important thing to me" (Newkey-Burden, 208, 207).

Creative expression and artistic endeavours are indications of how the Sun in this house can manifest, and indeed it did with Amy. Her mother said that Amy "was born with a vivid imagination and creativity bursting from her" (Winehouse Estate, 2023, 34).

As previously noted, the fifth house is also called the house of our inner child – i.e., the part of us which loves to play and which remains eternally young. The Sun in the fifth house also shows how Amy valued acting, drama and performance. It is unsurprising, therefore, that she went to several theatre and performance schools and participated in school productions, one being the musical, *Grease*.

The Sun in the fifth house can also indicate a love of children, and Amy made it evident to her friends over the years and to her last partner, Reg Traviss, that she wanted to be a mother. Given that she had bulimia for several years, it is possible that fertility may have been a challenge for her. This is because of the physical damage done to her body from the eating disorder and her relationship with food.

Her mother confirmed to author and documentary-maker Daphne Barak that her daughter had an irregular menstrual cycle, which sometimes included not menstruating at all (Barak, 2010, 83), something not uncommon with anorexics and bulimics. Reg Traviss told her father that Amy thought she had been pregnant on two occasions (Winehouse, 2013, 248).

Romance is also associated with the fifth house, as previously observed; and with the Sun in this house, it suggests that Amy loved to be in love and enjoyed the trappings of romance. Besides being heart-wrenching and passionate, romantic encounters can also enhance our sense of feeling special when we become the focus of attention for somebody else's feelings.

Love was certainly an essential part of Amy's self-dramatising nature, and she defined herself through it. She needed to be proud of her partner(s) and wanted the wider world to know about them. She would have expected them to be an attentive audience to her. We can certainly see this through the example of her relationship with Blake Fielder-Civil, who was never far behind her when she was performing on stage. Even when he was in prison, she would occasionally reference him to her audience. For example, when she performed at the Nelson Mandela 90th birthday concert in Hyde Park in 2008, sometimes she changed the words in the chorus to *'Free Blakey, My Fella'*, instead of singing the original line.

Venus, the planet of allure, is conjunct Mars, the planet of desire. The two planets blended together stir up charisma, passion and sensuality, and with both planets in Leo, it suggests that there would be plenty of drama in her life, which we know to be true.

Blake Fielder-Civil revealed in the 2015 film *Amy* that he asked her why she was promiscuous and why she was more like a man with sex. He said the reasoning behind his question was that he thought she may have been sexually abused as a child. He further added that Amy denied that was ever the case and she had never been a victim of abuse. Possibly, up until the point that Fielder-Civil had met Amy, he had never experienced sex with a woman who was highly passionate and who enjoyed sex as much as he did.

In terms of romantic liaisons, she needed somebody who stimulated her mentally. The Sagittarius descendant in her natal chart suggests that she needed a confident, enthusiastic partner. Somebody she could believe in and who could expand her world for her – be that on a mental or physical level, and with plenty of wanderlust.

In the aforementioned film, Amy comments on her relationship with Fielder-Civil and one of her revelations describes the Sagittarian qualities in action. She said, "Blake taught me that if you don't go for things, if you don't throw yourself into a situation in a big way, then you never know what might have been. Life is short" (*Amy*, Kapadia, 2015).

Certainly in her music partnerships, the people she chose to work with helped her to expand her creative and music capabilities. She commented once that she wanted to work with people who she could learn something from and who she respected: "I know it sounds a bit wanky, but I can't even work with someone unless they know more about music than me. I have to learn from them, or it's pointless" (www.faroutmagazine.co.uk). She also declared, "Success to me is having the freedom to work with whoever I want to" (Winehouse, 2014, 251).

Mercury in the fifth house denotes that she was entertaining and fun-loving and held a variety of interests throughout her life. Some of her interests were playing pool, ice-skating and cinema. Additional pursuits were clubbing, fashion, listening to music and probably a whole variety of other leisure activities, given that she liked diversity and stimulation.

The position of Mercury in the fifth house also shows potential for writing and an enjoyment of reading books, as well as other literary pursuits. For example, as a child she loved writing poetry and became obsessed with writing a Japanese style of poetry called 'haiku'. These were miniature poems consisting of three lines with five syllables in the first line, seven in the second and five in the third (Winehouse Estate, 2023, 19/20).

Her mother observed how when her daughter wrote her own poetry, and later her own lyrics, she always counted each syllable (ibid.), thus showing an attention to detail, creativity and developing her own style in song-writing.

As a child, she enjoyed being read to by her parents, with *The Cat in the Hat* by Dr. Suess being one of her favourites and Enid Blyton's *Noddy* books being others (Winehouse Estate, 2023, 46). When she was older, she was entertained by her father telling her ghost stories.

Amy's creative expression came mainly through song-writing, which predominantly was autobiographical and centred on aspects of her relationships. Written for the world to hear, they had a strong sense of atmosphere and drama which was mesmerising and unforgettable. The American magazine *Rolling Stone* commented on *Back To Black* and heralded Amy as "a nervy, witty songstress whom everybody can dig" (O'Brien, 2012, 394).

Healing Old Wounds

For Amy, song-writing was cathartic for the emotional pain she experienced in her life, but she always wanted to add something optimistic and upbeat to the lyrics.

The contact between Jupiter in the sixth house, the area of health and work, and Chiron in the twelfth house, the area of escapism, hidden emotions and healing, is indicative of this. Amy said of writing her songs, "If I haven't done it, I just can't put it into a song. It has to be autobiographical. It's an exorcism. I get all my stuff out there … If I didn't have this medium to get my experiences across, I would be lost" (Winehouse Estate, 2023, 182/183). This shows just how crucial her song-writing was to her well-being and creativity.

Her father recognised that part of the writing process for Amy involved tremendous soul-searching and honesty: "It was precisely because her songs were dragged up out of her soul that they were so powerful and passionate. The ones that went into *Back To Black* were about the deepest of emotions. And she went through hell to make it" (Winehouse, 2013, 52).

The twelfth house is also associated with disintegration and addiction (as well as other things); therefore, it could be argued that she was dependent on writing to help establish some kind of inner order and peace to make way for emotional and spiritual healing.

Her parents realised that "fame and her spiralling addictions also brought out her perfectionist and self-destructive tendencies ... Amy was her own worst critic" (Winehouse Estate, 2023, 232). Janis Winehouse said, "Amy was a perfectionist ... It was as if once she had got her thoughts and feelings down on paper or she had recorded them in an album, she was ready to move on ... Amy didn't even keep copies of her own albums at home" (Winehouse Estate, 2023, 24). The themes of craving and dependence show potential in the seventh house of her natal chart and will be discussed further on.

The Psychology of Fame

Jupiter is associated with fame – an area which often comes with a grave toil for celebrities and those in the spotlight, and Amy was no exception. The psychology of fame includes complex issues such as alienation, isolation, and mental health, including conditions such as anxiety, depression, body image concerns, and self-harming.

When she was thirteen, she wrote, "Mostly, I have this dream to be very famous ... I want people to hear my voice and just ... forget their troubles for five minutes" (Barak, 2010, 35). In later years, when she reached an iconic status, it was accompanied by the 'rock n roll lifestyle' in terms of being addicted to alcohol and drugs.

However, in the 2015 documentary Amy, pre-her *Back To Black* success, she commented, "I don't think I am going to be at all famous. I don't think I could handle it. I'd probably go mad" (www.thewalrus.ca).

Amy said that she wanted "to be remembered as someone who wasn't satisfied with just one level of musicianship, as someone who was a pioneer ... I've got all this time to make that happen. That's what's so exciting; I've got years to do magic" (Winehouse, 2023, 272/273). Her innocent teenage dream about being famous came to fruition, but it came at a price.

It is interesting that Jupiter is in the sixth house of her natal chart, the area connected with health and work. Abundance and excess are correspondences of Jupiter, and they are notable, given the wide-ranging problems that she had with her health. This doesn't mean, of course, that every person with Jupiter in the sixth house of their natal chart will be subject to many health problems.

Amy Winehouse.
(Credit: Picture Alliance/Photoshot/Bridgeman Images).

Mercury square (*see glossary*) Neptune in Amy's natal chart suggests a gift for creative compositions, images and music. In addition, it also alludes to the idea of escapism (Neptune) through writing (Mercury), which is echoed through the aforementioned contact between Jupiter and Chiron.

In addition, it suggests a gift whereby images and pictures can be painted by sound and/or use of the hands. This is borne out by Amy's ability as a lyricist and guitarist – music was a language that she intuitively understood. She said, "My music is the only area of my life where I'm fully confident, and I fully embrace everything" (Winehouse Estate, 2023, 261).

Earlier on in her career, she was reluctantly persuaded by her management team to stop using the guitar in her stage act, as they felt it was hindering her stagecraft in connecting with her audience – e.g., for not making sufficient eye contact with her audience and turning her back to the spectators. However, publicist Alan Edwards remembers how "She was absolutely lost in the music and avoided much eye contact, but it was a classy and magical performance. One knew one had been in the presence of greatness" (Parry, 2021, page un-numbered).

She cultivated her own iconic image: a great beehive hairstyle with heavy winged black eyeliner, synonymous with the style of the American sixties girl-groups which she was passionate about, such as The Ronettes. She said in an interview that The Ronettes (headed by Ronnie Spector) were her favourite girl-group of all time (*Amy Winehouse: Back to Black*, 2018, DVD). Other female groups from the sixties that she idolised included The Chiffons and The Crystals.

Amy said that what is attractive in a girl is a girl being herself and advised the public, "Don't be one of the crowd – be different" (Parry, 2021, page un-numbered). Indeed, Amy's personal and professional style was distinctive and unique. At times, she could be self-doubting about her looks and said in an interview, "I'm quite an insecure person ... I'm very insecure about the way I look ... The more insecure I feel, the bigger my hair has to be" (referring to her then beehive hairstyle) (*Amy Winehouse: Back to Black*, 2018, DVD).

On stage, Amy was usually bedecked in items such as jeans or shorts or designer dresses with high heels, which she referred to as 'pumps'. She wrote a track called *Fuck Me Pumps*, which appeared on the album *Frank* – a witty song about 'gold-digging' women who rely on their looks to get

Amy at *The Tonight Show* 2007.
(Byline: David Bjerke, Credit © NBC Television/Everett Collection/Bridgeman Images).

by in the world (the term 'fuck me pumps' is a slang expression for sexy women's shoes).

Amy's fifties pin-up girl tattoo was attributed to her late grandmother Cynthia. Other tattoos she had included 'Daddy's Girl', 'Blake', and a bird (and various others), which were also visible and part of Amy's image and self-expression. The ink art also illustrated how important love and family were to her. Tattoo artist Henry Hate inked seven of her fourteen tattoos; he said that "tattooing someone is a very intimate experience, and she told me all kinds of stories … We talked about addiction, and to me she was no different than any other 25-year-old who experimented with some of that stuff" (www.theguardian.com).

Returning again to the astrology and the aspect of the Mercury square Neptune. Another interpretation of it, which is pertinent to Amy, is that at times she could be prone to self-delusion. Mercury is associated with communication; and Neptune with illusion, glamorisation of the facts and distorting reality. The Mars trine Neptune aspect suggests (amongst other things) that Amy may have fantasised about her physical strength, which echoes the message about some of her misplaced confidence. Sun square Neptune in her natal chart can also be an indication of self-deception, which is illustrated in the aforementioned example regarding her health.

Many a time her response in critical situations surrounding her health was "Ah don't worry, I'll be alright," showing denial of the realism as well as absolute self-belief (O'Brien, 2012, 394). Her mother recalled how Amy often said, "Mum, don't worry. I have got this in hand and I have got that in hand." Janis commented that "With Amy, it is a case of we are living in 'Amyland' … It is very surreal" (Barak, 2010, 83).

Anger & Sexism

Author and astrologer Sue Tompkins observed that people with the Mars and Neptune contact in their natal chart, male or female, can often be heard talking about *'real men'* (Tompkins, 1989, 210). This is interesting given that (and as previously noted) Amy wrote the song *Stronger Than Me* from the debut album *Frank*, which was about her then on-off boyfriend Chris Taylor.

The lyrics reveal how she came to the conclusion that he wasn't manly enough for her and how their roles in the relationship had reversed (www.genius.com). The song stirred some controversy for its objectification of gender roles whereby Amy's lyrics insisted that her boyfriend act manlier and tougher (www.genius.com); some of the song's lyrics hold a conservative and sexist attitude towards masculinity and femininity.

In her song, *What Is It About Men*, Amy's lyrics partly draw upon her father's treatment of his wife, Janis, and his affair with Jane (who became his second wife). Janis Winehouse recalled that Amy missed not having her father around and perceived that it may be the reason why there is a lot of anger in her songs (Barak, 2010, 103). The rage, pain and susceptibility in her lyrics indicate some of the Mars and Neptune symbolism.

Venus is trine Neptune in her natal chart and echoes the theme of being a victim of fantasy and delusion. Her desire for love could easily have clouded her vision. It shows her yearning for love; it was like she lived for dreams and romance. Given that Neptune is also associated with addiction and is in the seventh house of her natal chart (the area associated with significant relationships), it could be argued that she was a relationship addict, drifting from one relationship into another.

The aspect between suggests that when it came to romantic relationships, she was in love with being in love and did not find it easy facing the reality of the other person, which included their flaws and imperfections. She may have been prone to idolising the object of her affections, but others may have deemed the individual unworthy of that level of adulation and devotion. This is certainly borne out in her relationship with Blake Fielder-Civil and what her family and close friends thought about him.

Such was Amy's yearning for affection that she may have seen her partner or significant other as a god to be worshipped and whom she placed on a pedestal. The aspect between Venus and Neptune also indicates that she may have seen her partner as a victim to be rescued or saved in some way and, by doing so, may have sacrificed herself for them. Equally, in her dark times she may have been perceived as a person who needed to be rescued or saved.

Her mother once said, "The need to rescue her is enormous … It's a case of where she has to take herself to that edge and say, 'Wow! Enough.'" Janis continued that "control is not possible, and you have just got to go with it" (Barak, 2010, 124). On many occasions she told her daughter, "I can't help you unless you help yourself" (Barak, 2010, 82).

In terms of Amy's capacity for devotion and forgiveness, this certainly manifested in her relationship with Fielder-Civil. Her father commented that "as far as Amy was concerned, Blake could get away with anything" (Winehouse, 2013, 107). His remark arose from the following incident.

Amy Winehouse, Blake Fielder, MTV Movie Awards
(Byline: David Longendyke, Credit Dave Longendyke/ZUMA Wire/Bridgeman Images).

Amy and Blake were at a party for a new fashion range. Amy was late for the event, and when she finally arrived, she found Fielder-Civil was ensconced with a model. Amy and Fielder-Civil had a blazing row in public, and he left the party with the model. He returned alone several hours later, and Amy forgave him (ibid.).

Another example of her refusing to face up to the realities of Fielder-Civil can be seen by the following. After he (and his friend Michael Brown) attacked publican James King, he was arrested and charged with grievous bodily harm with intent. He pleaded not guilty, and the case was transferred to the Crown Court. Amy was petrified that he would be imprisoned and rescheduled some tour dates so that she could be in court with him. Mitchell Winehouse said, "She refused to accept that he was guilty" (Winehouse, 2013, 114).

The fantasy and self-delusion themes seen in the two aspects of Sun square Neptune and Venus trine Neptune allude to the unobtainable, dreaming and yearning for the perceived ideal relationship. When she first got together with Fielder-Civil, he was already in a relationship, and apparently so was Amy.

He returned to his girlfriend, and the situation prompted the devastated Amy to write the song *Back To Black*, which was the title of her second album. Summing up that time, she said, "My ex went back to his girlfriend, and I went back to drinking and dark times" (Barak, 2010, 51).

When Amy was born, the Moon was in Capricorn. The Moon in a natal chart alludes to what nurtures us, reactions and responses, emotions and feelings, mood and sensitivity. It can also provide some insight into our mother and care-giver (as well as our own qualities as a nurturer), family and heritage. It is interesting that Amy's mother was born when the Sun was in Capricorn.

Her mother raised her single-handedly from when she was approximately nine years old; her father took more control of care and attention when Amy was older and dealt with many of the realities she experienced from addiction and bulimia. By this time, Amy's mother had developed multiple sclerosis, which was progressing quickly, and she was physically less able to be around for her daughter than previously. It must have been a challenging and worrying time for Janis Winehouse.

The Moon in Capricorn suggests that if Amy had ever become a mother, she may have been responsible and dutiful. Parenthood may have brought out maturity in her if addiction was not still a major player in her life. Her mother recalled how "Amy had looked out for me from a young age, in particular after the breakdown of my marriage to her father, Mitchell" (Winehouse, 2014, 11). In this situation we can see that Amy instinctively felt that she needed to take on the duty and responsibility of caring for her mother.

The lunar position coupled with the planetary activity in the fourth and fifth houses (associated with family and children, respectively) suggests that Amy may also have brought to her potential parenting role creativity, excitement, sociability, a generosity of spirit, and stimulation. Indeed, she was considered by some colleagues and friends to be motherly. A large group of close friends nicknamed her 'Mum' – Amy recounted that "at least ten of them call me Mum. They text me and say, 'Mummy, are you coming out tonight?'" (Newkey-Burden, 2008, 207).

Adeleye Omotayo, one of her backing singers, remembered that "she was always kind, trying to take care of us" (Parry, 2021, page un-numbered). Her flatmate, the aforementioned Catriona Gourlay, remembered that Amy fed her homemade chicken soup and meatballs (Parry, 2021, page un-numbered). Some American engineers and music recorders in the studio, along with Saalami Remi, also remembered with affection how Amy would make giant meatballs and tea for them (*Amy Winehouse: Back to Black*, DVD, 2018).

Returning to Moon in Capricorn in Amy's natal chart. This position also suggests that she may have been drawn to older people, be they older in years or in experience and wisdom. One obvious personal example of this is with her paternal grandmother, Cynthia. Professionally, she was elated to work with one of her idols from childhood, singer Tony Bennett, who was 57 years her senior.

The lunar position also suggests a need for security and tradition. Janis Winehouse commented that during the time when Cynthia's health was declining fast and her own health was uncertain, Amy's behaviour became more destructive as the family foundation was wavering. She continued that in an attempt to find "someone or something to secure her," sadly the only thing "she found was Blake Fielder-Civil and hard drugs" (Winehouse, 2014, 121).

The Moon is in the seventh house, the area of marriage, significant others and other one-to-one relationships. It suggests that she respected the tradition of marriage and also found herself in situations where one-on-one partnerships were nurturing. Some examples of the latter include working with her producers and collaborating with other singers as part of a duet.

Darcus Beese of *Island Records* observed that whilst Amy was close to her producer, Mark Ronson, it was her other producer, Salaam Remi, who was "a go-to person, kind of a father figure" (*Amy Winehouse: Back to Black*, 2018, DVD). Beese also recalled how Remi was good at getting stuff out of his artist, and that Amy would listen to him as she respected him.

Other engineers who worked with Remi and Winehouse commented on how they both worked in sync together, and Amy said that she and Remi were both insular people and that he helped her to push her creativity (ibid.). Amy's father commented on how Mark Ronson and Amy "inspired each other musically, each bringing out fresh ideas in the other" (Winehouse, 2012, 69).

The freedom and originality that she found in working with Remi and Ronson is a good example of the manifestation of the aspect Jupiter conjunct (*see glossary*) Uranus in the sixth house. Jupiter is associated with exploration and growth, Uranus with breakthroughs and uniqueness, and the sixth house is the area which governs health, work and co-workers.

Another interpretation of the aforementioned aspect which is pertinent to Amy is sudden fame, given that she was catapulted into fame in her early twenties. In the documentary *Amy*, she described fame as being "a scary thing" – this she said previous to her *Back To Black* days.

The Moon in Capricorn also suggests tradition, and some of the rituals that Amy loved included the Jewish custom of the Friday night dinner at Grandma Cynthia's home. The Winehouse family tradition of this meal was chicken soup, followed by roast chicken with roast potatoes, carrots and peas. Dessert was lokshen pudding made with baked noodles and raisins (Winehouse, 2012, 7). Occasionally, one or two of Amy's friends would be invited to the special family meal. For Amy, "being Jewish was all about being together as a real family" (Barak, 2010, 26) and less about being religious.

Being respectful to her family, she would accompany them to synagogue to celebrate Hanukkah (the Festival of Lights), which is in

November and December. Her family also went to the synagogue on Yom Kippur (the Day of Atonement), a one-day Jewish holiday which is the holiest day of the year in Judaism and occurs either in late September or early October.

Janis and Mitchell Winehouse wanted to ensure that their children were culturally aware; Amy attended cheder classes every Saturday, where she learnt about Judaism (Barak, 2010, 26). Traditional Jewish primary schools teach children the basics of Hebrew and Judaism. The word 'cheder' is Hebrew for 'room'.

Amy's family also sang Jewish hymns together, which she enjoyed immensely. When she was a toddler, she would sing and sing at the top of her voice until one of the other family members called out, "OK Amy, enough!" (Winehouse, 2014, 37). One of Amy's favourite hymns was *Ma'oz Tzur*, which means 'stronghold of rock', which references God. Her mother recalled how her daughter would "repeat it over and over again until she got the words right" (Winehouse, 2014, 76). This is another small example of Amy's perfecting nature.

Mr and Mrs Winehouse maintained a Jewish tradition of naming their children with the first letter of the name of a relative who had passed. Janis's grandmother Hannah was also known as Annie, so Amy was named in her memory. Amy's middle name, Jade, was attributed to Mitchell's stepfather, Jack (Winehouse, 2014, 20). Sometimes she wore her gold Star of David necklace, which she was given when she was a baby (Winehouse, 2014, 14), on and off stage. The six-pointed star is a symbol of Judaism and Jewish identity.

She kept her given name and never changed it, not even for a stage name. She was proud of being a Jewish North London girl and would often reference that in interviews. For example, she reflected upon going to drama school and how she had dreamt of going to one for a long time. However, she thought it would never happen to her: "I was a Jewish girl from North London, and things like that don't happen to Jewish girls from North London called Amy Winehouse" (Winehouse Estate, 2023, 54/55).

Her lunar sign, Capricorn, is ruled by the earth element and is associated with areas such as control, order and realism. Where her career was concerned, these characteristics were certainly evident in the earlier years. For example, she asked talent scout Nicky Shamansky to come and manage her and to leave *Brilliant 19* management, where he was contracted.

This was a subsidiary of the management company *19*, which was owned by Simon Fuller, who in the 1990s managed *The Spice Girls*. Shamansky declined, as by his own admission he felt he was insufficiently experienced and knowledgeable to manage her by himself (Winehouse, 2012, 65). In addition, it would have been incredibly disloyal to Fuller (*Amy*, Kapadria, 2015).

Amy objected vehemently to being managed by the aforementioned big money company, whom she perceived as having little regard for her authenticity and song-writing gifts. Being part of a celebrity culture was not for her. She said in the earlier part of her career, "I'm trying to continue being a musician in a time when everyone is very celebrity-led. I'm not Amy the star; I'm Amy the girl with the guitar" (Winehouse Estate, 2023, 242).

The Moon in the seventh house of her natal chart suggests that Amy may have tried to mother her partners and/or looked for maternal qualities in them in order to feel emotionally secure. She told author Daphne Barak that "I constantly want to look after people" (Barak, 2010, 41). An emotionally fulfilling partnership would have been vitally important to her.

The Moon contact with Pluto also suggests that she may have been passionate about being a mother, since some associations of Pluto include obsession and preoccupation. The pairing between the Moon and Saturn also suggests that potentially she could have been a responsible and conventional mother, since these are some of the qualities associated with Saturn.

Self-sacrifice, Compassion & Rescue

This position of the Moon in the area of relationships in her natal chart suggests that at times she may have lost herself in her partner, fitting in with their needs to such an extent that she may have forgotten her own needs. The theme is also connected with the aspect Sun square Neptune of her natal chart. It suggests escaping from the self and, as noted earlier, self-deception. The challenge of the square aspect with Neptune and its contact with the Sun and the Moon also suggests that she battled with what she wanted and what she thought she needed. Confusion, deceit and fantasy were part of the trial.

As previously noted Janis Winehouse recalled that once, when Amy was a teenager, she asked her if she had tried other drugs apart from cannabis. She was horrified when her daughter glibly replied that she had once tried heroin, but it wasn't for her (Winehouse, 2014, 101). However, when she was older, Amy privately and publicly claimed that previously to meeting her then husband-to-be, Blake Fielder-Civil, she had never taken a Class A drug.

After the album *Frank* was released, she would commence a performance at a gig by walking onstage, and as she did so, clapped and chanted, "*Class A drugs are for mugs.*" This she did repeatedly until the audience joined in, and then she would open with the first number of the gig (Winehouse, 2013, 58).

Tyler James recalled that it was soon after Amy and Blake started going out together that Blake introduced her to cocaine and heroin. Her mother commented that her daughter had "some hare-brained romantic notion she wanted to feel like he (Blake) was feeling, but she also needed him to need her." Eventually, she became more dependent on drugs than he was (Winehouse, 2014, 123).

This is one example of how she became lost in her partner and how her own principles regarding hard drugs were abandoned. Once in a relationship, Amy may have become excessively dependent on her partner. This message is echoed by the Moon and Neptune contact in the seventh house, which suggests at times she may have found it challenging to maintain her own boundaries.

Author Daphne Barak described Amy and Blake's partnership as being an "addictive but seemingly destructive relationship," and said that their relationship was "a co-dependency of two addicted people" (Barak, 2010, 62/63).

The Moon and Neptune pairing in her natal chart suggests that she was compassionate and sensitive to suffering. Two examples of this can be seen by the following. One evening when she was in a pub in the ladies' conveniences, she was approached by a woman who asked Amy if she would go and say *hello* to her friend who was a massive fan of hers. She obliged and went and sat down at the table where the woman's friend was. Amy observed that the friend was wheelchair-bound.

Amy spoke with her for a while and asked her if she was struggling financially, knowing full well that she was. Eventually, she ended up giving the stranger all her cash that she had on her (although the woman didn't want to accept it), which amounted to nearly £100, and left Amy with no money to settle her bar bill (Winehouse, 2013, 263/264).

Another example of her caring and generous nature can be seen in the following account. Amy befriended a man in St. Lucia called Julian Jean-Baptiste, whom Amy called George. He was in a desperate situation with his physical health. He had a ruptured hernia and was in agony, but neither he nor his family could afford to pay for medical care, which put his life at risk. He was left writhing on the beach in pain.

When Amy's father arrived on the island with plentiful money to pay various bills etc., Amy told him that they needed to get Julian (George) to hospital and that she would pay for his operation and aftercare. The sum of money that she paid to the hospital approximated to around 5,000 dollars (Winehouse, 2013, 220/221).

A further instance of her sympathy and kindness is borne out by the following example. On the island of St. Lucia, a man owned seven horses which he rented out to tourists so they could ride them up and down on the beach. It came to Amy's attention that the St. Lucian children who regularly played on the beach couldn't afford to rent the horses from the man.

Amy took immediate action; she rented all of his horses weekly from dusk till dawn for a month and let the children of the island ride them for free; she told the man that her father would pay him when he was next at the beach. She was so happy that she was able to help those children; her actions show not only her generosity but also an awareness of the injustice of the poverty on the island (Winehouse, 2013, 221) in taking some practical action.

The Mars trine Neptune aspect in her natal chart, along with Mars sextile the ascendant, indicates that Amy could fight on behalf of the underdog and put her ideals into action; we can see how this was borne out from the aforementioned examples. The aspect is also indicative of her strengths lying in areas such as compassion, empathy, imagination and sensitivity.

Potentially, there could be a sense of her 'emotionally drowning' as these themes are associated with the Moon and Neptune, respectively. However, she was able to offset her feelings through writing poetry and songs. Amy made no secret of the fact that when she was hurt and feeling wounded she would compose songs. Her practical nature (Sun Virgo and Moon Capricorn) illustrates that she was able to do something tangible and channelled those feelings, rather than just flounder with them.

The illusion of family being permanent must have been traumatic for her with at least two life-changing events: the death of her paternal grandmother, and also her father leaving the family home for another woman when she was nine years old.

Death, the Afterlife & Psychic Sensitivity

The Moon sextile Pluto also suggests that Amy had razor-sharp perception and strong gut feelings and hunches, which made her very intuitive and able to read undercurrents in a situation. She once commented, "I trust my instincts, and that's what has got me where I am, y'know?" (Winehouse Estate, 2023, 197).

The 2024 film *Back to Black* illustrates some of Amy's sensitivities in a scene whereby Amy and her father frequented the deceased Cynthia's old haunt, Ronnie Scott's nightclub. In the setting, it distinctly shows Amy sensing her grandmother's spirit and that she could feel Cynthia there. The film's director, Sam Taylor-Johnson, had obviously been made aware of Amy's sensitivities and wanted to share that side of Amy's nature in the film.

Amy owned a set of tarot cards (deck unknown), and she consulted them for her own readings and possibly for others. This was one way for her to channel her intuition and any psychic talents that she may have had. It's probable that Amy's tarot deck was inherited from her grandmother.

Cynthia was adept and experienced at reading tarot cards (Barak, 2010, 160); perhaps in using the tarot deck, it was a way of Amy still feeling connected to her grandmother. It's probable that Amy inherited her knowledge of the tarot from her grandmother. Cynthia was interested in the occult and spiritualism (Winehouse, 2014, 26) and had mediumistic tendencies.

Janis Winehouse recalled that each Tuesday a regular group of people would visit Cynthia at her flat to have tarot readings given by Cynthia, or she would conduct séances. For the latter, the select few would gather in a circle, and the lights were dimmed; they would talk amongst themselves until Cynthia received a message from the spirit world (Winehouse, 2014, 78).

When Amy was approximately four or five years old, one of the communications that Cynthia received was: "Someone always needs to look out for Amy." Janis elaborated that this was just one of several messages that Cynthia received about Amy, all of which advised that her granddaughter needed to be 'looked after' (Winehouse, 2014, 79).

Amy wrote a verse alluding to a sitter having her tarot cards read: *'She sits and knows, The Life she'll lead, She's told her fate, She's yet to be freed'* (Winehouse Estate, 2023, 135).

It appears that both Amy and her father inherited some of Cynthia's psychic abilities. Mitchell commented that Amy was "very spiritual." After his mother died, both he and Amy had a visitation from Cynthia in their dreams. She said the same thing to both of them: "I'm not happy with you" (Barak, 2010, 122/123). Amy's interpretation of her dream was that her grandmother was referring to her drug addiction.

One example of Mitchell's psychic ability can be seen by the following: when he was engaged to Janis, there was a time when she called the engagement off. He was devastated by it, so he decided to make up an excuse and call in sick to work so he could have some time with Janis to discuss their relationship.

The excuse that he made to his employer as to why he would not be going into work that day was that his grandmother had passed away, and on that same day his grandmother had actually passed away, but at the time he made that claim he hadn't been told that. Mitchell acknowledged the seriousness of his words and later said, "You've gotta be careful what you wish for" (Barak, 2010, 22).

Beliefs & Karma

Some insight is provided into Amy's beliefs and spirituality by her following quote: "I believe in fate, and I believe that things happen for a reason, but I don't think that there's a higher power, necessarily. I believe in karma very much, though" (Winehouse Estate, 2023, 125).

Given that Amy had a belief in karma, she may have been interested to know about the astrological karma points in her natal chart. The Moon's Nodes are the points where the Moon crosses the path of the Earth as it orbits the Sun.

The Nodes are karmic points which are believed to give you guidance on how to live your life in order to advance on your spiritual path. The North Node suggests the qualities one should develop, and the South Node qualities one should inhibit. Amy's North Node is in Gemini in the first house, and the South Node is in Sagittarius in the seventh house.

Amy's North Node position suggests that she needed to find a way to fully express herself in her life, uncovering her unique individuality and sharing it with the world – her karmic purpose being to develop herself unselfishly and to be wary about taking on too much.

Astrologer and author Judy Hall observed that many people with the North Node in Gemini "learn to communicate by means of writing for an audience" (Hall, 2006, 112), which is true of Amy's poetry and songwriting.

Her South Node placement suggests that in a previous life she put the needs of others first to the exclusion of her own needs and that being nice or being liked was more important than being true to herself.

Hall also suggested that those with the South Node in Sagittarius would have explored many philosophies and religions and asked innumerable questions. The challenge for those with this position is to be still and listen to the silent voice within that beckons to 'simply be' (Hall, 2006, 115).

The sixth house is the house of health, disease and service. Hall also wrote that when the outer planets are in the sixth house, they are major significators in the karma of disease and reveal the kind of body-karma a soul has around health, be it attitudinal and/or organic.

Amy had four of the five outer planets in the sixth house of her natal chart. Whilst the potential for disease may exist, it doesn't always follow that the disease will manifest, but in Amy's case it did. Hall's observations of those planets in the sixth house and their manifestations are pertinent to what we know of Amy's ill-health and disease (Hall, 2006, 146–147):

- *Jupiter* – karma carried through indulgence and abuse of the body – liver affected.
- *Saturn* – karma carried through depression – through one's own body or another's.
- *Uranus* – karma carried through the nervous system – electrical signals may misfire or chemical production malfunction – seizures.
- *Pluto* – karma carried through addiction.

Leaving the subject of karma now and returning to the subject of Amy and her grandmother Cynthia …

Amy's parents observed how much of a positive influence Cynthia was on Amy, and her father commented that "Amy's behaviour and attitude began to noticeably deteriorate after his mother's death in 2006" (ibid.), and she particularly missed Cynthia during the festive season.

One Christmas, she drank some Night Nurse on top of a large amount of alcohol and was crying hysterically; she sobbed, "I hate Christmas … I hate Christmas since Nan died" (Winehouse, 2014, 235). Janis Winehouse commented that "From a young age, Amy wanted to be like her grandmother, who must have always seemed glamorous and exciting to her." It must have been excruciatingly painful for all the family to see Cynthia deteriorate from lung cancer before she died.

Intensity & Intrusion

The depth of Amy's feelings is emphasised astrologically with the Moon and Pluto contact. The pairing suggests that she had an intense emotional life and that domestic crises were not uncommon (especially with her significant other) and that much was made out of ordinary everyday experiences.

One example of this can be seen where she was persecuted by the gutter press after she became famous and where it became physically apparent that she was an addict. The press permanently camped outside her home to take photographs of her. When she went outside of her front door for basic things, such as going to the local shop, for example, she was hounded by the paparazzi.

The press had violated her privacy for a long time. Reporter Charles Lavery claimed that her telephone and medical records were accessed by tabloid newspapers; however, he did not specify which newspapers did this. He added that they used hacking as a way of obtaining her arrival times at various clinics so that photographers could be called out to secure photographs of her entering and leaving her place of treatment (www.reuters.com/).

Her need (and entitlement) to privacy was such that even when her mother had consulted with Amy about having been approached by a literary agent to consider writing an autobiography, her daughter was vehemently against the idea and protested "Don't do it, Mum … I don't want people to know who I am." At that time, Amy was still alive and Janis Winehouse agreed not to undertake the project, but she did some years later after her daughter had died (Winehouse, 2014, 13).

Amy's father was also the recipient of his daughter's fury when he appeared on the popular morning television programme *GMTV* and participated in an interview about his daughter's drug addiction. His reasoning behind it was not to talk about the specific narcotics that she was addicted to; instead it was to raise awareness of addiction in the hope it would help other families who may also have a family member who is an addict. Mitchell said that there was a positive response from viewers (Winehouse, 2013, 110) and that what he said "helped them feel less isolated" (Winehouse, 2013, 111).

His daughter was in Europe at the time of the interview, but she found out that he had been on television discussing her addiction, and she was infuriated. When he questioned her about what she was so angry about, she said, "Dad, you said it's about a father's struggle to help his daughter or something like that. I don't want you talking about our problems on TV" (ibid.).

Nurturing & Parenting

Daphne Barak spent time interviewing Amy and her parents when they were all in St. Lucia (in approx. 2008/2009) and became aware of the different parenting attitudes that each of them adopted towards their daughter's problems. She commented that there was a controlling element to her father's approach in that he seemed to dedicate his time "to trying to save his daughter from her addictions." Amy's bodyguards were continuously reporting about her whereabouts to her father. In contrast, her mother's take seemed to be "a fatalistic view and her cold acceptance that only Amy can help herself" (Barak, 2010, 47).

Amy's mother jokingly commented that her daughter inherited the worst qualities of her parents, Janis with her "obsessive preoccupation with the world and his (Mitchell's) whirlwind drive and need for control" (Winehouse, 2014, 111).

Reflecting after Amy's death and having worked with children and parents at the Amy Winehouse Foundation, Janis Winehouse observed that "More often than not, parents of addicted children use denial as a coping mechanism before they are ready to face the truth; some never

Amy Winehouse arriving at Westminster Magistrates in London, 2009. (Credit: Associated Press/Alamy).

accept the problem, choosing to cover it up even after the person is dead" (Winehouse, 2014, 100). She finalised "the process of finding your way through the labyrinth of emotions that go hand in hand with coping with addiction is all-consuming" (ibid.).

Returning to the coupling of the Moon and Neptune in Amy's natal chart. There is also symbolism to suggest that Amy may have idolised her mother, as well as perceiving her as a victim. Certainly, she felt sorry for her mother when her father left the family home to live with another woman whom he had been having an affair with for some time.

Janis Winehouse spoke about the relationship breakdown in an interview in 2007: "We'd had a very agreeable marriage, but he was never there. He was a salesman, so he was away a lot, but for a long time there was also another woman, Jane, who became his second wife" (Barak, 2010, 27/28).

Amy penned *What Is It About Men* for the album *Frank*. The song was largely about her feelings towards her father and the breakdown of her parents' marriage. Given her mother's severe ill-health, Amy no doubt felt emotional pain and deeply sorry for her mother, who lives with the chronic autoimmune disease multiple sclerosis (MS), which affects the central nervous system.

Astrologer and author Sue Tompkins wrote about observations she had made surrounding the Moon and Saturn aspect, which are relatable to Amy. Firstly, she observed that there is something of the 'trapped child' within the personality (Tompkins, 1989, 142).

Physical and outward signs of this are borne out with the adult Amy when, at times, for example, she would sit on either her mother's or father's lap. She would suck her thumb, call her parents 'mummy' and 'daddy' and sometimes speak in a young child's voice to them. Mitchell also commented how at times when Amy was either high or drunk, she would call him from her flat, saying that she needed "kisses and cuddles," which he said was a phrase from her childhood (Winehouse, 2013, 125).

The aforementioned author and documentary maker Daphne Barak, who spent time with Amy and her parents in St. Lucia in approximately 2008/2009, wrote the following: "Amy still behaves like that nine-year-old kid, trying to grab her parents' attention. She needs it – craves it" (Barak, 2010, 31). At that time, Amy would have been around 25 years old.

Her mother said of her daughter that although her songs were mature, Amy was immature: "Her songs are very mature, but she is very childish, like 'I don't want to be a woman'" (Barak, 2010, 83). The Moon and Saturn contact illuminates craving nurturing, needing feelings of security (i.e., a family and home), as well as taking emotionality seriously.

Mental Health & Relationship with Food

In addition, astrologer Sue Tompkins observed that some women who had anorexia and bulimia also had the Moon and Saturn contact in their natal chart. The person may have been perceived as denying themselves food, controlling or not controlling their food intake, as well as overeating in an attempt to 'nurture' themselves, compensating for a period in their lives where previously they had not been 'fed' (Tompkins, 1989, 144).

The UK's eating disorder charity, *Beat*, defines bulimia as the following: "A serious mental illness where someone is caught in a cycle of eating large quantities of food and then trying to compensate for that overeating by vomiting, taking laxatives or diuretics, fasting, or exercising excessively" (www.beateatingdisorders.org.uk/).

In November 2006, Amy went on tour in the UK to promote her album *Back To Black*. Sadly, the reviews pivoted on her distinct change of appearance and weight loss; one commented that she had altered from a curvy teen to an "emaciated fitness addict" (Barak, 2010, 57). As ever, and in denial, she blamed her weight loss on her healthier lifestyle, which included going to the gym and having stopped smoking "£200 worth of weed a week; that's two ounces" (Barak, 2010, 56).

She continued drinking alcohol and freely admitted that her relationship with her then boyfriend, Alex Claire, made her aware that "she was a bad and violent drunk" (Barak, 2010, 57). She admitted punching Fielder-Civil too when she was drunk. Winehouse told *Bizarre* magazine in 2007: "I'll beat up Blake when I'm drunk … If he says one thing I don't like, then I'll chin him" (www.theguardian.com). Her relationship with Fielder-Civil has been described as a "tempestuous and often violent six-year on-off relationship" (www.standard.co.uk).

Amy had a hot temper as early as her schooldays, which she wrote about whilst she was still at school: "I hate my temper. At times it eats away at me so much that I get physically violent with those I love; however much I say 'I'm sorry', they can never forget." She revealed that it was little things that annoyed her and that she had to literally lie down to calm herself (Winehouse Foundation, 2023, 173).

In her natal chart, the position of Mars in Leo alludes to some anger issues, by virtue of Mars and Leo both being ruled by the fire element; this placement, amongst other things, is associated with enragement and fury.

When Amy first left home, she announced to her mother, "I've got this amazing new diet," and when Janis questioned her about it, her daughter laughingly replied, "It's called eating and throwing up!" (Winehouse, 2014, 131). She recalled how Amy gleefully explained to her, "Well, you get the food, and you chew it and get the taste of it; then you swallow the taste and spit it (the food) out" (Barak, 2010, 52).

By 2006, and after Cynthia's death, Janis observed just how thin Amy had become. She was reluctant to speak with her mother about her weight loss, and all that she would say to her was, "I'm dealing with it, Mummy; it's fine" (ibid.). Her mother commented that Amy's bulimia was never formally diagnosed throughout her life (Winehouse, 2014, 130). Her father tried in vain many times to seek treatment for her bulimia. He eventually sought counselling for her, and then for a short while in 2006 she was in therapy with an addiction counsellor (Barak, 2010, 53).

During his imprisonment, her husband, Blake Fielder-Civil, tried to support her, albeit from prison. Apparently, in a telephone call, he told her, "… you're taking drugs, not eating, and now you're fainting. You've got to eat properly and stop sticking your finger down your throat. Bulimia's taking a terrible toll on you" (Newkey-Burden, 2008, 189).

Medical Astrology and the Sixth House

Saturn in the sixth house of Amy's natal chart indicates that challenges and issues may have arisen in the area of health and the efficient functioning of the body. One of her health problems was related to depression, which is associated with Saturn in medical astrology. We know that as a teenager she took antidepressants; Nick Shamansky recognised it particularly after the *Frank* album tour had finished – he noted how she was depressed and melancholy (*Amy Winehouse: Back to Black*, DVD, 2018).

Reflecting upon her depression when she was younger, she commented, "I don't think I knew what depression was. I knew I felt funny sometimes, and I was different." She recognised that she was lucky in having a creative outlet through music to help channel her depression, and she commented that not everybody living with depression has a vent for it (Winehouse Estate, 2023, 249). She also said, "If I didn't have this medium to get my experiences across, I would be lost" (Winehouse Estate, 2023, 183).

Other Saturnian areas in medical astrology include the bones, joints, knees and the skin. Certainly, this was palpable when, at the height of her addiction, she had problems with her skin and teeth, and through weight loss her frame had diminished to a size 6 and she was able to fit into children's clothes (Winehouse, 2014, 216).

Saturn is in Scorpio in Amy's natal chart and indicates that she may have had some emotional problems and kept them well hidden from others. So much so that at times she could be difficult to help, through fear of opening up. One example of this can be seen through her addiction and reluctance to go to rehabilitation, the situation she wrote about in the legendary song, *Rehab*.

Counselling is often a core component in recovery programmes, and Amy vehemently believed that she did not need that element of therapy. Even her last doctor (Dr. Romete) revealed that Amy declined any psychological help and attributed it to Amy's fear that it would stifle her artistic expression. Amy wanted control over her life and treatment; Dr. Romente commented, "She was very determined to do everything her way, including her therapy. She had very strict views on that." (www.express.co.uk).

The contact between Saturn and Pluto in the sixth house suggests that Amy may have had a fear of death and also authority. This is because Saturn is associated with trepidation and Pluto with fatality and power. Both Saturn and Pluto are associated with life cycles and death. Compulsive behaviour and hard-to-break habits, as well as intense self-discipline and controlled use of power, are also possibilities of the Saturn conjunct Pluto aspect.

The planetary contact between these two planets can also be interpreted as a distrust of those in authority, which was certainly borne out in Amy's life through her attitude towards some executives in the music business, as well as in the formality of conventional education. Her father commented that his daughter "had a thirst for knowledge but hated school" (Winehouse, 2012, 19).

Another interpretation of the Saturn and Pluto conjunction includes lessons of survival, and given their position in the sixth house (the area of health and work), makes the explanation of the pairing between Saturn and Pluto more poignant when we consider that Amy nearly died from addiction-related ill-health and bulimia on more than one occasion.

Jupiter in Sagittarius positioned in the sixth house suggests that finding the right work for her was particularly essential to her happiness and that she could also foster cordial relationships with her colleagues. Given that the sixth house is also associated with health matters and Jupiter qualities of abundance, the advice given to her would be that she should avoid excesses. Sadly, we know that this did not happen in some areas of her life.

The natural position of Jupiter in Sagittarius indicates a generous, optimistic and philosophical slant to her nature; she may also have been drawn to different cultures and foreign travel, as these are also correspondences of Jupiter and Sagittarius. Aside from the foreign travel she experienced as an adult, she was also privileged as a child to travel abroad with family members; she visited places such as Cyprus, Florida and Paris.

Her philosophical nature is illustrated by the following quote, albeit ironic: "Life is short. Anything could happen, and it usually does, so there is no point in sitting around thinking about all the ifs and buts" (Winehouse Estate, 2023, 76).

Healing & Spirituality

In astrology, the asteroid Chiron in one's natal chart represents 'The Wounded Healer'. It is believed to help a person understand their deepest wounds and encourage them to try and heal the difficult aspects of their life, namely from their childhood. Amy's natal chart reveals that Chiron was positioned in the sign of Gemini in the twelfth house.

Chiron in Gemini suggests the core of her wound which needed to heal was in some of the following areas: communication, disruption in schooling, perception, a fear of being misunderstood, as well as struggling to be heard.

Mercury, Gemini's ruler, is also associated with guile, trickery and wiliness; it is interesting, therefore, that her father commented how as a child Amy "would know how to pull everyone's chain … She was quite clever, and she knew how to kind of manipulate people. But in a nice way" (Barak, 2010, 25).

Aged thirteen, Amy wrote, "All my life I have been loud, to the point of being told to shut up. The only reason I have to be loud is because you have to scream to be heard in my family" (Barak, 2010, 35). Being listened to is one thing, but being *heard* is something quite different. Chiron in Gemini includes making oneself heard, as well as speaking one's truths.

These areas may have seeped into areas such as her career, education (of which there were numerous schools), and social self-esteem. Amy wrote that when she was at school, she was aware of how people perceived her, and in her eyes it was because people were happy to think that she was "the nutter of the class" (Winehouse Estates, 2023, 173).

She described herself as being "a little eccentric and loud, weird also." She continued that she was pleased to be different: "I love having my own individual style. I love being loud and mouthing off to people; it's the way I am (ibid.). Amy recognised that she behaved differently at school than she did at home and saw it as a flawed way to be. She wrote, "… will somebody tell me why the hell I'm so different at school than I am at home? To me that's a bad thing" (ibid.).

Her recognition of herself as being different, creative and unique is symbolic of the characteristics associated with the Aquarius MC (Midheaven) and Leo IC. The MC is indicative of one's career-calling and vocation, and the IC is associated with heritage and roots. Certainly, she was distinctive and independent in the outside world and came from a family of creatives, e.g., her paternal grandmother Cynthia, her father, and jazz musicians in her mother's family.

The Leo IC also suggests that in her family there was plenty of entertainment and laughter, as well as commotion and drama in her own home when she was an adult. Uranus, the ruling planet of Amy's MC, is associated with rebelliousness, shocks and unpredictability. Amy gave her family and friends, fans and work colleagues plenty of this, especially when she became ill with a high level of addiction. Janis Winehouse's family nicknamed Amy '*Nooge*', which apparently is a Yiddish word and means Amy was always pushing the boundaries (Winehouse, 2023, 37).

Returning to Chiron again. Positioned in the twelfth house, it suggests that the wounding comes from a loss of union with the divine and that healing can take place if one is able to recognise oneself as divine and integrate that into everyday life.

We know about some of Amy's spirituality and that she had psychic and vivid dreams, as well as a strongly developed intuition. During her darkest times of addiction, and as part of trying to heal from that, she practiced yoga – at least for a short while. Participating in yoga would have involved breathing exercises and meditation, as well as specific physical posturing to help with her health and well-being.

Transpersonal sources, which involve esoteric mental experiences (such as meditation), could have helped Amy enormously in a creative and healing way, especially if she made it part of her daily routine. Altered states of consciousness she found through alcohol consumption and drug-taking, which quickly became an addiction.

Amy said that she did not believe in a higher force but did believe in fate and karma; she also honoured some of her family's rituals of Judaism, although she was not religious per se. The loss of union with any spark of divinity that she may have had possibly arose from her addictions. She may have no longer listened to her inner voice, the sacred voice that is without sound and which is present in each of us, along with our unique spiritual light.

In other words, she probably stopped listening to her higher self when the disease took over, partly because she was unable to due to the inner and physical effects. The twelfth house is also associated with institutions, and we know that Amy spent some time in hospitals and rehabilitation clinics and also had a private doctor visit her at home.

Potentially, she had the capacity to be able to help others heal, and she recognised this through her song-writing. Her curiosity, observation and communication skills are ideal qualities for being a healer, coupled with her brilliance and originality, as well as ceaseless probing and questioning, which may have taken her into areas where others may have feared to tread.

The Sun in Virgo, along with Jupiter, Saturn, Pluto and Uranus in the sixth house, the area of health and service, as well as Jupiter opposing Chiron, provides some indication that had she still been alive, Amy may have chosen to work in some form of healthcare and service.

Possibly she would have worked with younger people, given the strong Mercury energy in her natal chart. Certainly, her legacy through the Amy Winehouse Foundation echoes this possibility.

Closing the Gig

On the 23rd July 2011 (the day she died), there were two transiting (*see glossary*) planets and the asteroid Chiron aspecting natal planets in the sixth house of Amy's natal chart, which are of astrological interest and listed below. As previously noted, the sixth house is associated with health/ill-health, service and work.

- Transiting Uranus trine natal Jupiter
- Transiting Uranus trine natal Uranus
- Transiting Neptune trine natal Saturn
- Transiting Chiron square natal Jupiter
- Transiting Chiron square natal Uranus

At Amy's inquest, the Deputy Coroner, Suzanne Greenaway, concluded that Amy Winehouse died from alcohol poisoning and labelled the cause of death as misadventure (www.express.co.uk).

Transiting Uranus was at the eleventh house of her natal chart, the area associated with community, friends, groups, kindred spirits and projects. Uranus is associated with, amongst other things, shocks, accidents and suddenness. When she was found dead at her flat, the Camden Square community were indeed shocked when they saw her tiny lifeless body being brought out on a stretcher by the emergency services. She was pronounced dead at the scene when police first arrived at her home. The road was blocked off by police; fans and locals were captured on camera displaying their grief and upset, and they left candles, flowers and notes of disbelief and sorrow.

The transiting planets provide some astrological insight as to what was happening leading up to the period before Amy's death. Transiting Uranus trine natal Jupiter suggests that she was looking for new involvements with spiritual teachings and searching for new approaches to life; quite possibly this would have led to her being less materialistic.

Transiting Uranus trine natal Uranus suggests that she was looking to liberate herself from previous restrictions that were imposed upon her – freedom was everything. Amy may well have had a 'wake-up call' and experienced enlightenment as far as her health was concerned. She had freed herself from drug abuse but was still battling with alcohol dependency.

In terms of relationships, she may have been looking for new relationships which would better fit her needs. As far as we know, she seemed very happy with her new partner, Reg Traviss, and they had discussed marriage and having children, something she had dreamt of for a long while, even before she knew him.

Transiting Neptune was at the tenth house of Amy's natal chart on the 23rd July 2011. This area is associated with career, status and reputation. Like the other planets, Neptune has multiple correspondences. Some interpretations of transiting Neptune at the tenth house include the following: any vision of where she was heading career-wise may have been clouded, for she may have felt disappointed and disillusioned. At some point, she may have got confused and lost in any dreams about her future. Her reputation may have become cloaked in gossip and scandal, and she may have lost any respect that the media and some members of society once held for her.

Interestingly, Neptune also governs the following areas, which are relatable to Amy: alcohol, drugs, addiction, healing, poison, glamour, fashion, loss, sacrifice, pain, empathy, forgiveness, suffering, vulnerability and withdrawal.

The Neptune aspect created at the sixth house was transiting Neptune trine Saturn. Amongst other things, it can signify dreams versus reality time; equally, it could be seen as a dream coming to reality. Because of her vast experience, particularly in the area of health and ill-health, she may have come to the realisation of what she did and didn't need. Possibly, she thought that work was her best escape; working on her ill-health would certainly have given her a framework and structure to work within.

Chiron (the Wounded Healer) was transiting the tenth house and was square the natal Jupiter and Uranus in the sixth house. Possibly, she felt some constraints and tensions in a desire to expand her mind and follow her beliefs and ideals; part of this may have arisen from past traumas and wounds which were unresolved.

Amy Winehouse.
(Photo © Imago/Bridgeman Images).

The second transiting Chiron aspect is Chiron square natal Uranus; it suggests that potentially for her it was a time of putting past wounds into a new perspective. There may also have been a dramatic change of heart around this period; there may have been unexpected shocks and surprises and a time of major emotional triggers. This is borne out by her having entered a period of considerable sobriety, but then Amy relapsed just days before her untimely passing. She confessed this to her doctor, Christine Romete, on that night, just hours before her fatal drinking spree. Romete recalled their conversation and how Amy was "calm and somewhat guilty", as well as being "slightly intoxicated but still capable of engaging in conversation." It was during their final conversation that Amy realised the enormity of the situation and said to Romete, "I don't want to die" (www.express.co.uk/).

At the inquest, Suzanne Greenaway said of Amy that "She had consumed sufficient alcohol, and the unintended consequence of such potentially fatal levels was her sudden and expected death." The court also heard how Amy's blood contained 416mg of alcohol per 100ml, surpassing the lethal threshold of 350mg.

The influential and tragic legacy of Amy Winehouse reigns. She was one of the best vocalists of her generation, and she inspired many other artists, musicians, singers and song-writers, such as Adele and Lady Gaga. However, her accomplishments are/were largely overshadowed by a focus on her personal-life struggles, which included addiction.

Her authentic performances, sung with raw honesty and technical skill, were punctuated by her soulful voice, which had emotional depth. Her distinctive appearance, personality and style (which included retro fashions mainly of the 1950s and 60s) left an impact on those in the music industry, as well as fans around the world and her appearance and sound were instantly recognisable.

In her twenty-seven years of life, she became many things to many people: artist, fashion designer and icon, guitarist, poet, singer, award-winning song-writer and wordsmith. In her personal life, she was a granddaughter, daughter, sister, cousin, niece, friend, girlfriend, and wife, and probably a whole lot more to many people.

Amy's legacy lives on through her music, as well as the work of the Amy Winehouse Foundation, and through all those lives she touched on a personal and professional level.

CHAPTER TWO

Jimi Hendrix

Jimi Hendrix, c. 1967.
(Everett Collection/Bridgeman Images).

PART 1
THE STORY OF JIMI HENDRIX

Singer, Guitarist & Song-writer
(1942–1970)

"He was not only a brilliant and innovative player, but a riveting performer, and he took the Old World by storm."

– Eric Burdon.

Heritage

John (aka 'Johnny') Allen Hendrix (Hendrix/Mitchell, 2012, 6), who found fame in the spotlight as Jimi Hendrix, was born on Friday 27th November 1942 at 10.15am in Seattle, Washington, USA, at the King County Hospital (www.seattletimes.com/www.astro.com/databank).

His parents were Lucille Jeter Hendrix, born 12th October 1925, and James Allen Hendrix (aka 'Al') born on 10th June 1919. The couple first met at the house of a friend of Lucille's, and they went on to a local dance where jazz pianist Fats Waller was playing. The pair connected instantly, as both of them were passionate about dancing (as well as drinking). Al had found his perfect dance partner in the tiny Lucille, who was a jitterbugging whirlwind, as well as a talented singer.

Al was born to Bertran Philander Ross Hendricks (aka 'Ross') and Nora Rose Moore. Bertran was illegitimate; his mother was a woman of biracial heritage (black and white lineage) named Fanny. She was a former slave to a white merchant who once owned her. When Ross was born, on 11th April 1866, in Ohio, his mother was 40 years old and living alone (Cross, 2005, 16).

Bertran Philander Ross Hendricks Junior was named after his father. Bertran Senior's occupation is listed in the Census for 1870 as being a grain dealer with real estate valued at $135,000. Fanny's son gained no material privileges from his father (Shapiro & Glebbeek, 1991, 11).

Her son was formerly a special constable in the Chicago police (Shapiro & Glebbeek, 1991, 8). He made a distinct career change and joined a travelling vaudeville troupe called the *Great Dixieland Spectacle*, where he was employed as a stagehand (www.seattletimes.com).

The group performed in the *Alaska-Yukon-Pacific Exposition* (a global fair held in Seattle). There he met Nora Rose Moore, who was a dancer. Her father, Robert Moore, was Irish, and her mother, Fanny, was a full-blooded Cherokee princess; Nora Rose was born on 19th November 1883, and she was John/Jimi's paternal grandmother. Her birth name was Zenora, but everyone called her Nora (Hendrix, 2012, 32).

In approximately 1911, Nora Rose and her husband, Ross, gave up show business. They were tired of travelling and living out of suitcases. They decided to look for other opportunities and settled in Vancouver, British Columbia, where they raised a family. They had three sons and a daughter: Leon Marshall was born in 1913, Patricia in 1914, Frank in

1918, and James Allen (Al), the youngest, was born on 10th June 1919 (ibid.). In 1912, Ross changed his name and shortened Hendricks to Hendrix (Cross, 2005, 16).

Al Hendrix was raised in Vancouver and travelled to Seattle in 1940, aged approximately 21 years old. His employment included working in a nightclub and shining shoes, and he also undertook manual work at an iron foundry (www.seattletimes.com). Al inherited his love for dance from his mother, Nora, and his brother Leon.

Lucille (Jeter) Hendrix's parents were Preston Jeter and his wife, Clarice (née Lawson), and there was a nineteen-year age gap between the couple. They met and married later in 1915, and their marriage lasted 30 years. Before she married Preston, Clarice had been on a journey with her sisters to cotton-pick and was sexually assaulted, which resulted in pregnancy. She bore the child, and it was adopted (Cross, 2005, 12).

Preston came from Richmond, Virginia, and he worked as a docker and a coal miner near Whitesville, south of Charleston. He fled to Boston after an altercation with some local rednecks, which was racially motivated. He eventually settled in Washington State, where he worked in the mines (Cross, 2005, 11) and later worked as a landscaper.

Clarice worked in domestic service as a nanny, just as she and Preston were starting a family of their own. During the span of ten years, Clarice gave birth to ten children, two of whom died in infancy and two were adopted. Lucille was the Jeter's youngest child, born on 17th January 1894, in Little Rock, Arkansas. Clarice remained in hospital for six months after the birth of Lucille; this was due to complications from a tumour, as well as postnatal depression (Cross, 2005, 14).

By this time, Preston was 50 years old and living with his own health challenges, so the Jeter's other three daughters, Delores, Gertrude and Nancy, helped to raise their newborn sister. Sadly, Clarice faced further mental and physical health problems, and during this time the children were fostered to a big German family who lived in a predominately white area where, apparently, the Jeters were mistaken for gypsies (ibid.). However, by the time Lucille was ten years old, the family had been reunited again.

Returning again to Al Hendrix and Lucille – there was no time for the couple to enjoy a prolonged courtship, as there was apprehension and fear about what would happen next after the declaration of World War

II. After the Japanese bombed Pearl Harbour in December of 1941, Al received his draft papers from the American government in early 1942. The pair married on March 31st of 1942, six months before John (Jimi) Allen was born; his mother was just seventeen, and Al was 22 years old. They didn't even have the opportunity to co-habit before Al went into service.

He undertook his basic training in Oklahoma, then was sent to Fort Benning in Georgia, and by the time his son was born, Al was in military prison in Alabama. This was because although he was entitled to formal leave for the birth of his son, his superiors had denied him the opportunity to do so; the reason given was that his home was too far away.

He was angered by this, and the officers thought that he may try to escape. When he asked his sergeant why he was put in prison, the reply was "general principles" (Shapiro & Glebbeek, 1991, 13). Al commented that he was locked up for two months without trial, with no loss of pay, but he was denied the freedom to prevent him from going AWOL (absent without leave) to see his son.

Lucille had been living at home for part of her pregnancy but later lodged with Dorothy Harding, who was a friend of her sister, Dolores. Eventually, Lucille and her son had to move from there, as there was insufficient space. From there, she moved from one bedsit to another, as well as various hotel rooms.

In 1943, Lucille's father died, and her mother sold the family home to be with Lucille and help assist in raising her grandson. Lucille received no money from Al for nearly a year after he had been draughted into service; this was due to an administrative fault by the army. She tried to survive by waitressing; however, when she finally received money from Al, she was indebted to so many people that once she repaid them, the money had virtually disappeared (Shapiro & Glebbeek, 1991, 14).

The free-spirited Lucille was not cut out for playing the dutiful and faithful wife, waiting for her man to return from war. She was determined to still have a good time around the dance halls and nightclubs in Seattle; in addition, she became a hard drinker. She was unable to care for her child, and the care of her newborn son John/Johnny largely became the responsibility of her parents and various unofficial guardians.

For another short period, Johnny came under the care of a woman called Mrs Walls, until she unexpectedly died. Fortunately, Mrs Walls' sister, Mrs Champ, took responsibility of Johnny and took him back to her home in Berkeley, California. She wrote to Al Hendrix and informed him of the situation (Hendrix, 2012, 7).

Lucille was often seen in the company of a man called John Williams, who had moved from Kansas City to Seattle to work on the docks. The aforementioned Dorothy Harding described Williams as "a slime" (Shapiro & Glebbeek, 1991, 16). He mistreated Lucille and abused her physically; on one occasion she was taken to hospital after being savagely beaten by him. It was difficult for Dolores and Mr and Mrs Jeter to keep track of Lucille and their grandson's whereabouts, for Williams would take them all over the country with him.

At one point John, Lucille and Johnny were living on a housing estate in challenging conditions; her family tried to persuade her to return home with them, but Lucille insisted on remaining there with Williams and her baby. However, being moved from one cold and damp lodging to another took its toll on baby Johnny's health, and he contracted pneumonia (ibid.).

There was another occasion when Lucille had abandoned and neglected her baby, during the winter of 1942. Her mother was forced to visit her employer (who was like a friend to Mrs Jeter) with two-week-old baby Johnny. She had to make the visit to her because she had no nappies or bottle for the newborn.

She took the baby out in the freezing cold in a tiny blanket, and her employer scolded her for inadequately covering the infant. Johnny had wet himself, and such was the bitter cold that the nappy he was wearing had frozen and the urine had marked his skin (Shapiro & Glebbeek, 1991, 15).

Johnny Allen Hendrix had other names too. Approximately four years after he was born, his father legally altered his son's name to James Marshall Hendrix; the name 'Marshall' was in honour of Al's brother, Leon Marshall, who died in 1932.

This was when Al returned from the war in September of 1945, and he collected his son from Berkeley and took him back to Seattle with him. It was believed that Al wanted to change his son's name from John to James, as the name reminded him of the aforementioned John Williams, whom his wife had had an affair with (Shapiro & Glebbeek, 1991, 19).

It must have been a bewildering time for Johnny/Jimmy when Al Hendrix came to collect him from Mrs Champ and announced to his son that he was his father and that he was taking him away. Essentially, his father was but a stranger to him at that time. Being uprooted and taken away from the family where he had experienced routine and security must have been puzzling and upsetting for the young child.

Unaware of his wife's whereabouts, Al, now a single father, rented a flat in Seattle for a short while; that was until Lucille discovered where he was living, and then the three of them moved into Dolores' (her 'sister') flat. Al and Lucille were living together for the first time and were happy; they went out every night and enjoyed themselves. Dolores commented that she believed that "it was the only good life that Jimmy enjoyed. He had love and affection, and we were like one big happy family" (ibid.).

The family referred to Jimmy occasionally as "young Jimmy"; however, the child insisted on being called *Buster*. This was in admiration of the American actor, Buster Crabbe, whom he saw playing the leading man in the film serials of *Flash Gordon* at the cinema.

The young and indignant child refused at first to be called Jimmy; he found it confusing, having previously learnt to spell and write his name as 'Johnny'. Father and son used to row relentlessly about the child's name no longer being Johnny.

In the end, an alternative name was found – it was *Buster*, as it was obvious that his father would never agree to him being called Johnny again. However, as *Buster* grew older and felt more secure with himself and his environment, he became accepting of being called Jimmy (Hendrix, 2012, 10).

Later in his life, there came another modification in Jimmy's name; this was when he became prominent in the entertainment business in the UK. In 1966, his management, Chas Chandler & Mike Jeffery, decided that their client should drop the spelling of *Jimmy* and instead use the name *Jimi* – as in the stage name, *The Jimi Hendrix Experience*; the pair believed it looked and sounded more exotic. The other members of *Jimi's* band were Mitch Mitchell (drummer) and Noel Redding (bassist).

From here onwards, *John/Johnny/Jimmy* shall primarily be referred to as *Jimi*.

In 1947, Mr and Mrs Al Hendrix had secured their own rented property on an estate called the Rainier Vista Housing Project. A year later, on the 13th of January 1948, another son was born to Lucille and Al; they named him Leon Morris. Al found employment in a variety of low-paid jobs, as well as living off his army pension (Shapiro & Glebbeek, 1991, 20).

Leon recalled that when he was approximately two years old, his parents used to have parties daily in the family home, and when it got too crowded, he and his elder brother were instructed to go out and play. He commented that his mother and father were big drinkers, but once the alcohol wore off, then "life became a completely different reality. That's when the shouting and cussing started" (Hendrix, 2012, 5). As well as being a big drinker, Al also became a gambler, which sometimes was at the detriment of his children.

Al's niece's husband, Frank Hatcher, recalled that in 1953 Al asked them to live with him and take care of his children. "He just couldn't do it himself. He was drinking a lot, and gambling, and a lot of times he didn't even come home." For a short while, Mr and Mrs Hatcher were effectively the boy's parents; Grace Hatcher became one of his many mother figures (Cross, 2005, 41).

Domesticity and family life were stifling and unfulfilling for Lucille. At every opportunity, she would leave Jimmy and Leon in the care of her mother. She sought the highlife when and where she could, drinking and disappearing for days on end. Al frequently had to go looking for her, sometimes accompanied by his two sons; on occasion, she was found with other men (ibid.).

Nearly one year later, after Leon was born, another son, Joseph Allen, arrived; he was born with serious health problems, which included a cleft palate and one leg shorter than the other, and he also had a clubfoot (Hendrix, 2012, 8/9). He remained with his family for three years until they realised that the only way that their child could get the essential medical attention that he needed would be if they placed him into foster care – and that was what happened in the summer of 1952 (Hendrix, 2012, 13).

Earlier, in the autumn of 1950, Lucille gave birth to a daughter, who was born blind and was four months premature. She was named Cathy Ira; eventually, she was placed into foster care. Then, on 27th October 1951, Lucille gave birth to another daughter, whom she named Pamela Marguerite. Eventually, she was also placed into foster care (Hendrix,

2012, 9). The two daughters were born to Lucille before the divorce to Al came through in 1951 (Shapiro & Glebbeek, 1991, 22), and Al was cited as the father on both their birth certificates. After Lucille left Al, she bore another child, who was named Alfred (Shapiro & Glebbeek, 1991, 29).

Jimi Hendrix was fifteen when his mother died. Lucille (Jeter) Hendrix died on 2nd February, 1958, aged 32, in Seattle, King County, Washington. She died of cirrhosis of the liver and a ruptured spleen. Her ill-health and death were related to her years of alcohol abuse (www.findagrave.com).

In approximately 1966, Ayako ('June') Fujita met Al Hendrix through a mutual friend, Dolores Kurber. Ayako called herself June, as she was born in June, and in addition, people found it difficult to pronounce her name. She had five children from a previous marriage; four of them were all grown up, and Janie was the youngest, aged three years old. The couple married, and Al adopted Janie. In approximately 1986, Al and June amicably separated. Then, several years later, June died in 1999 (www.historylink.org).

Al Hendrix, Jimi's father, died on 17th April 2002, aged 82, in Renton, Seattle, Washington (ibid.). He died from congestive heart failure in Seattle (www.latimes.com). Al was 38 when Jimi's mother died, and 50 years old when Jimi died. Al was survived by his son, Leon, and daughter, Janie.

In 1995, Jimi's father established the *Experience Hendrix* and *Authentic Hendrix*. Today, it is known as *Experience Hendrix L.C.C.* and *Authentic Hendrix LCC*. After Al Hendrix's death, Janie Hendrix became fundamental in preserving Jimi's legacy; she is the president and CEO of the companies (www.jimihendrix.com). Janie L. Hendrix is also the president of JMH Productions (www.linkedin.com).

Leon Hendrix became an artist, musician and song-writer and produced multiple albums. In 2012, his autobiography (with Adam Mitchell) was published by Thomas Dunne Books, titled *Jimi Hendrix: A Brother's Story*, which he dedicated to his mother, Lucille Jeter Hendrix.

Education

Like Jimi's ever-changing home life, his education took place in various schools. It started in Seattle, then in Vancouver in British Columbia, and then again in Seattle; he also attended Sunday school in Seattle. When he returned to Seattle from Vancouver, he first attended Rainier Vista School and then Horace Mann Elementary School (Shapiro & Glebbeek, 1991, 24). Then he attended Garfield High School; it was multicultural, which included students from Chinese, Filipino, and Puerto Rican backgrounds.

Jimi excelled in art (particularly abstract art) and poetry; he mainly wrote poems about the natural world, and he did well, securing A and B grades. However, he was frustrated at school and left early, aged seventeen. He worked hard for a while with his father, who at that time was a landscape gardener. He stopped after a while, as Al wouldn't pay him for his labour. Jimi didn't see why he should be undertaking back-breaking manual work and not get paid for it. It's possible that his father was being frugal because of the poverty that the family was experiencing. Although he was employed, it was low-paid work, and it was extremely difficult to manage the cost of living.

Significant Relationships

Jimi was rarely without female company, be they confidantes, dalliances or live-in girlfriends. The key women most associated with Jimi appear to have been Betty Jean Morgan, Linda Keith, Kathy Etchingham, Sharon Lawrence, Devon Wilson and Monika Dannemann.

Betty Jean Morgan was also a pupil at Garfield High School, which is where she and Jimi met. She had been raised in the South and had a very thick Southern accent, which for African Americans was uncommon in Seattle. Her parents were conventional and insisted that if Jimi wanted to date their daughter, he must ask their permission first, which he did.

They liked Jimi because he was polite, and the couple started dating in the autumn of 1959 – the season when Jimi turned seventeen. In an effort to further impress Betty Jean, he would strum his Danelectro Silvertone guitar on the family's porch (Cross, 2005, 70). Originally, the guitar was white, but he painted it red and wrote the name *'Betty Jean'* on the front of the guitar (Cross, 2005, 73).

Betty Jean described how at that time Jimi "was a sweetheart" and how he adored Betty Jean's mother (ibid.). Leon Hendrix dated Betty Jean's younger sister, who was called Mattie B. (Hendrix, 2012, 84). He described Betty Jean as being the love of Jimi's life, and "the two of them were together constantly" (ibid.).

However, in May 1961, Jimi and a group of friends were hanging around with a stolen car and were joyriding. The Seattle Police Department arrested everyone and took them to the local detention centre. Jimi was released but was petrified at the thought of attending court the following week and what sentence the judge may give him.

Jimi had always been fascinated with the special *Screaming Eagle* patch worn by the military of the 101st Airborne Division. They were a light infantry of the United States Army which specialised in air assault operations; their patch emblem depicted an American bald eagle. The *Screaming Eagles* was made up of paratroopers and glider men (home.army.mil).

When the time came for Jimi to be sentenced, he was given the choice of going into the army or prison; he decided on the former and avoided a two-year prison sentence. It was agreed by the court that he could join the 101st Airborne Division.

The previous night, before Jimi was set to officially join the army, he proposed to Betty Jean at a dance. She agreed to marry him, and he gave her a cheap rhinestone engagement ring. The plan was for him to return from his eight-week basic army training in Fort Ord, California, and then they would marry. In 1961, he was Private James Marshall Hendrix of the U.S. Army Infantry Training Centre, 11th Battle Group, 3rd Brigade, Fort Ord, California (Roby & Schreiber, 2010, 2, plate 1).

Whilst he was in the army, Jimi wrote regularly to his father and usually to Betty Jean. He sent her money in his letters and penned a poem to her called '*Sweetheart*', and he inscribed it: "From the one who will always love you truly" (Cross, 2005, 92).

The first time that Jimi was home on leave, Leon described his brother's appearance: "… his carefully pressed army uniform and shined black shoes; I couldn't have been prouder. His hair was buzzed short, and all of his clothes were clean and neatly pressed" (Hendrix, 2012, 96).

By March of 1962, Jimi's respect for his division was waning. Mainly, he claimed, because they wouldn't let him play his guitar whenever he wanted to, particularly at weekends. The passion to play music was too strong for him, and he concocted a story which he knew would release him from the army.

Part of his bluff to ensure that he was released from the army included telling them that he had homosexual tendencies and masturbated, and

Jimi Hendrix – American Rock musician during his enlistment with the US Army in 1961. (Credit Pictorial Press Ltd./Alamy).

also that he experienced dizziness, pain and pressure in the left chest, and insomnia.

Eventually, they recommended that Jimi be released, and he was discharged in July, 1962. This was on account of his "homosexual tendencies" (Cross, 2005, 94). Jimi never told anyone the real reason the army dismissed him. If asked by reporters, he would say that on his 26th jump out of an aeroplane, he broke his ankle and also hurt his back. It was not until 1976 that same-sex sexual activity became lawful in the California and Washington states.

His military records reported that, "He has no interest whatsoever in the army" (Southall, 2012, 24), which by Jimi's admission was correct. He commented, "I hated the army immediately ... There's nothing more

Model Linda Keith modelling for milliner Edward Mann winter collection in 1963. (Credit photographer Smith Archive /Alamy).

monotonous than spending a whole day peeling potatoes" (Hendrix, 2014.22).

He never returned to Betty Jean after he left the military; he wrote to her and told her that he wasn't planning on returning to Seattle or to her. Jimi had begun a relationship with a woman called Joyce, and he sold his precious *Betty Jean* guitar to a local pawnshop (Cross, 2005, 95). Jimi later told Noel Redding, bass player in *The Jimi Hendrix Experience*, that the blues song *Red House* was written about his old high school girlfriend, Betty Jean Morgan (Cross, 2005, 175).

Linda Keith was a British fashion model best-known for her work with David Bailey, Ossie Clark, and Alice Pollock. Before she was a model, she worked at Vogue House delivering mail. She was also a blues fanatic, and for a while she was girlfriend to *Rolling Stones'* guitarist, Keith Richards, and later Brian Jones.

She described Richards as being "a blues aficionado", and it was through discussions on music that they bonded (www.theguardian.com/). Whilst being interviewed several years ago, she recalled how she banned Richards from playing *The Rolling Stones* on her record player. "He knew I was never a huge fan. I was hugely into Black music, so they sounded a bit pale by comparison" (bid.).

For a while, Keith lived in New York City and frequented the clubs in Greenwich Village. Initially, she invited Andrew Loog Oldham, the then manager of *The Rolling Stones*, to see Jimi play. He accepted her offer but after seeing him play decided that he was not going to manage him. Still resolute to make Jimi a star, Keith then persuaded Chas Chandler, the bass player with *The Animals*, to see Jimi play; Chandler was soon to leave *The Animals* to pursue a career in management and producing.

Speaking in 1973, Keith commented in an interview that when she saw Jimi perform when he was still playing as and with *Jimmy James & The Blue Flames*, his "indefinable qualities made me feel so incredible; it was amazing ... he was very shy ... unsure of himself – no confidence in his own creativity" (YouTube).

Eventually, Chandler signed and brought Jimi to Great Britain, and Chandler became Jimi's confidant, manager and producer until their business relationship ended in 1968. During the January of 1970, at the *Record Plant* studios, Jimi created the first draft of a track called *Send My Love To Linda* (www.jimihendrix.com/). The lyrics are poignant and acknowledge the impact and significance that Keith had on him. Before he died, Jimi gave Keith a Fender Stratocaster guitar as a token of his gratitude for everything she had done for him; she was indeed a major catalyst in his career.

Kathy Etchingham was born Kathleen Mary on 18th June 1946 in Derby, Derbyshire, UK. She worked in a chemist's when she first came to London and lived in Earl's Court, where she flat-shared (Etchingham, 1999, 47). She worked in a restaurant chain called *The Golden Egg* (Etchingham, 1999, 49). Her other employment included working as an apprentice hairdresser (Etchingham, 1999, 55), and she also worked as a DJ at *The Cromwellian Club* in Kensington and *The Scotch of St. James* in Masons Yard in Westminster (Etchingham, 1999, 54).

She was 20 when she met Jimi at *The Scotch of St. James* nightclub on the 24th September, 1966, which was the evening of his first day in London. There was an immediate connection between them. For a while, they shared a flat with Chas Chandler and his girlfriend at 34 Montagu Square, Marylebone, which was owned by Ringo Starr. The latter no longer lived there as he had bought a property in the country, and he offered to let the four live there (Etchingham, 1999, 84). Two months later, Etchingham and Hendrix moved to 23 Brook Street in Mayfair.

During the pinnacle of Jimi's rise to fame, their relationship blossomed, and they were lovers for approximately three years. Mitch Mitchell described Etchingham as being one of the two great loves in his life, the other being Devon Wilson (Mitchell, 1993, 160).

Etchingham commented that the name '*Mary*' in the track *The Wind Cries Mary* (it being her middle name) was crafted after a spat between her and Hendrix (www.musiclipse.com). Eventually, she left Hendrix and the flat in Brook Street in 1970; she was bored and tired with his endless philandering and had emotionally moved on.

Before she left him, she travelled to visit him at his hotel suite in New York, and she observed that he was like a different person. She commented that he was "trailing an enormous entourage like the colourful leader of some circus freak show" (Cross, 2005, 250). To Etchingham, the female followers seemed to be whores, and the men appeared to be drug dealers and pimps. When she asked Jimi who they were, he replied. "My friends" (ibid.).

She commented in approximately 1969 that "Jimi wanted a family as well … He just didn't know how to get it" (Cross, 2005, 251). Etchingham went on to marry somebody else and started a family; apparently Jimi was shocked and heartbroken by her actions; clearly it shattered his ego.

Before Etchingham met Hendrix, she already had a distinctive presence in London's Swinging Sixties. A sociable regular on the London club scene, she was friends with luminaries such as Brian Jones, *The Animals*, *The Who*, Zoot Money, and his wife, Ronnie. For a while, Etchingham lived with the couple in their large home in Gunnerstone Road, Fulham. She moved out of there when she and Jimi moved into the *Hyde Park Towers Hotel*, which was before the couple moved into Montagu Square (Etchingham, 1999, 65).

Such associations and networking enabled her to introduce Hendrix to many of her contacts, as well as provide him with her insights

Kathy Etchingham girlfriend of three years of Jimi Hendrix. (Credit Bridgeman Images).

and constructive viewpoints, particularly in the earlier part of their relationship. Etchingham was knowledgeable, observant and street-savvy; she also introduced him to some of the more fashionable parts of London, such as the Portobello Road market and Kings Road, Chelsea, as well as the traditional tourist sites (Etchingham, 1999, 69).

Her autobiography, *Through Gypsy Eyes: My Life, the 60s and Jimi Hendrix*, was published in 1998. It is a candid account of her earlier life and also provides insights into her relationship with Hendrix. *The Daily Telegraph* commented that the book had "an extraordinary life – spine-chilling descriptions", and *The Sunday Times* stated that it was "a morality tale about the consequences of the sexual and narcotic excesses of the 1960s, described with a touching lack of bitterness" (Etchingham, 1999, outside cover).

Etchingham has remained a key figure in the background of the Swinging Sixties rock history since Hendrix's death and has done much to preserve his memory. This has included engaging with a range of biographers, documentary makers and museums to ensure that the man – not only the music icon – became accessible to the world. She has also spoken at events and collaborated with initiatives which have aimed to remember Hendrix's contributions. Her endeavours have meant that her memories of Jimi Hendrix the man and his challenges, dreams and vulnerabilities are accessible to the world, providing a rounded perspective of him.

Sharon Lawrence was a journalist at the *United Press International* in Los Angeles. She specialised in pop music and film coverage. She went on to become a management, marketing and PR consultant for clients which included *Apple*, *Columbia* and *MCA*. She became an author and screenplay writer; she penned the book *Jimi Hendrix: The Man, The Magic, The Truth*. Lawrence was a trusted confidante to Jimi in his last three years, a genuine and reliable friend. Their relationship must have been invaluable to him, given the largely shallow and phoney circles that he mixed in, particularly in his last few years.

Devon Wilson was born Ida Mae Wilson in Milwaukee in October 1943 and died aged 27 in February 1971, when she fell from an eighth-floor balcony at the *Chelsea Hotel*, New York, under ambiguous circumstances. During her childhood, she faced challenges such as poverty and violence. She ran away from home aged fifteen and used the name *'Devon'* when she became a street prostitute. She was intelligent and beautiful and battled with substance addiction. (www.fr.wikipedia.org/wiki/.

Eventually, she found identity and power by becoming a groupie to some of the big names of the day in the music industry. They included not only Jimi Hendrix but also Eric Clapton, Miles Davis, and Mick

Jagger. Wilson's reputation preceded her; she was controversial and glamorous and was known (and self-identified) as a 'super groupie' (www.musiclipse.com/). She is believed to have been the inspiration behind Hendrix's track, *Dolly Dagger*.

It is uncertain as to exactly when she and Jimi first met, but is believed to be around 1967/1968 in Los Angeles. The couple had a turbulent affair, and she nurtured his excesses, providing him with cocaine, heroin and girls. As Hendrix grew more famous, she became increasingly jealous and possessive, which partly led to the breakdown of their relationship. Herbie Worthington, who knew the couple, said, *"She was a major groupie but also smart and loyal to Jimi. If you want to control someone, getting high together is a powerful way"* (ibid.).

Hendrix, apparently, felt smothered by Wilson and eventually separated from her. On the afternoon of the 18th September, when the two met in London, sadly, on that evening, Hendrix died. The distraught Wilson returned to New York and continued a life fuelled by substance addiction (www.fr.wikipedia.org/wiki).

Monika Dannemann was the last and brief girlfriend of Jimi Hendrix. She was a 25 year old German ice-skater and painter, and she first met him on 12th January 1969, at one of his concerts in Düsseldorf. Dannemann claimed that she took up with Jimi on 25th April, when she came to London and ran into him at the *Speakeasy Club*; they spent, just over a week together. Then, from 15th September 1970, she and Jimi spent the next few nights at her suite at the *Samarkand Hotel* at 22, Lansdowne Crescent, Notting Hill, London, and she was with him in his last hours (www.en.wikipedia.org/wiki).

Her book, *The Inner World of Jimi Hendrix by His Fiancée*, published in 1995, claimed that they were engaged, and she apparently promised him that she would help to convey his artistic message to others (Dannemann, 1995, front inside jacket). However, some of her story has since been discredited – some of it was declared as fraudulent by a court of law (Cross, 2005, 329). Mitch Mitchell commented that "Jimi was spending most of his last days with Monika Dannemann (sic), who – no offence to her – was not the great love of Jimi's life" (Mitchell, 1993, 160).

In 1996, and two days after Dannemann lost an ongoing court case with Kathy Etchingham where she was found guilty of contempt of court for repeating a libel case against Kathy Etchingham, Dannemann, aged

50, committed suicide. She was found dead in her fume-filled Mercedes and died from carbon monoxide poisoning (www.independent.co.uk/).

Children

The consequences of Jimi's promiscuity became evident, and Noel Redding hinted at the many illegitimate children Hendrix is believed to have fathered. He commented, "Judging by the amount of paternity suits, Jimi must have been the most potent man ever born, or else he just attracted chicks with their own future security in mind" (Redding & Appleby, 1990, 110).

There was a court case brought by Diana Carpenter, who claimed that her daughter's father was Jimi. The couple met in New York in the winter of 1965. Diana was a sixteen-year-old street prostitute who was a light-skinned African American, and Jimi told her that she reminded him of his mother (Cross, 2005, 126).

The couple started a relationship, and in early May, Carpenter discovered she was pregnant, and, at Jimi's insistence, she stopped working as a prostitute. However, Jimi's only income was made from the occasional gig, and by the late spring the couple were stealing to survive (Cross, 2005, 127). Secretly, Carpenter began working as a prostitute again to earn some money. Jimi found out and brutally beat her, in the full knowledge that she was pregnant. Unsurprisingly, after that, their relationship began to evaporate (ibid.).

After a concert in Oakland, California, on the 29th April, 1969, Hendrix and Carpenter were reunited for a very brief reunion at the airport before Jimi took a flight. She showed him a photograph of her child, called Tamika, and informed him, "This is your daughter … she is two years old." Jimi replied looking, at the snapshot, "She has my eyes"; he took the photograph of his daughter with him when he boarded his aeroplane (Cross, 2005, 252/253).

By early 1970, a paternity suit had been brought against Hendrix by Carpenter. Her solicitors made several requests for blood samples from Jimi, which he refused, and he denied in public that he had any children. He never met Tamika or financially supported her (Cross, 2005, 308). In 1972, Carpenter lost her legal case to have Tamika declared Jimi's heir.

The court ruled that during Jimi's lifetime, no blood tests were taken, and therefore paternity could not be proved. She tried again in 2002 to

Jimi Hendrix painting by Mark Hetherington. www.facebook.com/MarkHetheringtonArt and www.artpal.com/markhetherington#i6.

have her daughter established as Jimi's heir, but again was unsuccessful. However, Tamika did meet Al Hendrix on at least two occasions (Cross, 2005, 342).

In the early 1970s, lawyers who represented James Sundquist successfully got a Swedish court to recognise that he was an heir to Jimi Hendrix. His physical resemblance to his father was palpable, which in itself made it difficult for the authorities to challenge him. He and his mother, Eva Sundquist, filed two separate cases seeking a share of Jimi's wealth. In the late 1990s, Al Hendrix settled with James Sundquist and gave him a million-dollar payout. Eva Sundquist was a regular girlfriend of Jimi when he was in Sweden (Cross, 2005, 342/343).

In the 1990s, highly accurate parental testing became available, and PCR (Polymerase Chain Reaction) became the standard method for DNA parental testing, which was more accurate than previous methods of parental testing.

Health & Ill-health

Jimi experienced poverty and the effects from it throughout a large part of his life, some of which was overt. He once told his partner, Kathy Etchingham, "When you've been penniless, you never forget it" (Cross, 2005, 169).

Examples of some of his ill-health include contracting pneumonia when he was a baby, poor vision (which was never corrected by wearing glasses, even in adulthood), stuttering, nervous energy, ill-fitting clothes and shoes (his footwear causing damaged feet), malnutrition and hunger, as well as sleep deprivation from excessive touring and performance and also alcohol and substance abuse.

His recall was such that Jimi remembered being in hospital when he was a baby: "I had pneumonia when I was young and I used to scream and cry every time they put the needle in me" (Shapiro & Glebbeek, 1991, 16).

Jimi's father was a strict disciplinarian. He taught his young son that he must respect his elders and that he must not speak until an adult spoke to him first. Jimi later felt that was one of the reasons why he was so quiet (Hendrix, 2014, 16). One example of his father's tyranny included beating him senseless.

This was when Jimi placed a string on a broom handle, which was a way of trying to learn how to play a guitar (www.musiclipse.com). This was a technique that some of Jimi's blues heroes, such as Robert Johnson, also used before they could afford to buy a real guitar.

Returning to the younger Jimi again. Dorothy Harding, a family friend, recalled that Jimi was painfully shy, and for many years he had a stutter (Shapiro & Glebbeek, 1991, 28). Harding remembered that on one occasion Al and Lucille were trying to teach their three-year-old son how to tie his shoelaces. Jimi was so nervous with his father watching over him that he kept making mistakes; Al screamed at him for not being

The Jimi Hendrix Experience, 1967.
(Credit: Picture Alliance/Photoshot/Bridgeman Images).

able to do it. Harding interjected, screaming at Al: "He's just a baby! You'll make him nervous!" (ibid.).

When *Purple Haze* (originally titled *Purple Haze – Jesus Saves*) was released in 1967 and reached number three in the UK charts, Jimi was interviewed and questioned about a variety of topics, which included whether he smoked. His reply was, "If I didn't, I'd be as fat as a pig. My nerves are very bad" (Hendrix, 2014, 49). Speaking in 1968, Jimi commented, "This pop business is so much harder than people think. It's nerve-racking and mind-bending … We are constantly under pressure, and the workday is often 24 hours" (Hendrix, 2014, 101).

Possibly, the nervous strain was in connection with performance anxiety and scheduling, or maybe unresolved trauma from his childhood

– or both. In adulthood, he still had a tendency to stutter when he was nervous (Cross, 2005, 5).

Al Hendrix was religious, and he instructed the young Jimi to go to Sunday school, which he duly did. On one occasion, Jimmy was ordered to leave the church for wearing a suit with tennis shoes. The church considered it to be inadequate dress; he never forgot the experience, which then formed part of his attitude towards organised religion (Shapiro & Glebbeek, 1991, 34).

Press agent Tony Garland was preparing to write the first official press biography about him in approximately 1966. He commented upon Jimi's boots, and how they reflected his years of struggle: "When you saw the soles on those things … they were completely worn through" (Cross, 2005, 170). Some believed that the worn-out soles were what caused the peculiar way of walking, which was walking in a shuffle with both toes pointing inwards.

However, his pigeon-toed way of walking remained even after wearing a correctly sized new pair of square-toed Cuban-heeled boots. His friend Eric Burdon observed, "You could tell by the way he walked that he had the wrong sized shoes on as a kid, and that his gait was all screwed up … It was like his toes made a triangle as he moved" (ibid.).

Aged thirteen, Jimi's then girlfriend Carmen Goudy later observed how Jimi seemed poorer than poor. She recalled that, "He used to wear these little white buck loafers … He had a hole in the sole, so he'd cut these pieces of cardboard and put that in the bottom of his shoes" (Cross, 2005, 54). However, because he walked so much, the piece of cardboard would wear out rapidly; Jimi improvised and took to putting several pieces of cardboard in his pocket so that he had a supply to replace the piece of worn-out cardboard in his shoe.

Linda Keith commented on his look in the early days when she first met him when he was aged approximately 24: "He wore dreadful clothes – big Copacabana shirts with too-short bell-bottoms and shoes with holes in them" (www.guardian.com).

Speaking in 1968, Jimi acknowledged and commented upon his poor eyesight. He said, "My eyes are very bad, and sometimes I go into a club, and I might not see somebody, and they might get all funny" – meaning that they perceived that Hendrix was ignoring them because he had made the big time (Hendrix, 2014, 121).

When they approached him face-to-face, he would make an excuse and say something to the effect of, "Hello, I was thinking about something … I'm sorry." He refused to wear glasses or hard contact lenses (the latter were available in the UK from the early 1960s) to correct his vision; perhaps it was vanity.

As a child and young adult, Jimi experienced hunger and malnutrition – something that he understandably never forgot. He often commented when he was older about how essential it was for him to be able to eat properly and have a meal. Malnutrition also played havoc with his skin, as he developed acne. In his early twenties, he used Valderma face cream for the condition (Cross, 2005, 153).

Such was the food poverty when he was a child that at times he and his brother Leon were forced to steal because they were so hungry. One instance involved the brothers going to the grocery store, and Leon recalled, "Jimi would be smart. He'd open a loaf of bread, pull out two pieces, wrap it up and put it back. Then he'd sneak into the meat department and steal a package of ham to make a sandwich out of it" (Cross, 2005, 41).

At other times, the brothers would spend dinnertime with kind and trustworthy neighbours so they could be fed. Sometimes they would strategically plan to stay overnight so they could be fed supper and breakfast too (Cross, 2005, 45). When Jimi joined the army, he was for the first time in his life guaranteed consistent nutrition by way of having three square meals daily.

During an interview, Jimi revealed that since the band was formed, he and the *Experience* band members, Mitch Mitchell and Noel Redding, required a much-needed break: "We've hardly had a day off since the group was formed two years ago. None of us have had time to sit down and think by himself" (Hendrix, 2014, 124). Jimi also commented about needing a holiday, "We can't continue at this pace for long … I've had all kinds of bad hallucinations" (Hendrix, 2014, 116).

The relentless demands and their effects on the group are exposed in Jimi's commentary: "We are constantly under pressure, and the workday is often 24 hours. Every show takes its pound of flesh. I can hardly get anything to eat … even my skin is suffering from the lack of eating right. One often gets depressed. It's only natural that we need a stimulant sometimes … I need to slow down" (Hendrix, 2014, 101).

Noel Redding commented in his 1990 autobiography that Jimi had lost his light-heartedness and suffered from depressed panic attacks, and he believed that Jimi felt hounded and threatened; this was in 1968 (Redding & Appleby, 1990, 109). He also claimed that Jimi slashed his wrists, but the incident was kept very quiet. Concerned for his friend and colleague, he advised him to seek therapy for his depression (Redding & Appleby, 1990, 110).

The schedule of the band is documented in Mitch Mitchell's book, *The Hendrix Experience* (Mitchell & Platt, 1993, 172). It shows that between January and December in 1967 (including both national and international dates), the itinerary for concerts, club dates and television appearances totalled 212. Then, between the same months in 1968, the sum of dates was 121.

The dates of the more famous festivals where Jimi appeared were the 18th June 1967, at the Monterey Pop Festival, USA; 18th August 1969, at the Woodstock Festival, USA; and 30th August 1970, at the Isle of Wight Festival in the UK. It was at the Monterey Pop Festival, along with the success of his debut album, that Jimi finally became a musical success in America. Eric Burdon, lead singer of *The Animals* and friend of Jimi's, reflected: "To me, Monterey wasn't a pop festival. It wasn't a music festival at all, really. It was a religious festival. It was a love festival" (Bebergal, 2015, 55).

The spirit of the Monterey crowd inspired him to write the song *Little Wing*. He commented, "Everybody was flyin' and in a nice mood, like the police and everybody were really groovy out there … It's very simple. I like it, though. It's one of the very few I like" (Hendrix, 2014, 92). He continued the sentiment of the festival gathering by saying, "Those flower power people are really groovy" (Hendrix, 2014, 69).

Addressing the crowd at the Isle of Wight Festival, Jimi warmly greeted them: "Thank you very much for showin' man. You're all very beautiful and outasight" (Hendrix, 2014, 183). Reflecting upon the Woodstock Festival, Mitch Mitchell cynically commented, "People go on about Woodstock almost religiously, but really it was mud, no food, no toilets, and exhaustion" (Mitchell & Platt, 1993, 142).

Friend of Janis Joplin, Peggy Caserta, who accompanied Joplin to Woodstock, commented that by the time Jimi played *The Star-Spangled Banner* (the American national anthem), they and much of the crowd had left. However, those who remained described what he delivered as being 'spell-binding'. She later learnt that Jimi was able to "make his guitar sound as though bombs were bursting in the air" (Caserta & Falcon, 2018, 103). Astrologer and author Frank C. Clifford commented that the Woodstock Festival "became the template for subsequent gatherings and, indeed, for the arena rock gig" (Clifford, 2018, 18).

From the aforementioned gruelling schedules, we can see the immense pressure placed on the band and the expectation of performance. Clearly it was excessive and untenable, for in 1969, between January and December, the total sum of bookings was just 48. There were also the other significant commitments to consider, such as interviews, photo shoots and press calls, and recording dates and sound dates.

While each tour is unique, most involve a blend of biological, psychological and social stressors. For example, demanding performances, extensive travel and working in the different time zones after long flights, poor quality sleep or sleep deprivation, inadequate nutrition, and little privacy or solitude. Punishing tour schedules, such as those listed previously, would inevitably take their toll on the needs and limitations of the mind, body and spirit of those involved. Shortly, before Jimi died, he had complained of exhaustion for the prior two weeks, but in reality he had pleaded exhaustion for the last two years" (Cross, 205, 332).

Biographer Harry Shapiro wrote about the range of Jimi's alcohol and substance abuse in the biography *Jimi Hendrix: Electric Gypsy*. He smoked dope to keep mellow and snorted methedrine to keep himself going (Shapiro & Glebbeek, 1991, 104). He also took LSD (lysergic acid diethylamide) and STP (an abbreviation for Serenity, Tranquillity & Peace), which is part of the amphetamine family and is a powerful relative of MDMA (*Methylenedioxy-methamphetamine*) – more commonly known as ecstasy or molly (Shapiro & Glebbeek, 1991, 188/189).

Jimi was interviewed in 1969 by Jane de Mendelssohn of the underground newspaper *The International Times*. She commented that the interview was conducted with Jimi naked in bed, and she sat on the side of his bed. She observed that "on his bedside table there was the biggest collection of alcohol and drugs ... which included three different types of hash, grass, amyl nitrates, pills and lots of different kinds of bourbon and whisky ... He was constantly smoking joints" (Shapiro & Glebbeek, 1991, 346).

Shapiro commented on how a cocktail of drugs was used for different purposes, e.g., some were used to help wind down after the adrenaline rush of a great show, as well as deal with the post-show trauma of a bad gig. Also, using speed or cocaine to balance a tranquiliser or sleeping pill to take the edge off the stimulants (Shapiro & Glebbeek, 1991, 259) was also common practice; it was relentless.

Jimi Hendrix was pronounced dead on arrival at St. Mary's Abbots Hospital, Kensington, London, on 18th September 1970; he had been taken to hospital by ambulance. The emergency service was called by his girlfriend, Monika Dannemann, from the hotel suite in Notting Hill. She couldn't get Jimi to wake up, and she panicked as he had taken two of her barbiturate-type sleeping tablets called Vesperax. The normal dosage was half a tablet, but Dannemann routinely took one tablet.

The accident and emergency admissions officer commented that as the ambulance arrived at the hospital, the two ambulance men jumped out of the vehicle and rushed into casualty, where doctors tried to revive him but were unsuccessful. Sadly, Jimi had died in the ambulance; hospital staff then took him to the mortuary.

A top leading forensic scientist, Donald Teare, presented his autopsy report, and his findings revealed that he found the Vesperax in Jimi's body and "the coroner concluded that Jimi had taken about nine times the normal dose of Vesperax, as defined by Monika" (Shapiro & Glebbeek, 1991, 475). Teare's findings also revealed another barbiturate called Seconal, as well as 20mg of amphetamine, which was believed to have been taken at a party that Jimi attended in the early hours of the day.

There was no evidence by way of a suicide note to suggest that Jimi had committed suicide or anything which suggested that he had been the victim of foul play. The coroner concluded an 'open verdict' and the cause of death was recorded as "inhalation of vomit due to barbiturate intoxication in the form of quinal barbitone" (ibid.). Ironically, Jimi's last words that he penned on 17th September 1970 were in a piece called *The Story of Life*.

Working Relationships

After Jimi left the army, he moved to Clarksville in approximately 1962, and then he moved to Nashville, Tennessee. From there, he started gigging on the Chitlin Circuit. This was a group of live entertainment venues which catered to African American audiences and which booked Black performers during the segregation from the early twentieth century through to the 1960s.

Many celebrated Black performers of today started out on the Chitlin Circuit, including Sam Cooke, Otis Redding, and Ike & Tina Turner, and there were many others. It was through playing on the Circuit that Jimi secured a position in the backing bands of the Isley Brothers and Wilson Pickett. Later, he was with Little Richard's backing band until approximately 1965.

Jimi was a member of the *King Kasuals*, which he founded with Billy Cox after they both left the US Army in 1962, and was based in the Nashville area. Later, Hendrix became a member of other bands, such as *Curtis Knight & The Squires*. Ed Chalpin signed him to this band, which had disastrous ramifications once he became famous and successful.

Later, Jimi formed *Jimmy James & The Blue Flames*. He also jammed and performed with many other artists and bands throughout his life; his friend Brian Jones of *The Rolling Stones* was one such person (Mitchell, 1993, 81).

As previously noted, bassist Chas Chandler was on the verge of leaving the band *The Animals* and considering going into management. He persuaded Jimi to come to England, and in late 1966 he became Jimi's producer and co-manager, along with Mike Jeffery, who managed *The Animals*.

Jeffery changed the stage name, and his client became famously known as Jimi. A decision was made that Jimi would be part of a trio – Noel Redding (bassist) and Mitch Mitchell (drummer) were recruited, and the three became *The Jimi Hendrix Experience*.

In 1969, Jimi disbanded *The Jimi Hendrix Experience* and went on to form *The Band of Gypsys*, which comprised Jimi, bassist Billy Cox and drummer Buddy Miles. However, it became apparent that Mitchell and Redding's rhythm section had been essential components in the success of Jimi's previous work, and *The Band of Gypsys* ultimately could not attain the same criterion.

In early 1970, *The Jimi Hendrix Experience* reformed again, and Mitch Mitchell replaced Miles on drums, but Cox remained as bassist, although the group shortly disbanded again. Jimi's most significant musical

Jimi Hendrix in the Star Club in Hamburg.
(Credit © SZ Photo/Dietmar Gottschall/Bridgeman Images).

partner appears to have been Mitch Mitchell, and he was part of the trio that toured with Jimi in the final months of his life.

The last two years of Jimi's life were unstable financially and musically. He was involved in many multifaceted disagreements with management and record companies; some went as far back as contracts he had signed before *The Jimi Hendrix Experience* was formed (the Ed Chalpin lawsuit, for example).

Guitars, Amplifiers & Playing Techniques

Types of guitar that Jimi played during his earlier years of musicianship included the Epiphone Wiltshire in cherry with a rosewood neck, the Fender Duo-Sonic in white with a rosewood neck (used during the Isley Brothers period), and the Fender Jazzmaster in sunburst with a rosewood neck (used during his time with Little Richard). There was also the Fender Duo-Sonic in sunburst with a rosewood neck, which was used during the Curtis Knight period, which was then exchanged for a Fender Stratocaster in sunburst with a rosewood neck. It is believed to be the Stratocaster that Jimi brought to England with him (Cross, 2005, 629).

Other guitars that Jimi later used included a Gibson Flying V in cherry and also black, both with rosewood necks, a Fender Jaguar in blue with a rosewood neck, Fender Stratocasters, each in red, white or black, as well as a Gibson Les Paul, ES-335 and SG Custom all with rosewood necks and respectively in the colours of black, sunburst and white. There were many more, but the Fender Stratocaster was his mainstay guitar. Jimi said, "The Stratocaster is the best all-round guitar for the stuff we're doing. You can get the very bright trebles and the deep bass sound" (Hendrix, 2014, 87).

When Jimi lived in New York, he would frequently visit *Manny's Musical Instruments*, where he bought a variety of other models, such as Rickenbacker, Firebird and Mosrite (Cross, 2005, 631). Jimi used a variety of makes of amplifiers; these included Burns, Fender, Marshall, and Silvertone.

Some of the techniques that Jimi used included chording, finger tremolo, harmonics, octave playing, rhythm guitar, slide, string bending and tremolo arm (Cross, 2005, 635/636) (*see guitar-playing techniques in glossary for explanation of techniques*).

Drummer Mitch Mitchell commented, "He had these huge hands, and his thumbs were nearly as long as his fingers" (Mitchell & Platt, 1993, 18). Mitchell added, "Jimi could, and did, play anything – left-handed, right-handed, upside down, behind his back and with his teeth. He probably could have played with his toenails" (ibid.). Jimi got the idea of playing with his teeth when he played in Nashville, where the audiences were tough, very hard to please and wanted to see something different (Hendrix, 2014, 33).

Jimi commented after the Monterey Festival that when he is performing he forgets any physical pains he has; he referenced his thumb, saying: "Look at my thumb, how ugly it's become ... that's what it's all about, filling up the chest cavities and the empty kneecaps and the elbows" (Hendrix, 2014, 68).

Genres

Blues, R&B, rockabilly, psychedelia, and rock.

Inspired by Jeff Beck, Chuck Berry, Eric Clapton, Sam Cooke, Bob Dylan, Elmore James, Robert Johnson, Brian Jones, Albert King, B.B. King, Little Richard, Muddy Waters, T. Bone Walker, and Howlin' Wolf, as well as composers such as Bach, Handel, and Gustav Mahler, Jimi said that different music is meant to be used in different ways and added, "I believe the best time to listen to classical music is any time when it's very quiet or your mind is very relaxed. When you feel like daydreaming, maybe (Hendrix, 2014, 136).

Albums

The debut album was called *Are You Experienced* and featured *Hey Joe*, *Purple Haze*, and *The Wind Cries Mary*. The three tracks all made the top ten in the first six months of 1967. The album was hailed as a psychedelic work of genius and became a great success. *The Jimi Hendrix Experience* went on to record two more albums – *Axis: Bold as Love* and *Electric Ladyland*. These two albums were more diverse and experimental than *Are You Experienced*, as Jimi had greater creative control over them. Before his death, Jimi also worked intermittently on an album with a working title of *First Ray of the New Rising Sun*.

Studios, Studio Engineers & Record Labels

In 1967, Jimi paid tribute to Roger Mayer, stating, "The secret of my sound is largely the electronic genius of our tame boffin, who is known to us as 'Roger the Valve'" (Hendrix, 2014, 92). Studios that Jimi recorded in included *London Olympia Studios, Regent Studio Sounds, Mayfair Studios, Record Plant* and *Electric Lady Studios*. The latter is in Greenwich Village, New York City, and it was commissioned in 1968 by Jimi; it was his vision to have a permanent recording base.

Architect John Storyk designed the studio, and audio engineer Eddie Kramer (along with Jimi) made the vision a reality. Kramer commented, "I worked with Jimi Hendrix in the last three years of his life. Working with Jimi changed my musical, production and engineering career" (www.reddit.com).

Sadly, Jimi only got to use the studio for ten weeks before his untimely death (www.en.wikipedia.org/). Another engineer that Jimi worked with was Gary Kellegran. He had previously worked at *Mayfair Studios* but went to America to set up the *Record Plant* studios with his partner.

Record labels that Jimi was signed to at the time for *The Jimi Hendrix Experience* albums and singles were originally released by *Track Records* in the United Kingdom and *Reprise Records* in the USA. *Track Records* also issued the *Band of Gypsys* album; however, to settle an American dispute, it was released by *Capitol Records* in the USA.

Legacy

50 years plus after his death, Jimi Hendrix remains widely viewed as one of the greatest guitar influences in the music industry, and his story is compelling. Against the odds, he overcame his harrowing and poverty-stricken background and the racial segregation of the 1960s and transformed himself into something unique. A musical genius, he found success first in Great Britain and then in America.

Experience Hendrix L.L.C. is owned and operated by members of the Hendrix family and is the official family company. The organisation safeguards the image, likeness, music and name of Jimi Hendrix. As previously noted, Janie Hendrix is the President and C.E.O. of *Experience Hendrix L.C.C.* (www.jimihendrix.com).

One example of their more recent works has included a collaboration with *Strax AR*™ (augmented reality). The latter was granted permission to use content from *Jimi Hendrix*™ in support of the *Black Lives Matter* movement (www.jimihendrix.com).

In 1992, *The Jimi Hendrix Experience* was inaugurated into the *Rock'n'Roll Hall of Fame* in Cleveland, Ohio – a museum dedicated to the most influential bands, producers, and others who have significantly influenced the music industry, particularly in the area of rock'n'roll.

The Jimi Hendrix presence is found in another museum in Central London: the Handel Hendrix House. It is made up of two residences; Handel House at 25 Brook Street and the Hendrix flat at 23 Brook Street. The museum offers exhibition space for the public to delve into the lives of the two musicians and their time spent in London.

The Hendrix flat opened permanently to the public in 2016 and in September 1997 at number 23 Brook Street. It was selected for an English Heritage Blue Plaque, commemorating Hendrix's life and works. (www.handelhendrix.org). Kathy Etchingham was pivotal in the hanging of the blue plaque at 23 Brook Street and organised celebrations to mark the occasion.

When she and Jimi lived at the Georgian-styled property, it was Etchingham who found and secured the flat, which then was the equivalent of £30 a week to rent (Etchingham, 1999, 116). Jimi

Author's collection.

frequently remarked that "it was the only home I had" (www.musiclipse.com). Hendrix lived there intermittently from the summer of 1968 until 1970. When Hendrix discovered that Handel had lived at 25 Brook Street, he invested in copies of Handel's *Messiah* and also his *Water Music* (ibid.).

There is also a small museum in Jordaan, Amsterdam, named after Jimi's album *Electric Ladyland* (also known as the *Fluorescent Art Museum*), and it is devoted to fluorescence and making art with it. Visitors can experience the aura of the Flower Power generation and music of the 1970s, as well as psychedelic art.

Several blue heritage plaques have been erected in honour of Jimi Hendrix's name, representing different parts of his life. For example, there is a blue plaque that accompanies a mural (by artist Zabou) in Forest Gate, East London. The site is where *The Upper Cut* club used to be, and it is where not only did *The Jimi Hendrix Experience* play, but also where Jimi wrote *Purple Haze*.

Author, researcher and director of *Univibes* magazine, Caesar Glebbeek, ran the *Hendrix Information Centre* and co-wrote with Douglas J. Noble *Jimi Hendrix: The Man, The Music & The Memorabilia*, published in 1996. He also worked with biographer Harry Shapiro on *Jimi Hendrix: Electric Gypsy*, which was first published in 1990; many other biographies have also been written about Jimi Hendrix.

Author's collection. Artist Zabou @zabouartist/Zabou.me/.

There is a Jimi Hendrix Park in his hometown of Seattle, Washington. In addition, situated in the Capitol Hill area of Seattle, there is a bronze sculpture by Daryl Smith called *The Electric Lady Studio Guitar*, which depicts Jimi playing a Stratocaster guitar.

The film documentary *Jimi Hendrix: All Is By My Side* was released in 2013 and was directed and written by John Ridley; the part of 'Jimi' was played by American actor André Benjamin (aka André 3000 – rapper, singer and song-writer).

The digital age has seen the creation of many Facebook group pages for Jimi Hendrix fans, and there is also the official website: jimihendrix.com. There are many YouTube films of Jimi Hendrix performing at the great festivals, such as Monterey in 1967 and Woodstock in 1969, as well as the 1970 concert, *Rainbow Bridge*. Many have also been digitised on DVD for viewing.

In 1965, Curtis Knight wrote the prophetic *The Ballad of Jimi*, which was released as a 45 RPM single in 1970, after Hendrix's death. It was predictive, as apparently Jimi knew intuitively that he would be dead in five years' time, and Knight's lyrics reflect this: "Many things he would try, For he knew soon he would die … Five years this he said, He's not gone he's just dead" (www.songmeanings.com/).

In 2004, the *Power of Soul: A Tribute to Jimi Hendrix* album was released. Successful artists covered some of his tracks, which included *Sting* singing *The Wind Cries Mary*, and *Earth, Wind & Fire* singing *Voodoo Child (Slight Return)*, and Eric Clapton singing *The Burning of the Midnight Lamp*. Track one on side one of the album was *Gratitude*, sung by Jimi's father.

Artists Prince and Amy Winehouse, and undoubtedly many others, were also inspired by Jimi. Amy Winehouse said, "There is room in everyone's life for Jimi Hendrix" (https://www.musicradar.com).

Prince used to perform Jimi's 1967 track *Red House*; he performed it at his concerts from 1986 up to 2008. He commented, "I learned from Jimi Hendrix – they all wanted him to do the tricks, and at the end of his career he just wanted to play' (www.goldiesparade.co.uk/).

PART 2
WHAT JIMI HENDRIX'S NATAL CHART REVEALS AND THE ASTROLOGY IN ACTION

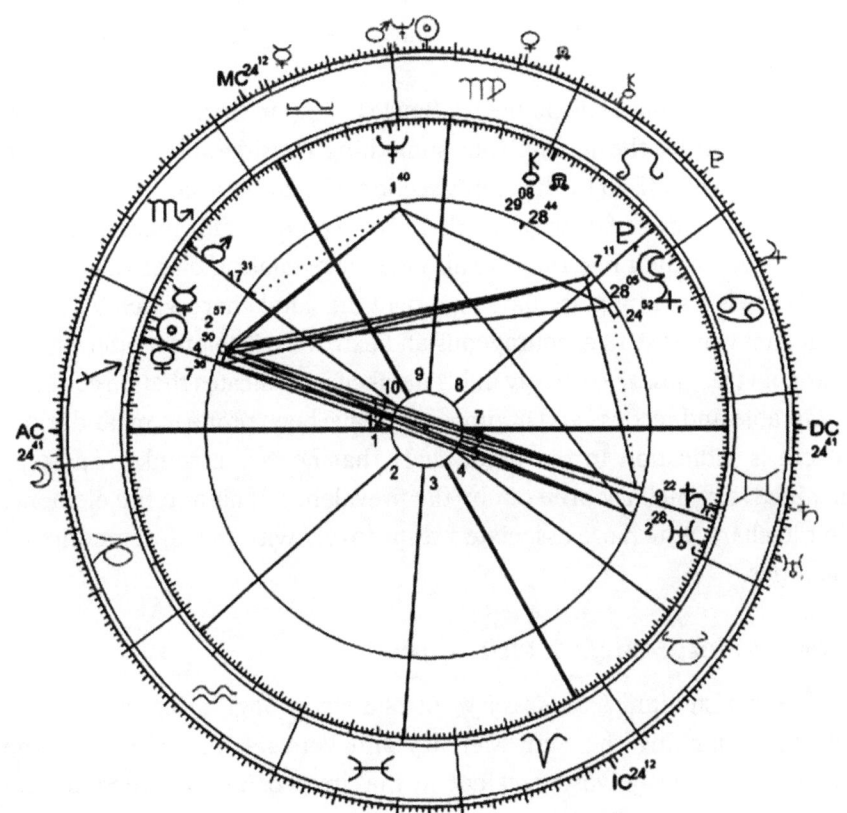

ASTROLOGY DETAILS

Jimi Hendrix's natal and transits chart via www.astro.com (Astrodienst).
Co-ordinates of natal chart: 122w20, 47n36.
Rodden Rating: AA.

Jimi Hendrix's Natal Chart and the Transits to it on the Day he Died on 18th September, 1970

John (Johnny) Marshall Hendrix, who became known worldwide under his stage name, Jimi Hendrix, was born on Friday, 27th November 1942, at 10.15am in Seattle, Washington, USA.

Like Amy Winehouse's natal chart, Jimi's has the shaping of the planets that is defined as being a Bowl. This is because the planets are virtually in one half of the natal chart, spanning from the fifth to the twelfth house (*see glossary*).

People who have the planetary Bowl shaping in their natal chart may feel agitated by the feeling that something considerable is missing in their life (symbolised by the empty section of their natal chart). By taking action and being self-motivated, there is the potential for them to fill that empty void in their life; they are also knowledgeable and self-reliant.

There is a strong masculine energy in the natal chart which indicates that Jimi was assertive, courageous and extrovert. The preponderance of mutable (*see glossary*) energy in his natal chart indicates that he could be adaptable and restless and at times may have been prone to meandering. There is indication in the natal chart that he was a thinker and was instinctive, which is borne out by the prevalence of air and fire elements in the chart, which are associated respectively with the aforementioned qualities.

Sagittarius, Beliefs & Philosophy

There is a stellium (*see glossary*) of planets in Sagittarius in his natal chart, comprising the Sun, Mercury and Venus. This shows that the Sagittarian energy was prevalent in the areas of excess, freedom and enthusiasm.

When Jimi was born, the Sun was in Sagittarius at four degrees, the Ascendant (*see glossary*) sign was also in Sagittarius at 24 degrees, and the Moon was in Cancer at 28 degrees. Once during an interview Jimi was asked to confirm if he was a Sagittarius; his reply was, "Constantly. Twenty-seventh" (Hendrix, 2014, 49), referring to the date in November when he was born.

The Sagittarius spirit is optimistic and forward-looking – it is the sign of the gypsy and the traveller who believes the whole wide world is home. During an interview in 1967, Jimi revealed, "I can't stay in one place too long. It drags me down, regardless of what's happening. I'm scared of vegetating. I have to move on." He concluded, "I haven't really got a home anywhere. The Earth's my home" (Hendrix, 2014, 79). His roaming Sagittarian spirit is also demonstrated through his following comment: "There's so much to see and so many places to go. I wish I could travel all the time" (ibid.).

The symbol of Sagittarius is the archer/centaur with the arrow aimed high into the distance; the archer's arrow symbolises high aspirations. The centaur represents half-horse and half-man, suggesting a love of wild nature and a world of philosophic contemplation.

Jimi loved the outdoor life, the natural world, and philosophy, as well as music. He once said, "My personal philosophy is my music" (Hendrix, 2014, 140). The aforementioned areas were subjects that he would often talk about when being interviewed. An illustration of this is when he commented, "I like to watch the lightning. Especially on the fields and flowers when I'm on my own" (Hendrix, 2014, 50).

A life full of adventures, education, freedom and liberty, opportunities, politics, religion, and long-distance travel, as well as a quest for the deeper meaning of life, are subjects which appeal to a Sagittarian. Monika Dannemann commented that "Jimi believed in himself and his inner faith in seeking a path to God" (Dannemann, 1995, 20).

As a child, Jimi experienced organised religion. His grandmother Clarice Jeter would take him to the Pentecostal Church of God in Christ on Sunday, where he learnt hymns. He commented, "I can't remember all the words now, but I can still hum the music." He also recalled how Clarice would pray for everyone, but especially Jimi's mother Lucille when she was missing (Lawrence, 2006, 10).

The Pentecostalists had holy dancing and music in their church, and as well as hymns, they sang songs which reflected the everyday experiences of the poorer working-class Black communities who largely made up the congregation of the Pentecostalists' Church.

Jimi's beliefs and metaphysical interests were vast and included subjects such as astronomy and science fiction, the afterlife, colour and dream symbolism, philosophy, UFOs, astral travelling, and life in other dimensions, as well as belief in the Voodoo religion.

Speaking in 1969, he discussed his strong belief that in the near future, Galacticans from outer space from a different galaxy and who held tremendous positive powers would come to Earth to help humanity in its struggle against evil (Dannemann, 1995, 133).

He was serious about his spiritual convictions – particularly reincarnation, the afterlife and Voodoo. He believed that there is more to our earthly existence and that we were not merely born to die. He believed that a thin veil exists between the physical and spirit worlds, where harmony and peace are the basis of the spirit world – as opposed to competition and conflict, which are prevalent in the materialistic world (Dannemann, 1995, 60/62).

Jimi commented, "When people fear death, it's a complete case of insecurity." He continued, "It's funny the way people love the dead. You have to die before they think you are worth anything. Once you are dead, you are made for life" (Hendrix, 2014, 190).

Through his lyrics and philosophy, he tried to persuade people to broaden their horizons and embrace their potential to become completely whole, human and spiritual beings. Jimi sought spiritual answers within himself, as well as having tremendous faith in the higher powers. Through this, we can see the Moon conjunct Jupiter aspect in action, since the Moon is associated with emotions and Jupiter with philosophy.

The tracks *Voodoo Child (Slight Return)* and *Belly Button Window* both reference the spirit world and reincarnation. *Life* magazine interviewed Jimi in 1969, and he told the journalist, "There's no telling how many lives your spirit will go through – die and be reborn" (Hendrix, 2014, 60).

Voodoo

Voodoo originated in West Africa and incorporates elements of two religions, Catholicism and West African Vodon, and is recognised as a formal religion. It is a spiritual and ancestor-based religion and considered a religious form of witchcraft. It came to the West Indies with slaves imported by the French. The word 'voodoo' is believed to have originated in Louisiana in the mid-1800s, possibly from the French word 'voudou'; today it is primarily practiced in Haiti (https://study.com/).

Within the Black community of the American South, voodoo worship had two prominent central figures: a high priest (Hougan) and Papa Legba. The Hougan had profound knowledge and experience. Papa

Jimi Hendrix, during a concert at Berkeley, California 1970. (Credit: Granger/Bridgeman Images).

Legba, one of the many *Iwa* spirits in voodoo, is believed to be an intermediary between humanity and a supreme being. Practitioners can call upon Papa Legba (or other spirits) for assistance and guidance.

Voodoo sorcery was available to those practitioners who wanted powerful charms and potions for both negative and positive purposes. This form of sympathetic magic was administered by men and women adept in voodoo lore. They were known as conjurors, gypsies, root doctors, shamans and witch doctors. High John the Conqueror root was an effective tool used along with items such as coins, bones, cats' claws, hair, teeth and herbs, which were used in conjunction with the root and wrapped in a small cloth bag and implemented, for example, to win back a wayward lover (Hendrix, 2014, 311). The track *Voodoo Chile* from the *Electric Ladyland* album makes references to voodoo, planets and nature.

Kathy Etchingham recalled that Jimi used to carry a lock of her hair in his shoe, stuck in a piece of Sellotape, which she said stemmed from his voodoo beliefs. She said he believed that "if he had a piece of me on him, then we were in touch with each other." When he started to wear hats, he transferred her lock of hair to the leather band inside the crown of the hat. Jimi discussed voodoo with her and told her about one of the practices which involved "… how people stuck needles into effigies of their enemies" (Etchingham, 1999, 68).

Through some of his songs we can see the influence of his metaphysical curiosity. Examples include *Astro Man*, *If 6 Was 9*, *The Valleys of Neptune*, *Scorpio Woman*, *The Stars That Play With Laughing Sam's Dice*, *Third Stone From The Sun*, and *Voodoo Chile*. Dannemann observed that "he had the wisdom of a philosopher although he was only in his late twenties" (Dannemann, 1995, 93). His long-time friend Billy Cox commented to *Guitar Player* magazine in 1985 that "Jimi's spirituality, his whole psyche, was that of someone from another planet. He felt that way about himself" (Dannemann, 1995, 12).

Faith, Politics & Racism

Regarding politics, it has been said that "Jimi's politics was the politics of love, music, spirit, and transcendence" (Roby & Schreiber, 2010, 183), but Jimi was also vocal about the politics of racism and violence, and he was no stranger to brutality, fighting, and violent behaviour himself.

The summer of 1967 was marred by the worst racial violence of the decade in parts of America. *The Jimi Hendrix Experience* played in Detroit in August, shortly after the race riots had destroyed much of the city and left 42 people dead. Jimi commented, "The Negro riots in the States are crazy. Discrimination is crazy. I think we can live without these problems, but because of the violence, these problems aren't solved yet. There's a lot of silly talk on both sides" (Hendrix, 2014, 76).

In addition, Jimi voiced his opinion about agitators and politicians who played their part in stirring the riots. He believed that "there is no such thing as a colour problem. It is a weapon for the negative forces who are trying to destroy the country. He believed that the establishment made Black and White communities fight against each other in the streets so that ultimately they could take control at the end by imprisoning people." Jimi concluded, "I wish they'd had electric guitars in the cotton fields back in the good old days. A whole lot of things would have been straightened out; not just for the black and white, but I mean for the cause" (ibid.).

On the subject of transcendence, Hendrix was once questioned about whether the teachings of the Maharishi Mahesh Yogi appealed to him. Hendrix's reply was, "I don't really believe that his transcendental meditation is much more than daydreaming. If you really believe in yourself, you can stick it out on your own. You don't need someone else" (Hendrix, 2014, 98).

The Hindu yogi introduced the practice of Transcendental Meditation (TM) to the West, and it grew in popularity in the late 1960s, when bands such as *The Beatles* and other celebrities followed his teachings for a short while.

Sagittarians are often enthused by potential and opportunities. However, where there is seemingly no meaning to life, then potentially this casts a shadow side to the Sagittarian's sunny disposition, as in depression, for example, which Jimi experienced. He penned the song *Manic Depression* for the debut studio album *Are You Experienced*. Jimi once commented on this song as being "ugly times music. It's so ugly you can feel it" (Hendrix, 2014, 62).

The sign has confidence and faith that everything will work out well in the end. However, at times, such belief can err on naivety, which can have challenging consequences, and Jimi was no exception to this. Eric Burdon remarked that, "the remainder of Jimi's life was a cascade of accidents, screw-ups, and bad decisions" (Burdon, 2001, 132). One example being his connection with executive and record producer, Ed Chalpin. The inexperienced Jimi signed with Chalpin when he was a member of the *Curtis Knight Band*, but he was still under contract when he left for Britain with Chas Chandler. After *The Jimi Hendrix Experience* broke up in 1968, Jimi lost a lawsuit that Chalpin had brought against him. Although Chalpin was not instrumental in Jimi's career and success, he made a fortune from the album *Band of Gypsys*, which was compiled and released purely to pay for the legal proceedings.

Jimi was also pressured in New York by *The Black Panther Party for Self Defence*. The political party was an African American revolutionary organisation with an ideology of Black Nationalism, Socialism, and armed self-defence, particularly against police brutality. They put pressure on Jimi to actively support their cause (unsuccessfully) and also used his name without permission in promoting one of their benefit concerts.

Speaking of the British police in an interview in 1967, he commented, "I think the British police are very groovy over here. They don't bother you very much" (Hendrix, 2014, 97).

In another interview with journalist Keith Altman, Jimi was once asked what he would change in the world; his reply was, "The colours in the street" (Roby & Schreiber, 2010, 183). He also commented on another occasion, "I don't look at things in terms of races; I look at things in terms of people" (Dannemann, 1995, 143). Jimi penned a song which was dedicated to all minority repressed groups, called *I Don't Live Today*, which appeared on the *Are You Experienced* album.

Clearly, his politics and philosophy about universal love were at odds with some of *The Black Panthers'* ideology. He said of *The Black Panthers*: "I naturally feel a part of what they're doing in certain respects ... But I'm not for the aggression or violence or whatever you want to call it. I'm not for guerrilla warfare" (Hendrix, 2014, 143).

The above comments by Jimi are in keeping with the Moon conjunct Jupiter aspect of his natal chart. It demonstrates his innate faith in life and all people, coupled with a belief system built around feelings of safety and security, as opposed to doctrine and dogma. He essentially believed that what unites humanity would always be stronger than what divides it. Eric Burdon commented after Jimi's death, "As young as Jimi was, he had a crystal-clear vision of international multicultural possibilities" (Burdon & Craig, 2001, 123).

Undoubtedly, Hendrix's comments about race come from his own experience of bigotry and segregation. This included being in the south of America and excluded from entertaining in certain clubs, and eating in specific restaurants, as well as experiencing second-rate travel with the 'Whites Only – No Blacks' ruling. On one occasion, Jimi was taken to jail for deliberately ignoring a 'Whites Only' sign in a Nashville diner, purposely sitting in that section.

When *The Jimi Hendrix Experience* was on tour with *The Monkees* in Jacksonville in the Deep South, their assigned limousine driver was a member of the *Ku Klux Klan*. The defiant Jimi sat in the passenger's seat next to the chauffeur to make a point. Mitch Mitchell recalled how racism occurred not only because Jimi was black but also because he was working and performing with white guys (Mitchell, 1993, 37).

He was involved with the beginning of the civil rights movement in the South and regularly attended Sunday demonstrations and marches with blacks on one side of the street and whites on the other (Roby & Schreiber, 38).

Jimi's American Indian ancestors were subjected to brutality by the white man, and of course there was the Vietnam War, which he narrowly escaped. All in all, it shows the yearning for peace and love, the principle of the Neptune in Libra generation into which he was born. It was the beginning of a new culture of youth, and justice and civil rights movements were making progress.

Jupiter, Style & Roots

Jupiter is Sagittarius' ruling planet and is associated with abundance, excess, growth, horizons, good fortune and fame. The colour associated with Jupiter is purple, and the gem which corresponds with Jupiter is turquoise. Interestingly, Jimi wrote a poem in 1970 entitled *Beam Me Up Jupiter*. The words suggest that he instinctively knew he didn't have much longer on the earth plane and that his new 'home' was the spiritual plane. Astrologically, Saturn (and Pluto) is associated with cycles of beginnings and endings, and these planets are referenced in the aforementioned poem.

Jupiter in Cancer suggests that Jimi enjoyed history and learning about the past. He was indeed absorbed with his family heritage and lineage. Eric Burdon said that Jimi had "an understanding of American culture and religion and had the knowledge of a shaman … later in his life he took counsel from the late great medicine man, Rolling Thunder" (Burdon & Craig, 2001, 123).

Jimi's last girlfriend, Monika Dannemann, commented that "he felt close to American culture and believed he had been an American Indian in a past life – Wasami, meaning thunder" (Dannemann, 1995, 73). His grandmother taught him stories about Indian laws, and he remembered that she said, "If you don't keep your balance, nature will make you pay. You can't defy nature. You can only respect it and work with it" (Lawrence, 2006, 147).

The ascendant (*see glossary*) position in a natal chart represents our outer appearance and the initial impression that we make on the outer world. Jimi strongly identified with his American Indian roots, and this was reflected significantly in the clothes that he wore as a young boy and also the stage persona of Jimi Hendrix the performer. His off-stage style was equally creative and visual, which is in keeping with a Sagittarian ascendant.

When attending school, he often wore the ponchos and shawls that his grandmother had made him, only to be ridiculed by his fellow students. He recalled how his grandmother, who still had "long silvery hair" (Hendrix, 2014, 15), gave him a little Mexican jacket with tassels. He commented, "It was real good, and I wore it to school every day in spite of what people might have thought, just because I liked it. I liked to be different" (ibid.).

After he became famous, he was asked, "Why is it necessary to be dressed peculiarly?" His candid reply was, "Well, I don't consider it actually necessary. This is the way I like to dress and look, off stage and on. I like shades of colour that clash" (Hendrix, 2014, 51).

Jimi's stage persona often reflected the roots of the Cherokee American Indians. He wore headbands, scarves around his legs, fringed jackets and trousers, as well as beautifully crafted silver and turquoise jewellery. Colour symbolism held tremendous importance for Jimi, as he saw his music in terms of colours (Dannemann, 1995, 110); this will be discussed further on.

His hairstyle was also distinct at the time; he was inspired by Bob Dylan's hair to style his own hair in a similar way – Jimi would carry pink plastic curlers in his guitar case. Linda Keith recalled that "he had processed hair that had spent the nights in curlers, so when he took the curlers out it remained in exactly the same form" (www.guardian.com). Jimi believed that the upright strands of his hair were vibrations. He described his hair: "I think this hairstyle is groovy. A mod Shirley Temple. A frizzy permanent" (Hendrix, 2014, 51).

Jimi was also inspired by Dylan's music and lyrics. Fans of the two singers will know that Hendrix covered *All Along The Watchtower* and

Like A Rolling Stone. Interestingly, Dylan and Hendrix both had the Sagittarius ascendant in their natal charts.

Kathy Etchingham recalled that Jimi "... liked bright colours and sumptuous textures like silks, chiffons and velvets." She also recalled how his Burberry-style raincoat was ill-matched with his wild hair, and as a couple they gained attention for his unusual appearance – not necessarily for him being famous (Etchingham, 1999, 69) or one half of a bi-racial couple.

She also recalled how he wore "satin shirts with voluminous sleeves, army jackets and bell-bottoms with scarves tied around the legs, long before anyone else." She enjoyed and indulged his original and flamboyant style.

His army jackets included a Hussars jacket from the Crimean War, which he purchased from the Portabello Road market. He also had an antique military jacket with elaborate gold braiding around the collar and sleeves with brass buttons, which was gifted to him by his friend, Eric Burdon (Burdon & Craig, 2001, 126). Etchingham commented that she bought him a black shirt with roses on it, which he wore regularly; it was at a time when men rarely wore anything so flamboyant (Etchingham, 1999, 91).

Before he became famous in his own right, Jimi was unable to develop and express himself in the way that he would have liked to. For example, when he worked with Wilson Pickett's backing group, he revealed that he (Jimi) "was shy, scared and afraid to be myself. I had my hair slicked back and my mind combed out" (Hendrix, 2014, 52). This certainly will have crippled his artistic and freedom-loving nature and inhibited the 'true' Jimi.

Care, Dependency & Nurture

The Moon in Cancer suggests that there was a considerable side to Jimi that needed to be nurtured and protected – a part of his nature that was dependent, needy, sensitive and vulnerable. The Moon conjunct Jupiter suggests that, emotionally, he was a 'big kid' – something which remained with him through adulthood. Mostly he fostered good relations with the mothers of his friends, girlfriends and band members.

He spoke fondly about his biological mother, commenting, "... my mother used to like dressing up and having a good time. She used to drink a lot and didn't take care of herself, but she was a groovy mother" (Hendrix, 2014, 15). Regarding his step-mother, June, and his stepsister, one article reported that his stepmother's relationship with Jimi was "cordial and familial." They developed a close bond, and Jimi was particularly pleased to have a younger step-sister in Janie (www.musiclipse.com). Jimi and Janie met several times before his untimely death in 1970.

Jimi was certainly dependent on women, perhaps more so than some. As a child, he had various women care for and mother him when his biological mother was missing and when his father had strayed away for days at a time. As an adult, he roused women who wanted to care and cook for him and, not forgetting, wanted to bed him. His girlfriend, Lithofayne Pridgon (aka 'Apollo Faye'), commented how she used to refer to him as 'the Baby'. She added that "he didn't like that term of endearment. The irony was that I really did feel like his mother at times." (Roby & Schreiber, 2010, 123).

Jimi's younger brother, Leon, identified with Jimi's song *Little Wing*. He interpreted it as his brother paying homage to "all of the wonderful loving women who took care of us over the years. He wrote it for his girlfriends, our aunties, and especially for our mama, who looked over us from high above in the afterlife" (Roby & Schreiber, 2010, 219).

There were, of course, times in his life when he demonstrated his own caring and nurturing nature, one example being towards Leon. His brother recalled their early childhood and revealed of Jimi: "Daily, he protected and watched over me. When I was hungry, he helped me find something to eat. Whenever our parents fought, he wrapped his arm around my shoulder and comforted me," showing the love between the two brothers and the responsible and tender side of Jimi's nature (Hendrix, 2012, 12).

For those with the Moon in Cancer position in their natal chart, home and food are usually seen as especially important. This is because they provide a great source of comfort; although, on occasion, when he was a child, sometimes he had to steal food to be able to eat. He never owned his own home, which many rock stars did, although he rented a flat with Kathy Etchingham.

Relationships, Freedom & Excitement

In Jimi's natal chart, the Moon is positioned in the seventh house, the area associated with significant partnerships, both personal and professional. This suggests that relationships, especially with women, may have been emotionally charged and that freedom-loving Jupiter, also in the seventh house, will have wanted to feel free.

Venus in Sagittarius (ruled by Jupiter) is another pointer that Jimi approved of 'free love' and open relationships, albeit on his terms. Venus is in the twelfth house, which (amongst other things) is associated with secrets; therefore, it can also be an indicator of clandestine affairs. Sagittarius is candid and open, so the position more suggests that Jimi was open about his other women, groupies included. His term for groupies was 'Electric Ladies', and the album *Electric Ladyland* was all about them (Hendrix, 2014, 113).

Girlfriend Carol Shirosky was quick to understand that there would never be a monogamous, long-term relationship with Jimi. She commented, "If you tried to hold him down, that's when you lost him." There were nights when he didn't come home, and although Shirosky knew he was with another woman, she would never question him, as he would have left. Like many of Jimi's women, she accepted and played by his rules (Roby & Schreiber, 2014, 147). Very broadly speaking, we could say, in Jimi's case at least, that Venus in Sagittarius is associated with an excess of women.

The Sagittarius ascendant coupled with the Gemini descendant (*see glossary*) in his natal chart suggests that he could be restless and therefore always in search of pastures new and would find it easy to have a variety of partners. It is believed by some commentators that he had casual affairs with women who were equally as famous as he was; for example, Brigitte Bardot (Cross, 2005, 264) and Janis Joplin (Amburn, 1994, 141).

Interestingly, his significant partner, Kathy Etchingham, was a Gemini, born on 18th June, 1946. After growing closer and more intimate with Jimi, she observed that "... he, like me, had never had a normal, cosy family life as a child and had been left feeling insecure and vulnerable" (Etchingham, 1999, 66/67).

Jimi is likely to have found satisfaction in a partner who could be not only a lover but who also offered him intellectualism, debate and exchange of ideas, and somebody to learn from, as well as somebody who was humorous and witty and who at times he could be playful and silly with.

Etchingham recalled that she and Jimi often visited the famous *Hamleys* toy shop in London and would buy games such as Monopoly, Risk, Scrabble and Twister. The latter game, she recalled, "used to have us helpless with laughter." Jimi also bought himself a car-racing Scalextric set, which was set up on the lounge floor, where they would compete with each other and race the cars (Etchingham, 1998, 68/69).

She commented that Jimi "... opened the door for me to become myself ... Together we made an anchor for each other, even though we were both independent, scared of commitment, and really too young to understand any of it" (Etchingham, 1998, 68).

Uranus positioned in the fifth house is associated with (amongst other things) romantic and sexual liaisons, often unconventional, which may be formed and broken off suddenly. One small example of this can be seen in the following account in Noel Redding's autobiography, where the shocking and unpredictable nature of Uranus is prevalent.

He commented that one drunken night in Sweden, Jimi had befriended a gay Swedish journalist, and Jimi suggested that the four of them (Hendrix, Mitchell, Redding & the journalist) have a foursome: "The Swede was pushing it, and the vibes got stronger and stranger ..." (Redding & Appleby, 1990, 73). Jimi made a pass at Redding, who declined, and the tension led to Jimi smashing up everything in his room. Redding continued that "it was terrifying to see – and very sobering. I hate violence of any kind. The journalist split" (ibid.).

Regarding the subject of marriage, Jimi had strong and defined views. He commented in an interview in 1967: "I have no intention of getting married ... Those are nothing but artificial rules ... Marriage certificates are only for people who feel insecure." He added: "You can give yourself to somebody, and you can take yourself away from somebody if you want to ... Freedom is the key word to this whole thing" (Hendrix, 2014, 96).

This shows his (then) unconventional view about marriage and how the idea of commitment is in conflict with his free-spirited nature, which is indicated by several astrological aspects in his natal chart, one example being the Venus opposition to Saturn.

Given his views on marriage, it is odd that his last girlfriend, Monika Dannemann, claimed they were engaged and she entitled her book, which was published in 1995, *The Inner World of Jimi Hendrix by His Fiancée, Monika Dannemann*. Journalist Mary Braid reported that after Hendrix died, Dannemann "built up a life based on their relationship. But in the end, Monika Dannemann was the victim of her own self-delusion" (www.independent.co.uk/), which suggests that being his fiancée was part of her fantasy.

Returning to the interpretation of Uranus in the fifth house, it can also indicate that a parent may be cut off or separated from their children, which certainly seems to have been the case with Jimi. When interviewed in 1967, he was asked if he liked children; he replied, "Yeah, I like kids. I guess I like them any age" (Hendrix, 2014, 98). Most likely, he was fearful of permanent responsibility where children were concerned, given his restless and freedom-loving nature and that it would also hinder his time for musical creativity.

Venus is in opposition to Uranus in his natal chart and echoes some of the themes associated with Uranus in the fifth house and also the Gemini descendant are, for example, the desire for social and sexual excitement, which may lead to on-off relating patterns, as well as changing partners frequently. If any relationships were going to flourish, then excitement, unpredictability and space for personal exploration and independence would have been necessary.

The aspect also suggests that Jimi may have alienated others by having an uncooperative attitude, a theme echoed by other aspects in his natal chart (such as the Sun opposing Uranus). Venus in opposition (*see glossary*) to Uranus can also suggest that there may be sudden changes of fortune, and as we know for Jimi, there was indeed that unpredictability surrounding finances.

The Sun opposing Uranus indicates that Jimi took pride in his originality and uniqueness and that for him freedom and independence were everything. He was uncompromising and cut across conservatism and tradition, and in return he met with resistance from mainstream society. His search for truth included wanting others to progress and seek and find their own truths. Those less spiritually enlightened may have regarded him as eccentric and rebellious.

Creative Freedom, Experimentation & Shockwaves

Uranus is positioned in the fifth house and is also indicative of his creative and genius guitar playing. This included playing the instrument with his teeth, behind his back and, of course, left- and right-handed. Jimi's legendary appearance at the Monterey Festival in 1967, where he kneeled before his guitar, having covered its body in lighter fuel, set it on fire and finally smashed it to pieces, is a good example of the shocking and unsettling energy of Uranus. Writer Michael Lydon described the act as "a pagan religious sacrament" (Bebergal, 2015, 55).

Interestingly, electricity is a correspondence of Uranus. In 1969, Jimi described the (then) band's music as "Electric Church Music," where they played a fusion of blues, jazz, and rock'n'roll with a lot of noise (Hendrix, 2014, 137). He philosophised that "Everything is electrified nowadays, so therefore the belief comes through electricity to the people." He likened the band's music to 'shock therapy' to spiritually awaken people (Hendrix, 2014, 139).

Here we can see the distinctive and progressive nature of Uranus at play. Jimi recognised that for some people it would be difficult for them to comprehend the name and its meaning and they would respond by either a "gasp" or 'exclaim" (ibid.).

In Jimi's natal chart, the Sun is positioned in the eleventh house, the area associated with friends, groups, hopes and wishes. This indicates scope for good leadership and being a natural leader in any group. An obvious example being his part in *The Jimi Hendrix Experience* and the *Band of Gypsies*, and he was a member of several backing groups before his success. Other examples of his teamwork include when he was a member of a basketball team at school, and also when he was a soldier in the US Army (the latter was less successful for him).

The position of the Sun in the eleventh house is often a position of 'freedom fighters'. Jimi often spoke about freedom, both personal and in a broader sense. When he autographed items for fans, he often wrote: 'Stay Free'. He also penned the song *Freedom*, which is on the *First Rays of the New Rising Sun* compilation album, and *Stone Free* from the *Are You Experienced* album.

He also recognised that artistic freedom (Venus in Sagittarius in the twelfth house) was important to all creatives and not just himself. His generosity and warmth of spirit towards his band, *The Jimi Hendrix*

Experience, was evident when he claimed that all three of them should be able to develop their own musical interests outside of the band, as well as having an opportunity to grow within the band.

Jimi commented in 1968 that he was uncomfortable with the band being called *The Jimi Hendrix Experience*. He would have preferred the group to be called *Experience* – he claimed that without Mitch Mitchell and Noel Redding, he would not have been successful as *The Jimi Hendrix Experience* (Hendrix, 2014, 123/124).

He said, "I've always insisted we were a three-piece group and should be acknowledged as such" (Hendrix, 2014, 140). He felt the spotlight shouldn't permanently be on him, as Mitchell and Redding equally contributed. Jimi believed in fairness and justice, which is in keeping with his Libra MC (*see glossary*); these areas are associated with Libra and its ruler, Venus.

Leadership, Political Ideology & Big Dreams

Pluto in Leo indicates that he was a powerful and magnetic leader and wanted society to transform for the better; he used his music to convey his message. The Pluto in Leo generation (1939–1958) made its mark with creativity, individualism and a desire for self-expression. This age group was born during or after World War II, and many of their fathers fought in the war. The generation experienced the rise of the civil rights movement and rock'n'roll, as well as an increasing emphasis on personal freedom.

The political idealism connected with Jimi's eleventh house in the natal chart also indicates his group's ideals for the future, coupled with respect for the cause or subject which united them. This can be construed through Jimi's bands, as well as the crowds that he drew at the hippie festivals. The philosophy of making love not war, and peace and harmony, was pivotal in the Neptune in Libra collective's future dreams for humanity's progress.

The themes of freedom, liberty, independence and truths are strong in Jimi's natal chart and are shown in the following areas: Mercury (in the eleventh house) and Venus in Sagittarius, Uranus in the fifth house, Neptune in the ninth house and Aquarius (ruled by Uranus) being the sign of the second house cusp – the area associated with earnings, possessions, resources and values, as well as various other aspects.

Many of Jimi's friends were also in bands. One example being the aforementioned Billy Cox, who was also in the 101st Airborne Division with Jimi. A musician himself, he later became a member of Jimi's group the *Band of Gypsies*. Cox said that Jimi always wanted to be in a band and be famous.

This was evident from the start when Jimi got his first guitar and told his father, "Oh Daddy, one of these days I'm gonna be big and famous; I'm gonna make it, man!" (Hendrix, 2014, 21). Through self-belief and determination, his goals came to fruition. Eric Burdon and Brian Jones were also loyal friends to Jimi. Acknowledging how important his friends were to him, Jimi said in an interview, "My friends are the people who give me a belief in myself" (Hendrix, 2014, 120).

One example of a wish coming true for him was having a permanent recording studio. This came to fruition as the *Electric Lady Land* studios in New York. Originally, however, Jimi wanted the premises to be in Hawaii. This was because he believed that Hawaii was the centre of the planet's entire positive energy. However, his manager Jeffery prohibited it, which is why the studios were finally built in New York (Burdon & Craig, 2001, 130), and Jimi's original dream for it to be in Hawaii was thwarted.

Truths & Unique Perspectives

Returning to the astrology again, there are several aspects that the Sun is making to other planets in Jimi's natal chart which suggest robust self-expression and willpower. The Sun conjunct (*see glossary*) Mercury indicates that he loved company and welcomed the exchange of ideas and viewpoints. He could communicate his ideas skilfully, although at times he may have been perceived as self-opinionated, and he liked to leave a lasting impression.

He was broad-minded with a unique way of perceiving things, certainly able to think outside the box. Mercury in opposition to Uranus shows a capacity for free speech, original ideas, and radical thoughts, and that he was a unique communicator; speaking this truth was important to him.

This position also indicates changes of mind and ideas, as well as bolt-lightning ideas which spontaneously came out of the blue. This is particularly relevant to the numerous times that he would receive sudden inspiration for riffs and song lyrics. He would quickly pen his ideas before he forgot them, putting his thoughts down on anything that was at hand: napkins, matchboxes, notebooks, postcards – whatever was available.

His unique perceptions included being able to see auras and identifying feelings with colours. He told Monika Dannemann that if he focused hard enough, he could see a person's aura, and that people with a developed sixth sense had this ability. Jimi also told her that when he astral-travelled, he had seen the auras of Jupiter and Saturn (Dannemann, 1995, 102).

He recognised that his observations may (then) have been vastly different from other people's, or, as he would have said, "far out and groovy." He commented that some feelings made him think of different colours: "Jealousy is purple, and I'm purple with rage or purple with anger. And green is envy" (Hendrix, 2014, 94).

Jimi had his own philosophy about the metaphysical meaning of colour and connected that with certain emotions and ideas. He revealed. "I want to get colour into music – I'd like to play a note and have it come out as a colour" (Dannemann, 1995, 110). And, as zealous fans will know, Jimi incorporated lyrics which included colour into his song lyrics. He also encompassed colour from his vivid dreams into his music; one example being *Purple Haze*.

Many people incorrectly believe that Jimi was writing about drug experiences, perhaps because 'Purple Hearts' (amphetamine tablets) were a popular drug of the time. The lyric and title *Purple Haze* pertained to Jimi travelling through various dimensions. In part of the dream he journeyed into different dimensions and was walking under the sea where he got lost.

Part of the song pertained to him being surrounded by a 'purple haze' which engulfed him and led to him getting lost (Dannemann, 1995, 44). Drawing upon his own colour philosophy and using colours seen in his vivid dreams in his music is in keeping with his experimental and unique nature, illustrated by Uranus in the fifth house.

Mercury is in opposition to Saturn, which suggests that at times he could also be contrary, defensive and opinionated; sometimes he may have thought differently from everyone else just for the sake of being different. He may have found it difficult to agree with others, compromise or negotiate, and, certainly, understanding another's point of view could have been challenging for him at times. Kathy Etchingham observed that as he became more famous, he became increasingly harder to live with. He refused to see anyone else's point of view or take anyone's advice apart from his own (Etchingham, 1999, 113).

Monetary Pandemonium and Valuing Art, Beauty & Music

Venus in Sagittarius also suggests a blasé attitude towards money: easy come – easy go. Aged 26, he commented, "I travel most places without any money, actually. I like to witness different types of life, rich and poor. If I starve tomorrow, it would just be another experience to me ... I'd still give money away to people if they needed it badly. What's money except a piece of paper?" (Hendrix, 2014, 141).

Venus is opposite Saturn in his natal chart and (amongst other interpretations) suggests there may have been barriers, delays, limitations, and obstacles surrounding his finances. A small illustration of this can be seen by the following example.

When he worked in Little Richard's backing group, he was asked by Richard to cut his hair, but Jimi refused and consequently was issued a five-dollar fine. On another occasion, Richard didn't pay the band for five and a half weeks, and because of that, Jimi left the band. He said, "I quit because of a money misunderstanding ... Everybody on the tour was brainwashed" (Hendrix, 2014, 35).

Venus is positioned in the twelfth house and can indicate confusion, deception, loss, sacrifice, and vulnerability. This is pertinent to what we know about Jimi, in terms of the aforementioned Little Richard examples, and also him losing the lawsuit against Ed Chalpin.

Some commentators have alleged that Jimi's co-manager, Mike Jeffery, syphoned off much of Jimi's income into his offshore accounts, although there has been no evidence to support this narrative. Jeffery died in 1973, in a mid-air collision over France, aged 39.

Monika Dannemann said of Jimi that "money meant nothing to him; he just didn't care about organising it" (Dannemann, 1995, 88). She added that "the 'chaotic' part of his career was almost entirely on the business side, never the artistic" (Dannemann, 1995, 88).

Another example of Jimi's disdain for money, as well as his generosity, can be seen in the following example. Aged nineteen, he was discharged from the army in July of 1962, and he had approximately 400 dollars in his pocket. He decided to visit a jazz club in Clarksville, stay the night, and return to Seattle in the morning. However, his generosity and high spirits got the better of him. After some drinks, he started to hand out money to anyone who asked him for it.

He left the club with a mere sixteen dollars; this was an insufficient sum to get him back from Tennessee to Seattle, as it was 200 miles away (Hendrix, 2014, 30). This example shows the Sun conjunct Venus in action and illustrates Jimi's extravagance and sociability, as well as his wanting to be seen as big-hearted and open-handed.

The Sun and Venus contact indicates that beauty was important to Jimi – not just in the sensual and physical sense, but also through art, music, and nature. He loved animals, and when he was a child living in Seattle, he had cats and dogs. He also described the deer and horses that he saw there as being "the prettiest" (Hendrix, 2014, 16). After touring in Sweden, he described it as "the most beautiful country on Earth" (Hendrix, 2014, 64).

He commented that when he was four years old, his first instrument was a harmonica and then a violin; he added, "I always dug string instruments and pianos" (Hendrix, 2014, 19). When he was approximately fourteen or fifteen, he started to play guitar.

In addition to these values, the concept of inner and outer peace held great significance to Jimi. However, although he sang and wrote about this, at times he could be brutal and violent, which will be discussed further on. An example of his pacifist stance can be seen in his anti-war song, *Machine Gun*, which was performed with the *Band of Gypsies* in New York City, 1969, at the *Fillmore East First Show*.

The Sweet-talker's Thirst for Knowledge & Stimulation

Mercury is also conjunct Venus, which indicates his love of learning, reading, languages, speaking, words, and lyrics. It shows that he was often thinking about Venusian themes such as love, music, peace and harmony, and at times he could be a charming 'sweet-talker'.

Although his experience of education was frustrating and unsatisfactory, it did not stop his thirst for learning and wanting to read. He revealed in an interview that he "read a lot of science fiction. And I love reading fairytales, like Hans Christian Andersen and *Winnie-the-Pooh*" (Hendrix, 2014, 50).

When Jimi was arrested in 1969 at Toronto airport for packing a small piece of heroin in his luggage, airport officials also saw a book of Jimi's, *You Can Change Your Life Using Psychic Power* (by Jo-Anne Chase and Constance Moon), in his bag. Fortunately for him, Jimi's confidante and music journalist Sharon Lawrence took the blame in court for the heroin being put in his bag (Burdon & Craig, 2001, 133). Musician Juma Sultan commented that by 1969, Jimi was intently reading the Bible (Cross, 2005, 293).

Other books that he owned included *The Tibetan Book of the Dead* and *Secret Places of the Lion: Alien Influences on Earth's Destiny*. The latter was about space aliens' involvement in human culture for centuries – a theory which Jimi believed. In addition, he also read *The Book of Urantia*, which was an alternative bible for UFO believers. It fused tales of Jesus with stories of alien visitations. During the summer of 1970, during the making of the film *Rainbow Bridge*, Jimi apparently took the *Urantia* book and also his Bob Dylan songbook everywhere with him (Cross, 2005, 307).

The aforementioned scope of reading material is a good example of the Mercury in Sagittarius position, which shows how broad-minded he was. Eric Burdon described Jimi as being "very spiritual, very searching and inquisitive" (Cross, 2005, 122). Mitch Mitchell said, "One thing I always found surprising about Jimi was that he'd not spent much time in the American school system ... Despite that, he was incredibly literate and in possession of a great deal of wisdom" (Mitchell, 1990, 24). Noel Redding commented that "Jimi had an open and loving mind" (Redding & Appleby, 1990, 130).

Fear of Authority and Control, and Optimism & Stamina

Jimi's freedom-loving Sagittarian nature was conflicted with Saturn, the planet associated with caution, limitation, discipline, and responsibility, which is shown by Saturn opposing the Sun in his natal chart. This aspect illuminates a fear of authority, control, and discipline and is borne out in what we know about his earlier life.

One example is that of Jimi's harsh and domineering father, Al. Jimi recalled that as a child, he twice ran away from his father's care because he was so unhappy. "I couldn't stand it at home ... Once, I ran away after a blazing row with my dad. He hit me in the face, and I ran away"

(Hendrix, 2014, 18). This particular example can be interpreted as the Sun opposing Saturn through Jimi's self-defence, which resulted in him escaping from home (although he did return).

In addition, his experience of the establishment – namely the army, church, education system, and politics – all added up to being limiting and obstructive. Certainly, these were testing areas for him, and being kept under strict control and surveillance would have frustrated him, as would discipline, organisation, and routine. Spontaneity was everything to him. However, endurance and stamina (correspondences of Saturn), coupled with the optimistic and wilful nature of the Sun, is an illustration of Jimi's determination and vision to get where he wanted to be, musically speaking.

This theme is echoed by the position of Mars in the tenth house of his natal chart. It shows that he had a burning desire to succeed in his arena and battled his way to the top with purpose and strength, albeit with trials and tribulations along the way.

Astrologer and author Sue Tomkins observed that for many with the Sun opposite Saturn in their natal chart, they are 'fame freaks'. Although they are desperate to be seen, they are conflicted in that they feel uncomfortable about putting themselves forward (Tomkins, 1990, 109). This is certainly borne out in Linda Keith's frustration when she first met Jimi. She perceived him as being apathetic in taking the lead to make himself a star, unmotivated and not recognising his own creative genius.

Ill-health & The Challenging Taskmaster

Saturn is positioned in the sixth house of his natal chart, which suggests that there were challenges with nutrition, health, and work. As Saturn is associated with being a taskmaster, it indicates that he had to work hard for his money, take any responsibilities seriously, and pay attention to detail in areas such as agreements and contracts.

It seems that nutritious eating was not a priority of Jimi's, which, to be fair, was difficult when travelling and touring. A small but telling example follows. Singer Etta James commented that she knew Jimi when they both played the clubs in Harlem. The performers and crew nicknamed Jimi '*Egg Foo Yung*' because he ate that same meal every night in a Chinese restaurant (Roby, 2010, 77).

Lithofayne Pridgon, one of Jimi's girlfriends in Harlem, commented that he developed an ulcer because of stress; he hardly ate, suffered weight loss and chest pains, was generally nervous, and chain-smoked. One brand of cigarettes that he liked to smoke was the menthol *Kools* (Lawrence, 2006, 146). Some of these medical conditions he apparently had from his army days (Roby, 2010, 86).

In addition, there was a more significant health problem which he refused to consult a doctor about. Pridgon revealed that Jimi liked to play his guitar on the bed and frequently fell asleep with his guitar lying on his chest. He had problems sleeping on his back and during the middle of the night would make choking sounds which were followed by muscle spasms. Pridgon would have to roll him onto his side to stop them. She said that she "wasn't surprised that he died from choking-related circumstances" (Roby, 2010, 87).

Gemini is the cusp of the sixth house, the area associated with health and ill-health. In the branch of medical astrology, Gemini and its ruler, Mercury, are associated with the lungs and nerves, as well as the arms and ribs. Fresh air, light and movement would have been helpful to Jimi. Uranus is also in Gemini and is an indicator that he could easily put pressure and strain on his nervous system, finding it difficult to relax and living on his nerves. The Sun opposing Uranus also indicates a nervous disposition and that he could be irritable and highly strung, and he may have experienced highs and lows. His erratic behaviour may have alienated those he felt closest to.

Lunar Emotionality & Feeling It

The Moon rules Cancer, and in Jimi's natal chart, it is at home by the Moon being positioned in Cancer. In medical astrology, Cancer/Moon rules the breasts and stomach and is also connected with emotions, suggesting sensitivity in these areas. By nature, the Moon is changeable, and in astrology it is associated with emotions and feelings; therefore, it could be argued that Jimi may have been prone to mood swings.

The Moon conjunct Jupiter in Jimi's natal chart suggests that he may have been prone to huge emotional outpourings. This is certainly borne out by channelling his feelings into his lyrics, singing and guitar playing, which all in all makes for an explosive performance.

He revealed in an interview in 1968, "I feel everything I play. It's a release of all my inner feelings – aggression, tenderness, sympathy, everything" (Hendrix, 2014, 86). He also said, "True feelings are really the only qualities worth listening for in a voice" (Hendrix, 2014, 115). This reveals that for him, in performance and vocals, there must be real emotion to make it an authentic experience for the listener.

Linda Keith recalled when she first saw Jimi play at the *Cheetah Club* in New York: "He was astonishing – the moods he could bring to his music, his charisma, his skill and stage presence" (www.theguardian. com). Her comment reveals how Jimi was aware of feeling, mood and emotion in his performance way before he became famous. He once said, "Technically, I'm not a guitar player. All I play is truth and emotion" (Lawrence, 2006, pre-chapter 1, quotation).

This also pertains to a manifestation of the Moon square MC aspect in his natal chart. It suggests that he was emotionally invested in his career, perhaps to the detriment of personal relationships; there may have been an emotional disconnect where he pulled away from developing personal relationships and remained emotionally distant. Jimi said in 1967, "In the end, there has to be a complete marriage between words and music" (Hendrix, 2014, 61). Jupiter square MC suggests that he experienced a wealth of challenging times and hard work as he strove to achieve his goals for his career.

Lithofayne Pridgon commented that, to many observers, "Jimi was perceived offstage as quiet, contemplative, polite, absentminded, even ethereal" (Roby & Schreiber, 2001, 133). However, another Harlem-based girlfriend (originally the partner of Curtis Knight), Carol Shiroky, remembered being subjected to Jimi's frustrations and mood swings, particularly after gigs (Roby & Schreiber, 2010, 146).

Courage, Independence, Survival & Trauma

The Aries IC (*see glossary*) and Libra MC (*see glossary*) suggest that from a very early age Jimi learnt to be independent – a theme echoed by Uranus being positioned in the fifth house. He had to make his own way, as his home life was often intense, and often survival was the name of the game.

Themes such as anger, control, lust, and violence, as well as impulsiveness and risk-taking, were prevalent in his home life. In turn, he is likely to have learnt how to charm and negotiate in order to get what he wanted as part of his 'survival kit'. He may have harboured repressed anger and trauma from his upbringing, where he often experienced abandonment and observed domestic violence and infidelity.

Mars (the ruler of Aries) is positioned in Scorpio and is unaspected in Jimi's natal chart. This means that Mars has no relationship with any of the other planets, so the energy of the planet is able to work at its optimum and purest form. It can lead to unique developments and is sometimes powerful enough to dominate one's personality.

From what we understand of Jimi's short life, we know the following, which are in keeping with the correspondences of Mars/Aries. He was assertive, courageous, impulsive, motivated, daring, and certainly a survivor. He was a soldier, a leader (in music), and the firstborn child to Al and Lucille Hendrix. Jimi was perceived in his career (tenth house) by many as being independent, wilful, dynamic, and sexy.

Mars in Scorpio, coupled with Pluto in the eighth house, also indicates that he was a survivor, was driven to succeed, and was determined to reach his goals at the cost of being ruthless if necessary. This astrological data shows potential for an intense sex life, an insatiable sex drive, as well as a compelling presence, which would have been difficult to ignore. Kathy Etchingham described him: "Jimi oozed a sexuality that seemed dangerous and exotic" (Cross, 2005, 5).

The energy of Pluto (ruler of Scorpio) in the eighth house illustrates Jimi's tremendous inner strength and that he had exceptional willpower, with an ability to overcome any crisis and trauma, which may have been hidden from others. One example of a childhood trauma which was buried deep down is that of him being subjected to sexual abuse. The darker side of the human condition is also associated with Pluto and includes themes such as control, abuse of power, violation, and the taboo.

Biographer Charles R. Cross claimed in his Hendrix biography, *Room Full of Mirrors*, that Jimi had been sexually abused. Jimi told a girlfriend that he was sexually abused as a child and would only confide in her that the perpetrator was "a man in uniform". The conversation had arisen when his girlfriend described her childhood sexual abuse to him, and "Jimi broke down in tears" (Cross, 2005, 50/126). Clearly, he empathised with her, and it must have been a huge release for him in being able to share his secret with her.

Controlling Behaviour, Unpredictability & Violence

According to Lithofayne Pridgon, Jimi tried to control her behaviour and movements. An extreme example was when he physically restrained her in a New York hotel room. He tied her up by her arm and ankle, and when she started screaming, he tied one of his shirts around her mouth.

Pridgon claimed that "Jimi's temper was often uncontrollable" (Robey & Schreiber, 2010, 133). After that and other similar events, he would say, "I don't know what came over me. I really can't understand." He would grab his hair or cry. Pridgon also recalled how he used to get into fights with various band members (Robey & Schreiber, 2010, 134), and that Jimi "… used to always talk about some devil or something that was in him that he didn't have any control over" (Robey & Schreiber, 2010, 133).

Kathy Etchingham recalled that Jimi "… had a fierce temper that would occasionally flare, particularly when fuelled by alcohol, and heaven protect anyone in the way when it did" (Cross, 2005, 5). She wrote that they had many fights, and on one occasion Jimi kicked her in the face, and her nose was broken in three places (Hermon, 1982, 123). Eric Burdon recognised the conflicting nature and duplicity of his friend, commenting, "… one minute he is on stage singing about the masses of underdogs in America, and the next he's kicking the hell out of some poor chick in a back alley" (ibid.).

Noel Redding recalled that any conflicts which he and Jimi had were mainly about women. He recalled one occasion where he went home with a girl that Jimi was strongly attracted to: "Jimi freaked and hit her. Next day, all was forgotten – except by the poor girl, I guess" (Redding & Appleby, 1990, 48).

These examples of aggression, control, and jealousy show the intense downside nature of unaspected Mars in Scorpio with the exacerbated energy of Pluto in the eighth house.

The Venus trine Pluto aspect in Jimi's natal chart is also associated with compulsive affection, crisis, and trauma. It could manifest through intense feelings of jealousy, possessiveness and controlling behaviour – which was indeed the case in some of Jimi's relationships, as we already know. It must be said, however, that it does not follow that everyone with these aforementioned astrological positions in their chart will manifest as Jimi's did. Astrology is not fatalistic, and there are multiple interpretations to astrological information – one's behaviour is one's choice. Interestingly, Janis Joplin, like Jimi, had an unaspected Mars in the tenth house, as well as the Moon and Jupiter in Cancer.

Venus opposing Saturn suggests that Jimi may have wanted proof of affection in his relationships – and at the same time may have been fearful of love. What he interpreted as love may have been very different to that of his partner's. Venus is also opposing Uranus in Jimi's natal chart and suggests that he could be unpredictable and unsettled in relationships. In order to keep him interested, a budding partner would have needed to give Jimi his freedom and also bring excitement and surprise to the relationship.

Amusement, Laughter, Wit & Rapport

Another side to Jimi's nature was that of his sense of humour, which several people close to him commented upon. Mercury is associated with mentality, humour, and wit, and in Jimi's natal chart it is opposing Saturn and Uranus, which suggests a dry, original, and quirky sense of humour, as well as having a good sense of timing.

The Sun is conjunct Mercury, and the Moon is trine Mercury. This suggests that Jimi lived off his wits, had a sharp and quick silver tongue and was fun-loving and playful to be around when he was in the right mood. Eric Burdon commented, "That's probably the one thing people didn't realise about Jimi – he was hilarious" (Burdon & Craig, 2001, 148).

Bandmate Noel Redding wrote that he and Jimi "swapped jokes all the time – including racial ones. He'd tell us the jokes black people told about whites ... and we took it for what it was – humour. We shared a lot of humour" (Redding & Appleby, 1990, 130). Redding also commented on how he turned Jimi on to the British radio comedy programme, *The Goon Show*, and that Jimi "really appreciated their humour" – they were a favourite of Jimi's (Redding & Appleby, 1990, 110).

The Moon trine Mercury also indicates that Jimi had a need to discuss feelings through speech or writing, and that he also had a good recall of past experiences, which is good for jokes and story-telling. The aspect also indicates that, through acute observation of everyday life, he could find the comedic where perhaps others didn't.

Jimi Hendrix, USA c. 1970.
(Unknown photographer, 20th Century, Bridgeman Images).

The aspect is also indicative of how Jimi was able to generate a real rapport with his audience; he commented, "I know how to play by the way they react, by the feeling with the audience. It gets me in the right mood" (Hendrix, 2014, 58), showing how he could connect with the crowd.

Introspection, Privacy, Imagination & Inspiration

Jimi valued introspection, solitude and privacy when and where it was possible (shown by Venus in the twelfth house). He often referred to this as 'daydreaming time', and it was a time when he was receptive to inspiration and when his imagination was fertile (Hendrix, 2014, 59).

In addition to this, he also placed great worth on his vivid dreams – some of which were prophetic. He also commented on how his dreams were vivid and in colour and that the closest he had to a black and white dream was in pastel colours (Hendrix, 2014, 99). Venus in the twelfth house shows that he could draw sustenance from inner resources and could transcend himself through creative expression – especially art and music – and that he was very imaginative.

Interestingly, when he was a student at Garfield High School, Jimi had aspirations to be an actor or painter; he enjoyed abstract art, and amongst other subjects, he painted scenes on other planets, naming them with titles such as *Summer Afternoon on Venus* and *Martian Sunset*. He also wrote poetry – mainly about flowers, nature and people wearing robes (Hendrix, 2014, 17). In 1966, whilst being questioned as to what his professional ambition was, he replied, "I want to be the first man to write about the blues scene on Venus" (Hendrix, 2014, 50).

Foresight & Prophecy

Two examples of his prophetic dreams include one about his mother, which was in different shades of green and yellow. In it, she was saying farewell to him – and approximately two years after Jimi's dream, she died (Hendrix, 2014, 16). The second example of his predictive dreams is where he frequently used to see the digits '1966' in dreams.

He recalled that he felt "very strange that I was here for something and I was going to get a chance to be heard" (Hendrix, 2014, 21). As we know, 1966 was the year that Chas Chandler brought Jimi over to England, where he found fame and eventually became successful in America.

Jimi predicted his own death in the summer of 1970, when he said to Melinda Merryweather (art director of *Rainbow Bridge*) that he would be 'leaving' his body, "I won't be here anymore" (Cross, 2005, 308). Jimi penned *Scorpio Woman* as a tribute to her – Scorpio being her zodiac sign. This foresight remained with him, for in early September 1970, he told a Danish newspaper, "I'm not sure I will live to be 28 years old" (Dannemann, 1995, 153).

Chuck Wein (director of *Rainbow Bridge*) asked him days after this comment if he would play again in Seattle. Jimi's prophetic reply was, "Next time I go to Seattle, it'll be in a pine box" (Cross, 2005, 308), which sadly materialised on 18th September of 1970. Evidently, Jimi's clairvoyant ability was not confined to his dreams.

There are several aspects in Jimi's natal chart which indicate potential for the aforementioned artistic, imaginative and spiritual expression: the Moon trine Neptune, Mercury sextile Neptune, and Mercury conjunct Venus. Neptune is in the ninth house, and, as previously noted, Venus is in the twelfth house.

Reincarnation & Old Wounds

Given that Jimi believed in reincarnation and had a mild interest in astrology, he may have been interested in the area of astrology that addresses reincarnation and past lives, which is about the positioning of the Moon's nodes – the North Node and South Node (known to the Chinese as the Dragon's Head and Dragon's Tail). The Moon's nodes are the points where the Moon crosses the path of the Earth as it orbits the Sun.

The Nodes are karmic points which are believed to bestow guidance on how to live one's life in order to advance on one's spiritual path. The North Node suggests the qualities one should develop in this incarnation, whilst the South Node advises the qualities one should inhibit, which are residues from previous incarnations.

The North Node is in Leo at the eighth house, and the South Node is in Aquarius at the second house in Jimi's natal chart. Astrologer and author Victor Olliver observed of this nodal pairing, "You're happy to work in teams but may find that you're suppressing a natural talent that is hidden in collective actions. In this life, no matter your circumstances, allow your star quality to shine. Time to step up" (Olliver, 2022, 48).

Certainly, Jimi shone, roared and was heard once he came to England and was spotlighted in *The Jimi Hendrix Experience* with his unique and stand-alone performances. His journey and struggle for success, which originated in his homeland, included being unable to shine his light and express himself freely whilst he was part of many backing bands. It must have been exceedingly frustrating and inhibiting for him. This latter experience may well have been a residue left over from a previous incarnation from which he had to release himself, metaphorically speaking.

Astrologer and author Steven Forrest commented that for those with this nodal configuration, they must be able to appeal to the unconverted. Part of that includes being able to appear convincing, non-threatening, and plausible, as well as sending out a 'message' through one's clothing, language and word choices (Forrest, 2012, 108). Jimi certainly achieved that in his creative expression and theatricality.

The North Node in the eighth house is a transformative position that encourages deep self-exploration. It is also associated with death, sex, wills, inheritance, and money that is made with another person's resources. In terms of the latter, Jimi transformed himself through his manager's financial resources. They backed him, which helped him to achieve his goal, albeit to the detriment of his health, largely because of the intense touring schedules. Jimi was no businessman, and after his death, the Hendrix family had much to fix and organise from his estate.

In astrology, the asteroid Chiron in one's natal chart represents 'The Wounded Healer'. It is believed to help a person understand their deepest wounds and encourage them to try and heal the difficult aspects of their past – namely from their childhood. The North Node is conjunct Chiron in Leo in the eighth house in Jimi's chart.

Jimi's inner child wounds may have included feelings of inadequacy and being unseen and unappreciated for who he truly was. Any feelings of a lack of validation may have resulted in a need for external corroboration in adulthood.

The North Node in Leo position encourages Jimi to embrace his full potential and unique gifts and talents, expressing himself creatively without fear of judgement, which would have been a powerful process for the Chiron wounds. Healing through performance using creative avenues such as performing arts, leadership and public speaking would have helped to build his confidence and self-esteem. By doing this, he could have integrated the positive aspects of the Leo energy – i.e., charisma, generosity, and warmth.

Certainly, he achieved much of this in his shortened adulthood. He followed his inner star's powerful calling to authentically shine his light and inspired others through his actions and creativity. By doing so, he transformed (a quality associated with the eighth house) his life from a childhood of inadequacy and sparseness to a world where he was externally validated as a performer and song-writer; more so after his death (another theme associated with the eighth house).

Closing the Gig

According to a police report, Jimi died from an overdose of alcohol and sleeping pills, and an autopsy concluded that "Hendrix aspirated his own vomit and died of asphyxia while intoxicated with barbiturates" (www.americansongwriter.com).

On the 18th September 1970, the date when Jimi died, some relevant transits (*see glossary*) were making aspects to his natal chart which are pertinent, given what we know about the later years of Jimi's life.

Transits

- Transiting Pluto sextile natal Moon
- Transiting Neptune trine natal Moon
- Transiting Jupiter square natal Pluto

Transiting Pluto sextile the natal Moon suggests that Jimi was undergoing intense emotional change where raw emotions, fears, and inherited matters from the past may have been brought to the fore, forcing him to face that which had been buried for a long time. These profound changes may have enabled him to change some of his behaviour and habits, which potentially could have led to him confronting his inner self and making the necessary changes needed to find inner satisfaction.

Transiting Neptune trine the natal Moon indicates that Jimi may have found spiritual and platonic relationships more satisfying than in previous years. His time spent with Monika Dannemann was exceedingly short-lived, and by the time Jimi had matured, he was in search of a new approach, shedding the 'wild man' image that had previously been created for him.

Dannemann commented that she believed it was her "... destiny to help reveal Jimi's personal and spiritual essence" (Dannemann, 1995, 9).

Her book, which includes her painted portraits of Jimi, as well as her explanations about them, reveals a lot about the essence of the man, alongside her interpretations about his lyrics. There appears to have been a mutual spiritual understanding between the couple, however temporary their relationship was.

It was also a period when Jimi's imagination may have been stimulated towards a more poetic leaning. After his death, poetry and verses were discovered and were later published. His psychic abilities may have become more prolific, which could have included an even greater interest in the occult, psychic studies, and the afterlife.

His psychic attunement may have included dreams with prophetic undertones, as well as experiencing dreams which may have brought clarity, healing, closure, and guidance.

Given what we already know about Jimi experiencing prophetic dreams and the value that he placed upon his dreams, possibly he dreamt of his own death. We know that in his dreams he often dreamt of numbers, digits, and years (e.g., 1966), and that colour in dreams had a language of its own to Jimi.

Under this transit, Jimi may have felt emotionally vulnerable, as if he was emotionally drowning, and thus felt drained of energy; subsequently, his needs may have changed. Delusions, loss, and illusions are possibilities under this transit. Neptune is ambiguous by nature, and it is also associated with drugs as well as suffering, confusion, deceit, and scandal. This is pertinent to Jimi, certainly in terms of his death.

The Times newspaper reported on the 29th September 1970 that Jimi "died after inhaling vomit. He had taken nine sleeping tablets, but there was no evidence of drug addiction" (*The Times*). The Coroner, Mr Gavin Thurston, recorded an open verdict. Pathologist Professor Donald Tearle said that "Mr Hendrix died because he inhaled vomit due to barbiturate intoxication" (ibid.). His death prompted claims by some that he committed suicide, and another story was that he had been murdered by gangsters.

Transiting Neptune sextile the Moon also suggests that Jimi may have experienced increased sensitivity to the world and those he cared about, as well as holding a greater compassion and sympathy for and understanding of others' feelings and moods.

He certainly felt the loss of his friend, Brian Jones, who died in 1969. Mitch Mitchell observed how deeply Jimi was affected by this and commented that Jones' death "hit Jimi really hard" (Mitchell & Beazley 1993, 83). Jones' death must have triggered Jimi to consider the similarities of their lives, and in doing so, reflect upon his own mortality. Jones died aged 27, which may have influenced Jimi's thinking and comments about not living a long life.

Given Jimi's fearless belief about death and the afterlife, it could be argued that the transit of Pluto sextile the natal Moon was a period in Jimi's life when he was experiencing a rebirth. Pluto is associated with death – be it physical or metaphoric – as well as transformation. In his inner knowing, he would have been aware of the oncoming inevitability of passing into a new life. It is interesting that the Moon is associated with home and security, for Jimi died in a place where he felt at home and with a woman who tried to care for him, Monika Dannemann.

Another significant transit that Jimi had been experiencing at the time of his death was transiting Jupiter in the tenth house square natal Pluto. Jupiter is associated with fame, and Pluto with death. The transiting Jupiter was positioned at the tenth house (this area is associated with career, status, and reputation), whilst the natal Pluto is in the eighth house.

Therefore, it could be argued that Jimi's death reached a wider range of people than perhaps ordinarily it would have, producing greater professional recognition and worldwide prominence for him. *The Times* newspaper carried an obituary for him headed *'Jimi Hendrix: A Key Figure in the Development of Pop Music'* (*The Times*). In addition, and as noted in Part One, Jimi left a great legacy which inspired and motivated others – he also became an early member of what is known in today's pop mythology as the *27 Club*.

Other possibilities with transiting Jupiter in the tenth house include increased property, expansion of a business, and travel in connection with business or work. However, over-expansion in business can lead to problems in the future, as well as arrogance. Overestimating accomplishments is also possible. Although it would have been a favourable time for Jimi to expand his power, there may have been a tendency to ignore important details.

The aspect of transiting Jupiter square natal Pluto can also manifest by way of becoming involved with a project that could involve building or transforming a property – and this was certainly true of the *Electric Lady Studios*. Pluto's energy can be obsessive at times, and so it is possible that Jimi may have become compulsive in wanting his vision brought to reality.

Whilst his course of action was commendable in terms of being determined to achieve his ambition, when it came to business and property matters, Jimi lacked the necessary knowledge and experience needed. As we know from Part One, there was a range of legal conflicts surrounding his estate after he died.

Another manifestation of the aforementioned aspect pertains to philosophical, religious, and metaphysical views being turned upside down and undergoing a profound change. This is certainly true in terms of Jimi's future plans. Part of his dream included him wanting to learn and write music, find a new style, and work with a big band.

At the end of 1968, he referred to his music as 'sky church music', called so because he believed that music of the correct kind could unite people by drawing them towards God and spiritual realms. Whilst he had no faith in the institute of the Church, he was absorbed in spirituality and what he believed it could do for the progress of humanity (Dannemann, 1995, 30).

His vision was to combine playing rock blues with classical music and perform it outside. He described it as follows: "It'll be like a sky church sort of thing. You can get all your answers through music, and the best place is through open air" (Hendrix, 2014, 152).

After Jimi's death, *The Who*'s Pete Townshend paid homage to his genius: "*He had a kind of alchemist's ability … When he was on stage, he changed. He physically changed. He became incredibly graceful and beautiful*" (Hendrix, 2014, 183).

The Times obituary reported that, whilst Bob Dylan liberated pop music verbally, where originally the only subject was about teenage affection, Jimi Hendrix was largely responsible for whatever musical metamorphosis had occurred in the last three years (*The Times*).

Jimi's final public appearance was in *Ronnie Scott's Jazz Club* in London on 16th September 1970. At an impromptu jam, he sat in and played with Eric Burdon and the American band, *War*. He performed renditions of *Mother Earth* and *Tobacco Road* (www.guitarplayer.com/). Two days later, he was dead.

Prior to the 18th September, 1970, aged 27, Jimi Hendrix glibly commented in an interview, "When I die, just keep playing the records" (Hendrix 2014, 190).

CHAPTER THREE

Janis Joplin

Janis Joplin, 1960s, from the documentary 'Janis' released in 1975. (Credit: Everett Collection/Bridgeman Images).

PART 1
THE STORY OF JANIS JOPLIN

Singer, Musician & Song-writer
(1943–1970)

"From Janis, I learned that to make it as a female musician in a man's world is gonna be tough, and you need to keep your head held high."

– Stevie Nicks.

Heritage

The birth certificate for Janis Joplin shows that she was born Janis Lyn Joplin on 19th January 1943, at 09:45am in Port Arthur, Texas, USA, at St. Mary's Hospital (www.astrocom/databank). She came from a liberal middle-class background and as a child lived in the conservative and deeply segregated South.

Her father was Seth Ward Joplin, who was born on 19th April 1910, in Lynn, Texas, and he was the younger of two children. He later moved to Port Arthur from Amarillo. He died on 10th May 1967, in Yavapai, Arizona.

He was a mechanical engineer at the *Texaco* (previously *The Texas Company*) oil refinery in Port Arthur. Suffering with agonising arthritis, he changed his job when he was older and became a supervisor in the package division at *Texaco*; he was employed at *Texaco* all his working life. Seth Joplin married Dorothy Bonita East on 24th October 1936, in Jefferson, Texas.

Laura Joplin (Janis' sister) described her father as "a strikingly handsome guy with a square jaw and a wry grin" – apparently, he had the bluest eyes in his school and was also a flirt. However, at times he could be excruciatingly shy and spent a lot of time alone. Laura also described her father as having lived "a risqué life, smoking marijuana" – which was not widely legal when he was a young man (Joplin, 2005, 25).

Dorothy Bonita East was born on 15th February 1913, in Dewey, Oklahoma. She died on 13th December 1998, in Yavapai, Arizona, aged 85. She was the eldest of her parents' four children, and in addition to Dorothy, there was Gerald Wayne East (born 1917), Barbara Jean (East) Irvin (born 1919), and Mildred Irene (East) McBride (born 1923).

Like her husband, she also moved from Amarillo to Port Arthur, aged 22 years old. Seth Joplin courted her for a year before the couple married in 1936. She worked as a businesswoman and also as the registrar at a local business college (Friedman, 1974, 8). Before she moved to Port Arthur, she worked at the Amarillo radio station, *KGNC* (Joplin, 2005, page 6 of plates, second plate top right-hand).

She enjoyed singing and apparently sang like the great operatic soprano and actress Lily Pons; she also enjoyed singing Broadway show tunes and loved the songs of Cole Porter (Joplin, 2005, 23) and had aspirations to be a Broadway singer (www.dailymirror.co.uk).

Dorothy had a reputation in Amarillo as being a free spirit. This she heightened during the 1930s – the era of the 'flapper'. She created scandal and shocked her parents by cutting her long hair into a bob. In addition, she wore figure-hugging dresses, high heels, and hats. She caused further controversy in the neighbourhood when she smoked cigarettes, which was still illegal for women in many of the states (Joplin, 2005, 25). Janis inherited her mother's blue-nickel grey-coloured eyes.

Janis's paternal grandparents were Seeb Winston Joplin, who was born in Lynn, Texas, on 12th June 1880; he died in New Mexico in 1962, aged approximately 81. He was married to Florence Elizabeth (Porter) Joplin, born in Burleson, Texas, on 1st December 1887; she died on 10th July 1956, in Sierra, New Mexico. The couple married on 24th June 1907, in Williamson County, Texas.

Seeb Winston's father (Janis's great-grandfather) was Charles Alexander Joplin, born in Texas on 15th November 1853. He died on 10th March 1928, in Lamb, Texas. He was married to Margaret Elminor (White) Joplin, who was born in Hood, Texas, in 1863. She died on 29th November 1942, in Lubbock, Texas. The couple married in 1878. Charles Alexander was the person in the Joplin family to drop the 'g' from the surname 'Jopling' (Joplin, 2005, 18); his father was Benjamin Jopling (Joplin, 2005, page 1 of platelets, 1st photograph).

Janis's maternal grandfather was Cecil Walter East, born in Mason County, Illinois, on 31st July 1889. He died in Whittier, Los Angeles County, California, on 24th June 1962. He was married to Laura Mildred (Hanson) East, born on 5th April 1890, in Henry County, Iowa. She died in Los Angeles, California, on 29th May 1958. The couple married on the 4th August 1910, in Clay Center, Clay County, Nebraska.

Her (Janis') maternal great-grandfather was Ulysses Simpson Grant East, born in Macon, Illinois, on 9th May 1864. He died in November 1944, in Fairfield, Clay County, Nebraska. He was married to Anna Belle (Bowman) East, who was born on 1st February 1871, in Logan, Illinois. She died on 17th November 1959, in Adams, Nebraska. The couple married on 21st October, 1888, in Dewitt, Illinois (www.wikitree.com).

The first of Janis Joplin's maternal ancestors to reach America was Hezekiah Hore in 1633. He was a pilgrim from England who was determined to escape the oppression of the Church of England and the English government. He flourished in the Massachusetts Bay Colony and helped found the town of Taunton. He lived amongst Puritans (although they were not the minority of the community) and prospered as a businessman and farmer (Joplin, 2005, 12).

William Ball, an ancestor on Janis' father's side, originated from Chesapeake Bay in Virginia, where he built his Georgian-style mansion, Millenbeck. He became the grandfather of the US President, George Washington.

Phillip Sherman was Ball's son-in-law; he was a defiant supporter of American Indian rights, and he lived amongst them and learnt their language. Sherman became a Quaker and a farmer and became involved in the 'Great Awakening'. This was a series of religious revivals where spirituality was believed to come from within, so that each person could experience the ecstasy of a spiritual rebirth (Joplin, 2005, 13).

Siblings

Janis had two younger siblings: Laura Lee, who was born in 1949, and Michael Ross in 1953. When their big sister died in 1970; Laura was 21 and Michael was seventeen years old. Neither had any experience of the music business, but they undertook the management of Janis' estate after her death.

Laura Joplin wrote an intimate biography about her elder sister called *Love Janis*; it was inspired by the hundreds of letters that Janis wrote to her family throughout her career. She also appeared in the 2015 documentary *Janis: Little Girl Blue*, where she appears as herself. Laura Joplin is also a former education consultant, and she organised a *TEDx Talk* in her hometown of Chico, in California. A *TEDx Talk* is a showcase for speakers presenting innovative, well-informed ideas in less than eighteen minutes. She has a master's degree in psychology and a Ph.D. in education.

Michael Joplin is a glassmaker and, along with his sister, still manages Janis' estate. He was recently invited to *The Royal Albert Hall* in 2024 to see the production (before the previews) of *A Night with Janis Joplin, The Musical*, starring Mary Davies, Bridget Davies, and Sharon Sexton at the *Peacock Theatre* in London. The show is a musical journey which pays homage to Michael's sister and her biggest musical influences.

Education

Janis was educated at Woodrow Wilson Junior High School (Amburn, 1994, page 8 of platelets, 3rd photograph), which was near to the family home, Griffing Park, Port Arthur; previously the family home was at 4048 Proctor Street, Port Arthur (Friedman, 1974, 8). From there, Janis attended the 'old' Thomas Jefferson High School and graduated from the 'new' Thomas Jefferson High School in 1960. During the summer of 1960–61, she attended Lamar College of Technology in nearby Beaumont, Texas, as well as the Port Arthur Business College.

In summer of 1962, she enrolled as an art student at the University of Texas in Austin; however, she did not complete her studies. Instead, she chose to spend the majority of her time socialising with the in-crowd of the growing folk scene. It was during this time that she taught herself to play the autoharp.

Her distinctiveness and originality did not go unnoticed and earned her a headline in *The Summer Texan* (the university newspaper) with the headline: '*She Dares to be Different*' (Joplin, 2005, page 12 of plates, bottom photo). In May of 1965, she registered to study sociology at Lamar Technical College – and just as before, she did not complete her studies.

Inspired By

Janis was brought up in a family home where music and song were regular features; the family listened to show tunes constantly, one example being *Mack The Knife* from *The Threepenny Opera* (www.newyorker.com/). Michael Joplin commented that their mother had always wanted to be a Broadway singer and that the whole family could play instruments and sing. Mr and Mrs Joplin encouraged their three children "both academically and musically" (www.mirror.co.uk/). Clearly, musicality and song were in Janis' DNA.

When she was an adult, Janis was inspired by artists such as Bob Dylan, Aretha Franklin, Billie Holiday, Jimi Hendrix, Odetta, Leadbelly (also spelt Lead Belly), Otis Redding, Bessie Smith, and Big Mama Thornton. She was also inspired by the traditional American folk music performers, *The Carter Family* (www.cookephoto.com/index.html).

They recorded between 1927 and 1956, and their music had a profound influence on other musical genres such as bluegrass and country, as well as on the US folk revivals of the 1960s. Possibly, *The Carter Family* music was played in the Joplin family home when Janis was a child.

During Janis' teenage years, it was the aforementioned Leadbelly, Bessie Smith, and Big Mama Thornton who really turned Janis on to the blues. Speaking in an interview, she recalled that the first record she ever bought was one of Leadbelly's – although she could not remember which track it was (*Janis: Little Girl Blue*, Berg, 2016).

Her short-term partner, Jae Whitaker, recalled that when they were at the Monterey Folk Festival in May 1963, Janis saw Bob Dylan off-stage. She ran up to him and said, "Oh Bob, I just love you; I'm gonna be famous one day" – to which, he wryly replied, "Yeah, we're all gonna be famous" (ibid.).

Instruments & Music Genres

Janis played autoharp, piano, and guitars, which included a Gibson J45 and Gibson Hummingbird acoustic guitars with six and twelve strings. She often played Latin American percussion instruments, such as the guiro, as well as claves and maracas. Janis had mezzo-soprano vocals – a female singing voice that falls between a soprano and contralto, which gives a range that sits in the middle register. Her musical genres were blues & blues rock, country, folk, and soul.

Cover Versions

Janis's most popular songs were her numerous cover versions, indicating where much of her inspiration came from. These include (along with the original artists and their performance/release dates) the following tracks:

- *Ball & Chain:* Big Mama Thornton (1968).
- *Cry Baby:* Garnett Mimms & The Enchanters (1963).
- *Down On Me:* Eddie Head & Family (1930).
- *Maybe:* The Chantels (1957).
- *Me & Bobby McGee:* Kris Kristofferson (1970).
- *Nobody Knows You When You're Down & Out* was recorded by Bessie Smith in 1929, but the first artist to record it was Blind Bobby Baker (Bobby Lecan) in 1927 (www.udiscovermusic.com).

- *Summertime* was written by D. Heyward & G. Gershwin, from *Porgy 'n' Bess*, the opera, and sung by Abbie Mitchell, who played *Clara* in the production (1935). Billie Holiday released a version in 1936; it was the first version to be recorded for 78 records (jazzhistoryonline.com/).
- *Piece Of My Heart:* Erma Franklin (elder sister of Aretha) (1967).
- *Tell Mama:* Etta James (1968).
- *To Love Somebody:* The Bee Gees (1967).
- *Trouble In Mind:* Nina Simone (1960).
- *(Try) Just A Little Bit Harder:* Lorraine Ellison (1967/68).

Song-writing & Arrangements

Janis' song-writing was not immense, but she did pen the tracks *What Good Can Drinkin' Do; Daddy, Daddy, Daddy; One Good Man; Move Over; Kozmic Blues,* which was co-written with Gabriel Mekler; and *Mercedes Benz,* which was co-written with Michael McClure. She also created the arrangements on some of the tracks, which included *Down On Me* and *Hesitation Blues.*

Nick Gravenite wrote several songs for Janis, which included *Work Me Lord* and *As Good As You've Been To This World* for the album *I Got Dem Ol' Kozmic Blues Again Mama.* In addition, he also wrote the unfinished instrumental track, *Buried Alive On the Blues,* on the *Pearl* album (www.facebook.com/). He became the lead singer of the reformed *Big Brother & The Holding Company* (without Janis) between 1969 and 1972 (en.wikipedia.org/wiki/).

On the Move

In 1960, Janis left home, discarding the small-town values that she found so limiting. She began singing in Houston bars and clubs, where she earned a few dollars for entertaining. Her first big break was securing a regular gig in Austin, where she performed at a gas station-turned-bar, which was run by Kenneth Treadwell; the venue was a hangout for country music outlaws.

Janis had majored in art at college but dropped out in 1963 and headed out from Austin, Texas, for San Francisco, California. For a short while, she experienced communal living with Chet Holms (founder of

Big Brother) and her soon-to-be band *Big Brother & The Holding Company* in rural Lagunitas.

This was in their small Lagunitas house in Marin Bay, California; inevitably there was conflict "over standards of cleanliness and tidiness and over late-night noise" (Echols, 2001, 156) amongst the housemates. Prior to Janis formally joining the band, the group was in residency at the *Avalon Ballroom*, which was a psychedelic dancehall that produced other bands.

Eventually, she moved to Haight-Ashbury, San Francisco, where she found a community of kindred spirits. The neighbourhood became the birthplace of the mid-1960s hippie counterculture movement, and in 1967, many American youths (sometimes referred to as the 'flower children') moved there for what became known as the *Summer of Love*.

The majority of them came to protest about the Vietnam War and the materialism of mainstream American society. In addition, many wanted to expand their minds through the means of exploring alternative religions, psychedelic rock music, experimenting with hallucinogenic drugs (such as LSD) and free love (www.britannica.com).

Janis' addresses in Haight-Ashbury included 123 Cole Street, 122 Lyon Street, and 635 Ashbury Street. Other famous people who lived in Haight-Ashbury in the 1960s included the groups *The Grateful Dead* and *Jefferson Airplane* (ibid.).

She returned to Austin in 1965 to detoxify from the excesses of Haight-Ashbury; however, in 1966, she was drawn back to California, and it was at this time that she joined the Haight-Ashbury-based *Big Brother & The Holding Company* (janisjoplin.com/).

During her short-lived career, apart from her many concerts and outdoor festival performances in the US, Janis also toured Canada, Denmark, and France. Her only British solo performance was at the *Royal Albert Hall* on 21st April 1969, where the rock group *Yes* supported her. (https://www.royalalberthall.com/). She enraptured the audience, and several months after her appearance there, she was voted the World's Top Female Singer by readers of the *Melody Maker* publication (*The Times*, 06/10/1970).

Working Relationships

Big Brother & The Holding Company was formed in San Francisco in 1965. The line-up eventually became: vocalist Janis Joplin, guitarists Sam Andrew and James Gurley, bassist Peter Albin, and drummer Dave Getz. They played blues and rock. *The Kozmic Blues Band* was formed less than a year after Janis left *Big Brother* in 1969.

Her final band, *The Full Tilt Boogie Band*, was more soulful-sounding with horns – and this was a step further into Janis' musical evolution and her determination to find her own sound. The band's line-up included musicians such as keyboardist Stephen Ryder, saxophonist Cornelius 'Snooky' Flowers, as well as *Big Brother & The Holding Company's* guitarist Sam Andrew, and *The Full Tilt Boogie Band* bassist Brad Campbell (www.last.fm/music).

The Full Tilt Boogie Band was a Canadian rock band that was originally headed by John Till in 1969, and later by Janis up until her death in 1970. For a short while, the band was known as *Main Squeeze* and later became known as *Joplin's Full Tilt Backing Band*. Aside from Janis, other members of the band included pianist Richard Bell, drummer Clark Pierson, organist Ken Pearson, the aforementioned bassist Brad Campbell, and guitarist John Till (www.last.fm/).

They played their first session together in April 1970, at the *Fillmore West Studios* in San Francisco, and then from 28th June to 4th July 1970, they all joined with the *Festival Express*, performing alongside bands such as *The Band, The Grateful Dead,* and *The Buddy Guy Blues Band*. They toured through Canada, giving free concerts where they stopped. The tour was called *Festival Express*, which was named after the train.

Management, production, road crew, and song-writing personnel that she worked with through her successful career included Bert Block, Mike Bloomfield, John Cooke, Joe Crowley, Clive Davis (president of *Columbia Records*), Bennett Glotzer, Albert Grossman (manager of Bob Dylan), John Hall, Johanna Schier, Chet Helms, Julius Karpen, Eddie Kramer, Gabriel Mekler, Mike Nubrit, Paul A. Rothchild, and Bob Shad (founder of *Mainstream Records*).

Before she found fame with *Big Brother & The Holding Company* and her *Kozmic Blues Band*, she performed on the folk scene with *The Waller Creek Boys*. They were from Austin, Texas (fellow University of Texas students), and formed in 1962 but disbanded in January 1963.

The folk blues trio comprised of 20-year-old Janis Joplin on autoharp, Lanny Wiggins on guitar and vocals, and Powell St. John on vocals and harmonica. Songs that Janis sang with the group were *Careless Love* and *Black Mountain Blues* – both of which had been recorded by her idol, Bessie Smith.

In November 2009, St. John attended the *Rock 'n' Roll Hall of Fame*, where he was invited to a tribute concert honouring Janis Joplin (www.powellstjohn.com/biography.html). During her career, Janis occasionally sang with legends. One included Tom Jones on the TV programme *This is Tom Jones* in 1969; they sang *Raise Your Hand*. In November of 1969, she collaborated with Tina Turner at Madison Square Garden and sang *Land of a Thousand Dances*.

Albums, Singles & Record Labels

November 2021 saw the release of the album *The Waller Creek Boys featuring Janis Joplin* on the *Lysergic Sound Distributors* label in America. The album includes the songs *Daddy, Daddy, Daddy* and her version of *Nobody Knows You When You're Down And Out* (written by Jimmie Cox in 1923 and recorded by Bessie Smith in 1929).

Jefferson Airplane's guitarist, Jorma Kaukonen, and Janis first met in 1962, at a hootenanny at the *Folk Theatre* in San Jose, California. During June of 1964, the two practiced at Kaukonen's home for a fundraising event at *The Coffee Gallery* in San Francisco. The rehearsal of the couple's duets was recorded on a reel-to-reel recorder.

Miraculously, the recording remained in existence and was released on an eight-track album: *Janis Joplin and Jorma Kaukonen: The Legendary Typewriter Tape* (the signature title came from Kaukonen's wife, who can be heard in the background typing). Janis' vocals on the blues country album include the songs *Trouble In Mind* and *Nobody Knows You When You're Down And Out*.

Janis released two albums with *Big Brother & The Holding Company*: *Big Brother & The Holding Company featuring Janis Joplin* was the debut studio album, released in August 1967, and the second was *Cheap Thrills*, released in August 1968.

The album was a commercial success and reached number one on the US *Billboard Top LPs* chart for eight non-consecutive weeks. After that, she left the band to go solo and formed her own backing groups – the first was the *Kozmic Blues Band*, and the second was the *Full Tilt Boogie Band*, as previously noted.

The debut solo and third studio album, *I Got Dem' Ol Kozmic Blues Again Mama*, was released in September 1969, and it reached number five on the *Billboard 200* chart. The single *Kozmic Blues* was part of Janis' set at the Woodstock Festival in 1969; its peak position in the US *Billboard Hot 100* was 41.

In January 1971, three months after her death, a second solo album, *Pearl*, was released; it was her final studio endeavour. The album was her only album with the *Full Tilt Boogie Band*, and it topped the album charts at number one on the US *Billboard 200*, securing that position for nine weeks. The album also yielded Janis' only number one single, which was her version of *Me and Bobby McGee*, written by Fred Foster and Kris Kristofferson.

It was released in January 1971, and it topped the *Billboard Hot 100*. The B-side of the single was *Half Moon*, which was written by the aforementioned John Hall and his first wife, the former Johanna Schier. Hall commented that the track was influenced by Janis' friend, Jimi Hendrix, and that it "was numerological and astrological in nature" (www.faroutmagazine.co.uk).

Joplin's record labels were *Columbia Records* and *Mainstream Records*; the latter contracted Janis and the *Big Brother Holding Company*, and the former was responsible for the two later albums.

SIGNIFICANT AFFAIRS & RELATIONSHIPS

Powell St. John

Powell St. John of *The Waller Creek Boys* commented when Janis joined the Austin, Texas, band in the early 1960s that she "instantly became one of the boys" (*Janis: Little Girl Blue*, Berg, 2016). He recalled a two-week affair with her as being "intense and unforgettable, really something." It ended when Janis went off with somebody else. St. John commented, "I loved Janis; I always did and I always will." He was aware that the relationship was going to be short-lived and reflected, "She wasn't ready for any commitment, and neither was I" (Echols, 2001, 62). Laura Joplin commented that St. John was "attracted to Janis' brash, outspoken nature. He liked her *because* she was different" (Joplin, 2005, 115).

Powell St. John went on to have a successful music career, which included forming a rock band called *St. John & The Conqueroo*; he also co-founded the band *Mother Earth* with Tracey Nelson. He married and raised a family (www.powellstjohn.com/).

Peter de Blanc

Peter de Blanc and Janis had been seeing each other during her earlier spell in San Francisco, between approximately 1963 and 1965. De Blanc was described as a 'speed freak', and it was evident that Janis' speed use increased dramatically whilst she was in a relationship with him. Speed was easily available and cheap in the circles they moved in. She became malnourished and sleep-deprived, and her weight plummeted to "less than ninety pounds" (Angel, 2010, 31).

During 1965, Janis moved back to the family home in Port Arthur for detoxification purposes. She made an effort to try and take some control of her life; part of that (as noted earlier) included her enrolling to study sociology – she was determined to straighten her life out.

During her recovery period, she chose to wear traditional long-sleeved dresses (which would hide the needle marks on her arms) and tamed her wild hair by wearing it in a bun. De Blanc had also returned to his homeland of New York in order to detoxify.

 The couple became engaged, and De Blanc visited Janis' father and asked him for her hand in marriage. Seth Joplin agreed, and Janis and her mother began to prepare for the wedding. However, shortly afterwards, De Blanc stopped visiting Janis and also replying to her letters. He had been deceiving Janis; when she telephoned his home, a woman answered the phone, and it was made clear that De Blanc was living with this person and was in a relationship with her (*Janis: Little Girl Blue*, Berg, 2016).

De Blanc called the engagement off (Willett, 2008, 55), and Janis returned to San Francisco to pursue her music; her return to that community caused her parents to be fearful of her future and wellbeing.

Peter J. de Blanc later made a name for himself in the world of computers and travelled extensively for his work, where he eventually became "an acknowledged technical genius." He died in 2002, aged 57, after battling cancer; he was survived by his wife, children and eight grandchildren (https://web.archive.org/web).

Jae Whitaker

Janis met Jae Whitaker in the spring of 1963 in North Beach at a gay bar called *Gino and Carlo's*, and during 1963 and 1964, Janis was hanging out with a lesbian crowd. Janis decided to move in with Whitaker, but just two months into their relationship, things turned sour. She would take off for days at a time hitchhiking, but Whitaker was never sure if Janis was with friends or lovers. In early 1964, the couple broke up, and Janis moved out; Whitaker saw her on a few occasions after they split – and that was when Janis needed money.

Whitaker commented that once Janis started going with men and taking heroin, she avoided her. She commented, "Janis was a walking contradiction" – adding that Janis would say that she wasn't gay, but "you could take everything that Janis said, turn it backwards, and that would be the truth too" (Echols, 2001, 86/87). Linda Gottfried, a friend of Janis', described Whitaker as being "so cute … She had a real short Afro and looked like an androgynous guy. She was really sweet and loved Janis" (ibid.).

Apparently, Whitaker was considered a catch in the lesbian community, and she believed that was one of the reasons why Janis was drawn to her; that, plus she was black and knew a lot about the old blues and R&B. Whitaker perceived that they were both rebels; for her, it was because she was attracted to white girls (ibid.). Whitaker remarked that Janis "needed stroking all the time … being on stage, it made her feel like somebody" (*Janis: Little Girl Blue*, Berg, 2016).

Joe McDonald (of Country Joe & The Fish)

In 1967, Janice had a relationship with Country Joe McDonald (the leader of *Country Joe & The Fish*), who hailed from Berkeley. He was politically minded and "he often wore flowers at political benefits and protest buttons at hippie dances" (Joplin, 2005, 225). According to McDonald, their partnership lasted for "a month or two", and for a while he lived with Janis at her flat in Haight-Ashbury (YouTube.com). Laura Joplin commented, "They broke up in a very touching way; in love but unwilling to compromise their individual pursuits" (Joplin, 2005, 226).

Speaking after her death, he said that Janis was always searching for love, and when she became a superstar it only gave her what she wanted in terms of fame, but nothing in her personal life (www.youtube.com).

James Gurley

James Gurley and his wife Nancy moved to San Francisco in 1962, and he joined *Big Brother & The Holding Company* in 1965, where he became lead guitarist. His fearless, wild guitar playing gave the band a reputation for *far-out* psychedelic experimentation; between 1966 and 1968, Janis fronted the group.

Gurley and Janis started an affair shortly after she joined the band; he left his wife and son to be with Janis, which lasted only a couple of weeks. His wife forgave him, and he moved back home to be with his family. Nancy Gurley and Janis remained friends, just as they had been previously to Janis joining the band. James Gurley remarked that he thought he and Janis were "a couple of desperados ...". He added that he had grown up feeling 'uptight' about sex and said, "He had a lot of learning to do" (Echols, 140, 2001).

Both of the Gurleys were heroin users; Nancy was struggling to cut back on heroin when she became pregnant, and James was grappling to get clean (Echols, 2001, 259). In 1969, Nancy died of a heroin overdose. Gurley was charged with murder for injecting the drugs into her, and he spent two years fighting the charges before he was finally sentenced to two years' probation (en.wikipedia.org/wiki).

Janis was devastated by the news of Nancy's death and sent James Gurley 25,000 dollars to help pay for Nancy's legal expenses. In honour of the deceased, Janis dedicated the album she was then working on (*Kozmic Blues*) to Nancy: 'to Nancy G. love' (www.janisjoplin.net/). Gurley remarried and raised a family and went on to have a successful music career. He died in December 2009, from a heart attack, at his home in California.

Peggy Caserta

Peggy Caserta and Janis met in approximately 1966; they began a friendship and were on-and-off lovers. Caserta openly identified as lesbian at a time when visibility was rare; when she met Janis, she was already in a partnership with another woman. Janis met Caserta in her boutique, *Mnasidika*, which was at 1510 Haight Street, Haight-Ashbury; she owned the business and also worked there full-time.

Janis came into the shop and wanted to purchase a pair of jeans but didn't have the full amount of money to pay for them. She offered to put down a deposit and then to pay an amount weekly until the full amount was paid off. Caserta was overjoyed to meet Janis and gave her the jeans as a gift, and eventually the two became friends (and later lovers).

The shop became a social hub for the counterculture and hippie movements of the 1960s. Caserta recalled how the community grew and that hugely diverse people were moving daily into the once-little neighbourhood. She remembered how the dawn of a new era and easy access to LSD "… made Alice's adventures in Wonderland pale" (Caserta, 2018, 20).

Caserta reflected on the time when a new shop owner had moved into Haight Street: "He sold incense, Madras bedspreads, imports from India, incense holders, and beads – all the inexpensive and groovy accoutrements to the LSD-tripping youth cavorting around the area." The heady and potent scent of "marijuana, patchouli, and sandalwood wafted in the air" (ibid.) and was inescapable. Customers of her store included *Jefferson Airplane, The Grateful Dead, Jimi Hendrix, Kris Kristofferson,* and *Sly Stone.*

At Janis' invitation, Caserta attended the Woodstock Music and Art Fair in 1969, in Bethel, New York. This was Janis' first big performance without her band, *Big Brother & The Holding Company*; this time she was backed by her new band, the *Kozmic Blues Band.*

David Niehaus

In February of 1970, Janis travelled to Brazil in order to try and overcome her heroin addiction. She met Niehaus, a middle-class American traveller, on Ipanema Beach in Brazil. They fell in love and began a relationship. Niehaus helped her kick her heroin habit, albeit short-lived. The couple split when Janis' relationship with alcohol and heroin relapsed and intensified.

He remembered his relationship with Janis as being wild and liberating, as well as delicate when he saw her during her most tender and vulnerable moments. He described Janis as being "the girl who inspired me to be whoever I wanted to be … she set me free" (*Janis: Little Girl Blue*, Berg, 2016).

Seth Morgan

Seth Morgan was Janis' fiancé at the time of her death in October 1970. He was the son of soap fortune heir and poet George Fredrick Morgan and Constance Canfield. He dropped out of UC Berkeley in 1970, and it was later that year that he met Janis. They started a relationship and became engaged; Janis talked casually to her friends about the possibility of marriage and having children (*Janis Joplin: Her Final Hours*, Kilback, 2007).

After Janis' death, he married twice. He worked in strip clubs, exhorting the venue to passing members of the public. He developed a heroin addiction, and in order to support the habit, he apparently committed armed robberies. During one of the robberies, he was caught by the police and sentenced to 30 months' imprisonment. After his release, he returned to working in strip clubs.

He penned a novel called *Homeboy*, which was published in 1990 by Random House, New York (ISBN 0394575776). The book was partly autobiographical and was about criminals and heroin addicts in San Francisco. One of his characters was a flamboyantly dressed prostitute, whom he apparently based on Janis; he also started a second novel which was never completed.

Morgan died aged 41, along with his girlfriend, Diane Levin, in a motorbike accident, in October 1990. His autopsy revealed that his blood alcohol content was nearly three times the legal limit and that he also had cocaine and Percodan (a painkiller) in his system (en.wikipedia.org/wiki).

Jimi Hendrix, Kris Kristofferson and Jim Morrison

All three had casual affairs and liaisons with Janis.

Jimi Hendrix and Janis met at Monterey in 1967. "The chemistry between Jimi and Janis was immediately apparent … after the festival, she would become erotically involved with him, as well as with another member of his group, *The Jimi Hendrix Experience*" (Amburn, 1994, 141). It has been suggested that aside from their mutual affinity for the blues, heroin and sex, "perhaps his strongest attraction for Janis was the colour of his skin" (Amburn, 1994, 143).

Kris Kristofferson met Janis in 1970, shortly before her death, at her home in Larkspur, California, where a party was being held. Bob Neuwirth introduced Kristofferson to Janis, and he caught her eye immediately. "She thought he was a honey" (ibid.). Like Janis, Kristofferson was a heavy drinker, and the two developed an alcoholic co-dependency. Initially, he wanted to leave, but he allowed himself to become helpless and dependent on Janis. Apparently, he "was the only man who could drink her under the table" (ibid.). He introduced her to the song *Me and Bobby McGee,* and wanted her to record it for the album *Pearl* (Amburn, 1994, 279/80).

Jim Morrison slept with Janis in 1967 at a party she held at her flat in San Francisco. Her friend, Dave Richards, recalled that they were locked in her bedroom for hours (Amburn, 1994, 147). Some days after this, she told her friend, Henry Carr, "I don't like Jim Morrison. He was okay in bed, but when we got up the next morning, he asked for a shot of sloe gin." This was a derogatory remark implying that by her standards his choice of drink was for the feeble (Amburn, 1994, 148).

The bedroom in her San Francisco flat was described as follows: "Janis' boudoir was a soft and seductive seraglio with velvet, satin, lace, and silk everywhere. Bob Sideman's nude poster of her adorned one wall, and there were incense, lubricating lotions, booze, dope, water pipes and needles" (Amburn, 147, 1994). Janis' friend and roommate, Linda Gravenites (wife of singer and song-writer, Nick Gravenites), said of Janis, "There were women who turned her on, but her main focus was definitely men" (Byrne Cook, 2014, 112).

Style

Janis' mother, Dorothy, was a gifted dressmaker, and as a child Janis enjoyed wearing the many dresses that her mother made for her. These included dresses for special occasions, such as an Easter outfit, as well as matching outfits for both of her daughters. During prep school, Janis' dress style was visibly different from those of her peers; for example, she would wear her skirt much shorter than her peers and didn't wear the customary 'bobby-sox' and loafers (Joplin, 2005, page 10 of platelets, bottom picture).

In the early 1960s, Janis wore the iconic *Beatnik* clothes: a black turtleneck jumper, gold medallions, blue jeans, and pumps, and she kept her hair short. During her junior year at high school, she often wore black to emulate the *Beat* artists.

The University of Texas at Austin wrote a profile about her, stating that "She goes barefoot when she feels like it, wears Levis to class because they're more comfortable, and carries her autoharp everywhere

Janis Joplin American Rock Singer (1943–1970).
(Unknown photographer, 20th Century/Superstock/Bridgeman Images).

she goes so that in case she gets the urge to break into song, it will be handy" (vinepair.com). However, when she returned home to detox in the mid-1960s, she returned to dressing conservatively and wore her hair up, pulled into a bun.

Nancy Gurley, wife of guitarist James Gurley, was believed to have "had a profound influence on Janis in Aquarian ideas and hippie fashions" (Amburn, 1994, page 3 of platelets, bottom photo). Nancy has been described as being an "Earth Mother figure and a vision of a modern woman to Janis ... she inspired Janis' clothing. She emulated Nancy's look of granny gowns – hand-me-down dresses redone into Earth Mother fashion" (www.janisjoplin.net).

In the late 1960s, Janis loved capes and wore them for all sorts of occasions, including for promotional shots. She enjoyed wearing designs

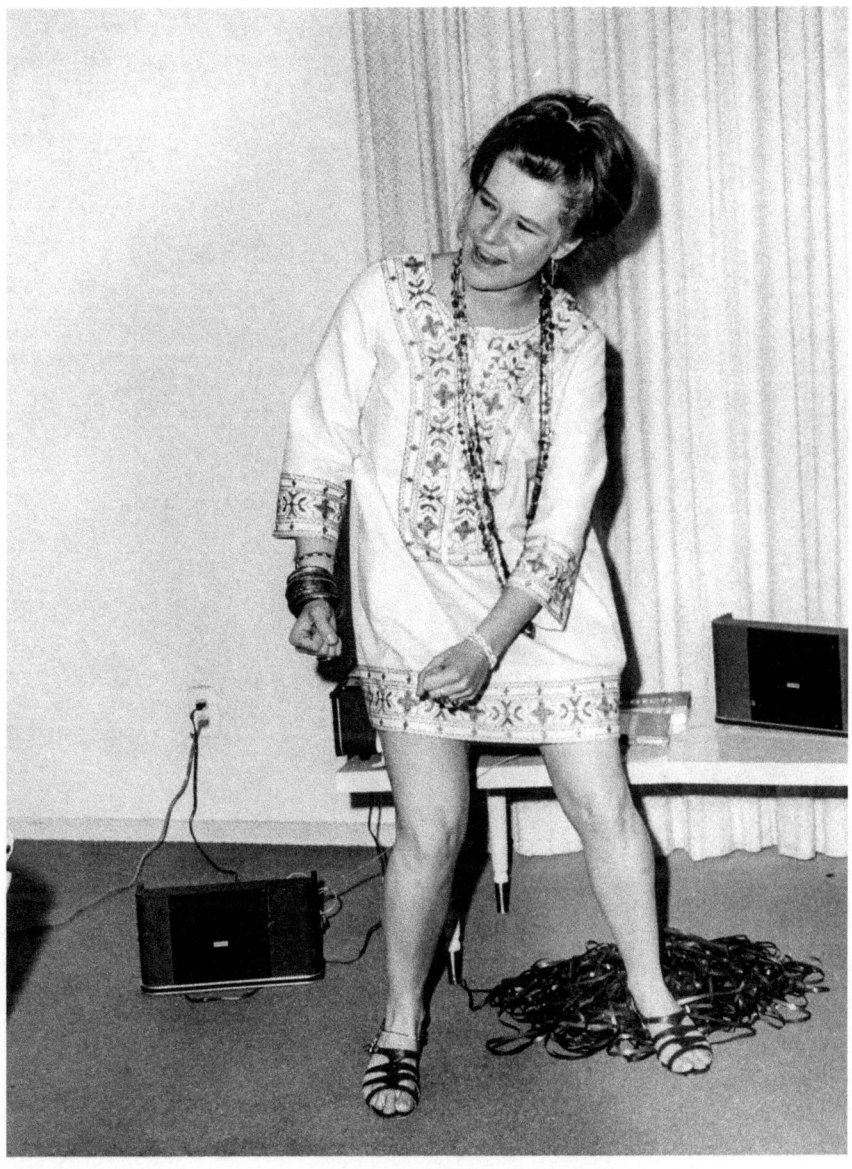

Janis Joplin, 1960s.
(Credit: Bridgeman Images).

which were specifically made for her and which emphasised her unique style. One example of this is of designer Jeanne Colon (a clothes designer for rock stars), who made Janis "a poncho of antique Moroccan fabric over velvet peony pants" (Joplin, 2005, page 5 of platelets, top left-hand photo).

Janis Joplin, c. 1965–1970.
(© SZ Photo/Röhnert Ursula/Bridgeman Images).

As she became more successful, Janis' stage image became increasingly sexy. Her friend and roommate of three years, Linda Gravenites, became Janis' costume designer, creating elaborately embroidered stage clothes for her, some of which revealed her cleavage. One example of her Gravenites work is a black, crushed velvet dress with beaded flowers sewn on the bodice (Joplin, 2005, page 5 of platelets, top photo). Janis wore it at the Newport Folk Festival in 1968. Off-stage, Janis also liked to wear bell-bottom jeans and red satin pants.

Another illustration of Gravenites work and styling for Janis was a handbag she made for her in approximately 1967. It was made of goatskin with silk embroidery (chain stitch) and glass beads, measuring 18x12 inches. Janis asked her to make a handbag for her "big enough for a book and a bottle" (O'Brien, 2012, 89).

Speaking to *Vogue* magazine and discussing Gravenites work in 1968, Janis commented that "Linda Gravenites turns them out slowly and turns them out well, and only turns them out for those she likes" (www.overdressedforlife.com/). For a short while, Janis had an interest in making items using leather; in a letter, she told them, "I've been making things out of leather lately. Made a beautiful blue and green Garbo hat and a pair of green shoes" (Joplin, 2005, 235).

Janis loved crafting with beads; she made her necklaces on a loom using antique beads and knotted leather (Amburn, 1994, page 7 of platelets, full page). On- and off-stage she wore bracelets, rings, ankle bracelets, long earrings, necklaces, and shoes with hourglass heels.

Her friend, Peggy Caserta, recalled that during the earlier part of Janis' career, she was famous for wearing "cheap, gaudy jewellery" (*sic*) and that the cheap rings stained her fingers green (Caserta, 2018, 119). She also wore chains, bells and spangles around her waist; Linda Gravenite commented, "If Janis saw a look or a style that she liked, she immediately copied it" (Friedman, 1974, 136) but ultimately made it her own with effortless style.

When she performed at the Monterey International Pop Festival in 1967, Janis was bedecked in a tunic-style gold sequined dress with matching bell-bottomed trousers and gold slingback kitten heel shoes. She rhythmically stomped her feet defiantly as she performed her five-track set.

Mama Cass and Michelle Phillips of *The Mamas & The Papas* were amongst the audience. Footage shows Cass watching Janis' performance with astonishment; she visibly mouths 'wow' (*Janis: Little Girl Blue*, Berg, 2016). Evidently, she was impressed by the incredible Janis. Cass smiled in awe, as if she had experienced something truly amazing happening right in front of her.

Janis Joplin, 1960s. (Credit: Everett Collection/ Bridgeman Images).

Janis said of the Monterey audience, "Those were real flower children. They were beautiful and gentle and completely open, man. Ain't nothing like that ever gonna happen again" (Cooke, 2014, 35).

Her iconic performance and distinctive gold outfit helped establish her as a compelling force and cemented her place in music history. When she played at Woodstock, she wore tie-dyed velvet bell-bottoms and a royal blue blouse, matched with a cape-sleeved loose open jacket in royal blue.

Myra Friedman, publicist in the Albert Grossman office, was instrumental in Janis' look of wearing a three-quarter-length coat and matching hat made of Russian lynx for her cold-weather travelling wear. She proposed that, as Janis generated publicity for the *Southern Comfort Company* by telling reporters that *Southern Comfort* was her favourite drink, they should repay Janis in some way. Friedman secured a deal with *Southern Comfort* for Janis to visit a fur warehouse in New Jersey to select whatever she wanted; the fur coat and hat was the outfit chosen by Janis (Byrne Cook, 2014, 140).

Her last memorable look was one of her wearing large circular sunglasses, two-toned in pink and purple; in her wavy, thick, long hair she wore multi-coloured feather boas and green, hot pink, and purple feathers, which created a kind of ostrich tail effect.

Janis also had lots of tie-dyed velvet items, which included tie-dyed satin sheets that she described to a friend as "the most beautiful fuckin' sheets in the world ... I started makin' it with this cowboy, and he shredded them up with his cowboy boots. Three hundred dollar satin sheets shredded by cowboy boots. I loved every minute of it!" (Dalton, 2000, 231).

The singer used Lyle Tuttle, a psychedelic tattoo artist, for her body art. For her, he inked a small heart on the area of her heart, a bud on her right heel and a three-coloured bracelet on her left wrist (Amburn, 1994, 283).

Author David Dalton recalled that when he was with Janis on her last tour, on one occasion, as she rummaged through her handbag looking for her cigarettes (probably *Marlborough's*), a cascade of seemingly random junk tumbled out. As well as "an antique cigarette holder", there were "several motel and hotel keys", "cassettes of Johnny Cash and Otis Redding", and there was also the mandatory "bottle of Southern Comfort (empty)" (https://vinepair.com).

Distinctions

Her posthumous hit *Me & Bobby McGee* from the album *Pearl* became a major hit with over 15.5 million albums sold in the US. In 1995, she was inducted into the *Rock 'n' Roll Hall of Fame*. Then in 2005, she won a Grammy Lifetime Achievement Award. In 2009, the *Rock 'n' Roll Hall of Fame Museum* honoured her as part of its annual *American Music Master* series. In the same year, Janis was the honouree at the *Rock Halls American Music Concert and Lecture* series. In 2008, *Rolling Stone* magazine rated Janis as number 28 in its list of the *200 Greatest Singers of All Time*.

Philanthropy

One example of Janis' generosity is illustrated through her and Juanita Green paying the cost for a headstone to be laid at the graveside of Bessie Smith in August 1970. Green did housework for Smith when she was a child and clearly remembered her with affection. Prior to that, Smith's grave had remained unmarked for over 30 years. Janis and Green both chose the words for the headstone; the epitaph (near Philadelphia) reads: *'The Greatest Singer In The World Will Never Stop Singing'* (https://www.udiscovermusic.com/).

Another illustration of Janis' charity can be seen by her performing solo with an accompanying acoustic guitar at a benefit evening in Austin; this was for the blues singer and guitarist, Mance Lipscomb, who was in ill-health (en.wikipedia.org). And, as previously discussed, there was the instance where she paid a considerable sum of money towards James Gurley's legal case after his wife died from an overdose and he was initially accused of murder.

Health & Ill-health

Janis became addicted to alcohol, heroin, and speed; in addition, she occasionally experimented with LSD (lysergic acid diethylamide) and regularly smoked marijuana, and also made several attempts at sobriety. Her sister commented that for a significant period, Janis had been heavily into pills. Substances she listed included Quaaludes and Demerol (as well as heroin and speed) (Joplin, 2005, 158).

Her main taste in alcohol was beer, *Southern Comfort*, and tequila. Linda Gravenites said that a friend of Janis' revealed to her that they would go to bars and drink tequila; she described Janis: "She'd lick her thumb with salt and squeeze lime down her throat and shoot tequila. She had this ritual down" (O'Brien, 2012, 89).

Interviewed by author and journalist David Dalton in approximately 1970, Janis reflected on her mood when she first arrived in San Francisco in 1963: "I'd've fucked anything … I did … I'd lick it, smoke it, shoot it, drop it, fall in love with it" (Herman, 1982, 37).

By 1965, her friends were extremely worried about her, as she was severely underweight; this was during the time she lived with Peter de Blanc and developed speed abuse. They held a collection to buy Janis a bus ticket home, as they were deeply concerned about what would happen to her if she remained in San Francisco. Janis complied and returned to the family home in Port Arthur.

During her time back at Port Arthur, she received counselling and was also prescribed Librium, which was an early anti-anxiety medicine. Janis continued with the tranquilizer for a while after she returned to California; she wrote to her family and told them that she "liked its calming effect" (Joplin, 2005, 159).

Conditions and illnesses that she experienced during her short life, aside from her addictions, included acne affliction (for which she later sought medical attention), anxiety, depression, mood swings, and also bronchitis. When she hit puberty in her teenage years, she also had poor body image, which is believed to have originated from her schooldays. Author Lucy O'Brien commented that Janis was "a heavy girl with a gutsy voice who wanted to make her space in the world; she found it difficult to squeeze into the rigours of decorative small-town femininity" (O'Brien, 2012, 88).

Laura Joplin observed that Janis' school years "were marked by periods of peace broken by instances of outrageous behaviour that led to confusion, panic, and yelling at home" (Joplin, 2005, 68).

After she left home and was in a physical relationship with Powell St. John of *The Waller Street Boys*, Janis became pregnant with his child. Sadly, she had a 'spontaneous abortion' and by that time their relationship had transformed into a platonic one (Joplin, 2005, 116).

In her early twenties, Janis was concerned about her mental health, and in an attempt to take control of her life, she tried to admit herself into a hospital as a psychiatric patient. She was rejected, as she was not deemed to be mentally ill (Angel, 2010, 31).

Given her promiscuity, Janis may have also been concerned about her sexual health and been tested for STIs (sexually transmitted infections). During the *Summer of Love* in 1967, the rate of venereal disease went up by six times. 50,000 people ventured to San Francisco (O'Brien, 2012, 89) in search of free love, peace, and sex.

When she had therapy with Bernard Giarratano, a counsellor and psychiatric social worker who worked for Children and Family Services in Beaumont, one of the things she confided in him was that "she wanted to be like normal people" (Joplin, 2005, 157). She wanted to be true and sincere to herself, without generating negative attitudes towards her.

Following several appointments and tests that Janis undertook, she was relieved when results indicated that she was not anaemic, there was nothing wrong with her blood or liver, and that there were no genealogical problems.

However, Giarratano believed that Janis may have had a hormone imbalance because Janis had never been pregnant and added that if she had any further problems, he would probably prescribe her some hormones. Janis wrote to her family that she felt embarrassed talking about it, "as if I weren't really a woman or enough of one or something" (ibid.).

He counselled her to accept herself and to experiment to find what she described as a balance between a creative and straight life (Joplin, 2005, 158). After her therapy sessions finished, he referred her to an agency in Austin where she could continue in therapy; he did not want her to "lose the self-awareness she had gained" (Echols, 2001, 129).

Giarratano remembered from their consultations that chiefly "Janis' intense concern was meeting the challenge of her family's conventionality" (Echols, 2001, 94), and that "singing was Janis' only relief from despair" (Echols, 2001, 128). For a while, life looked different for Janis while she was in recovery.

However, once she returned to California, she reverted back to using heroin and drinking heavily. Linda Gravenites commented on Janis: "… she was in serious need of protection, if not rehab. There wasn't a lot of rehab in those days – no-one thought anybody was going to die from it" (O'Brien, 2012, 91).

January 1968 was a significant time for Janis. Close to her 25th birthday, she had a termination in Mexico; terminations only became legal in the US in 1973 (www.plannedparenthoodaction.org/). She confided to her friend, Linda Gravenites, that she regretted having the abortion – she was at the height of her fame, and a child would have interrupted her career.

Sadly, two days after the procedure, and literally minutes before she was scheduled to go on stage in Los Angeles, Janis could barely walk (Echols, 2001, 181). Despite her being in excruciating agony, with obligation and professionalism, she nonetheless went on stage and performed; the audience would not have had any inkling that she was unwell, according to an observer. It was a case of 'the show must

Janis Joplin with Big Brother and the Holding Company (Studio Brass Section) c. 1967. (Unknown photographer, Bridgeman Images).

go on'. The reason for her sickness was due to the clinic in Mexico making mistakes during the abortion, for which Janis haemorrhaged and endured agonising pain. She was eventually confined to bed for a week and a half and had to cancel three days of work (Joplin, 2005, 256).

The father was a young man whom Janis had had a casual affair with, which was unlikely to be anything more than that. For a while, Janis toyed with the idea of having the baby but realised that, whilst she was at the height of her career, it would be impossible and impractical.

On the 1st October 1970, Janis completed her last recording, *Mercedes Benz*. Two days later, she visited the studio to listen to the instrumental track for *Buried Alive In The Blues*, and was exceptionally pleased with the sound. They all decided that on the following day Janis would return to record the vocals for the track.

Janis died of an accidental heroin overdose on 4th October 1970, aged 27, in room 105 of the *Landmark Motor Hotel* in Los Angeles,

California, where she had been staying. Janis and the *Full Tilt Boogie Band* musicians had been recording at the nearby *Sunset Sound Recorders*.

Unusually for Janis, she did not arrive for recording on the 4th October, so her friend and road manager John Cooke was sent to look for her at the hotel. There inside her room, he found Janis dead on the floor.

According to official records and statements from the office of Thomas T. Noguchi, the chief medical examiner of the County of Los Angeles, Janis died of an accidental overdose of heroin (Friedman, 1974, 321), which converts to morphine after it enters the body. Alcohol was present in her blood, and her liver showed the effects of long-term heavy drinking. Noguchi's record lists that there was no evidence of injury or violence.

In the spring of 1974, during an insurance trial connected with Janis' death, it was revealed that the amounts of morphine found in her body were not significantly large and that the quantity of morphine stated did not rule out that an actual overdose occurred. This would have been from an amount that was more than her body could tolerate and/or the heroin that she injected was almost pure. It is also possible that alcohol played a contributing factor in her death (Friedman, 1974, 322).

The immediate members of the Joplin family attended a private service on 7th October 1970, and according to her wishes, Janis was cremated, and her ashes were scattered by air along the coastline of Marin County, California.

Recently, a writer for an American healthcare institution, *FHE Health*, which specialises in addictive disorders and other behavioural health diagnoses, commented, "It is believed that Joplin had manic depression, attention deficit disorder and body dysmorphia" (www.fherehab.com/).

Legacy

Janis was a heavy drinker and drug user who enjoyed relationships with many men and several women; she also pushed back the gender boundaries. Janis was known as much for her rock 'n' roll lifestyle as she was for her musicianship. She could out-swear and out-drink any man under the table and was proud of being able to "hold her liquor, Texan-style" (O'Brien, 2012, 91).

She was one of music's most electrifying performers, free-spirited and totally uninhibited. When she performed, she really gave her all – inside out, back to front, and upside down. When she performed, she gave her fans her best and was agonised and loud. She remains the undisputed queen of rock 'n' roll, and her powerful bluesy vocals remain unmatched.

Singer, song-writer and actress Debbie Harry observed that "people do (Janis) even when they don't know they're doing her." She added that "the people 'doing Janis' are guys in heavy-metal hair bands" (Echols, 2001, xvi). Author and biographer Alice Echols commented that "Led Zeppelin's Robert Plant was the man most responsible for the Joplinesque quality of heavy metal vocalizing" (ibid.).

Steve Tyler, singer, song-writer, and lead singer of *Aerosmith*, confessed to what a huge influence Janis had on him by helping him to develop his confidence as a singer. He recalled that as a teenager in the late 1960s, he was mesmerised by her rebellious and unconventional presentation. She was wearing "bangles and beads ... drinking *Southern Comfort*, and she's spitting and using the F-word, smoking cigarettes – nobody did that" (https://faroutmagazine.co.uk/).

Her decadence certainly impacted on Tyler; both artists became well-known for living a life of excess – both chemically and sexually. He remains a fan of Janis and regularly covers her songs *Mercedes Benz* and *Piece Of My Heart* (ibid.).

Female singers such as Melissa Etheridge, Joan Jett, Stevie Nicks, Joss Stone, and Florence Welch of *Florence & The Machine* are clearly all influenced by Janis. Etheridge has frequently commented how Janis has inspired her, both personally and professionally. In 1994, she released a CD album called *Melissa Etheridge Sings Janis Joplin*, and in 2005, she and Joss Stone took to the Grammy's stage and performed a tribute to her.

Joan Jett said of Janis' singing, "I remember thinking that Janis Joplin sang like Mae West spoke ... When I first heard the primal scream in *Piece of My Heart*, I was hooked." Jett continued, "I couldn't help but go to the mirror and pretend I was a wild woman like Janis in a rock band" (https://www.azquotes.com/).

Speaking in 2025, Stevie Nicks, singer and song-writer with *Fleetwood Mac* and a solo artist, declared in a tribute to Janis: "From Janis, I learnt that to make it as a female musician in a man's world is gonna be tough, and you need to keep your head held high" (https://faroutmagazine. co.uk/).

Florence Welsh of *Florence & The Machine* described Janis: "She was vulnerable, self-conscious, and full of suffering. She tore herself apart, yet on stage she was totally different. She was so unrestrained, so free, and she wasn't afraid to wail" (https://www.ellecanada.com).

Before musician, singer, song-writer and actress Suzi Quatro moved to England, she was courted in Detroit by the record label *Elektra* and also the British producer Mickie Most, who was in America on business. She recalled, "*Elektra* wanted to make me into the new Janis Joplin, but Mickie said, 'I'm going to make you into the first Suzi Quatro.'" She added, "Obviously, I went with Mickie because I thought, 'OK, you see me.' I mean, I'm nothing like Janis Joplin" (www.choicemag.co.uk/).

Janis would have valued Quatro's need to be recognised for her individuality, talent and who she really was, not marketed as a copy of Janis (or anybody else). During 2011, Quatro explored the life of Janis Joplin in her BBC Radio 2 weekly documentary series, *In Search of Janis Joplin*. She interviewed some of Janis' family and friends, lovers and musicians to unearth the woman behind the image. Other subjects of Quatro's documentary series included Patsy Cline, Jim Morrison, Elvis Presley, and Otis Redding (www.bbc.co.uk).

After Janis' death, several of her contemporaries paid their respects by penning accolades to her. These included *The Mamas & The Papas'* tribute to Janis from their *People Like Us* album, the track called *Pearl*, The Grateful Dead did *Bird Song*, and Leonard Cohen's ode *Chelsea Hotel #2*.

Sculptor Doug Clark captured Janis in a variety of poses for a bronze statue of her that was donated to the City of Port Arthur and which is part of the Port Arthur Historical Collection at Lamar University in Port Arthur (Joplin, 2005, platelet opposite page 267).

Books, documentaries, films, and musicals about Janis have been written and produced since her death. The films include *Janis: Little Girl Blue*; *The Way She Was,* directed and edited by Howard Alk & Seaton Findlay; and *Janis Joplin: Her Final Hours*, produced by Katherine Buck and John Vandervelde.

There have been several biographies written about Janis, including *Love Janis*. This was written by Laura Joplin and was pivotal in helping to develop the off-Broadway play of the same title by Randal Myler (Joplin, 2005, author section). Grace Slick, singer/song-writer from Jefferson

Airplane described the biography as "A loving but balanced look at a wrenching struggle for freedom of expression" (Joplin, 2005, outside back cover).

The production *A Night with Janis Joplin, the Musical* (as previously mentioned) was first performed on Broadway in 2011 and then toured internationally. Its UK premiere was performed at the Sadler's Wells *Peacock Theatre* in London, 2024. In March 2016, the production (part live gig – part play) *Full Tilt* was staged at *Stratford East Theatre* in East London.

The Times newspaper obituary was headlined: '*Janis Joplin: Foremost Female Blues Singer of Her Generation.*' They added, "Her harsh delivery and sensual stage act put her in direct line with Bessie Smith … She had the tough, hard-boiled exterior which hides the tensions and fears inside all women who choose to sing the blues for a living" (*The Times*, 06/10/1970, 14).

Beyond the raucous and wild woman image, Janis' family and closest friends found her to be all of the following: caring, kind, experimental, fun-loving, intelligent, needy, sensitive, uninhibited, original, unpredictable, and witty, but mostly unashamedly herself.

PART 2

WHAT JANIS JOPLIN'S NATAL CHART REVEALS AND THE ASTROLOGY IN ACTION

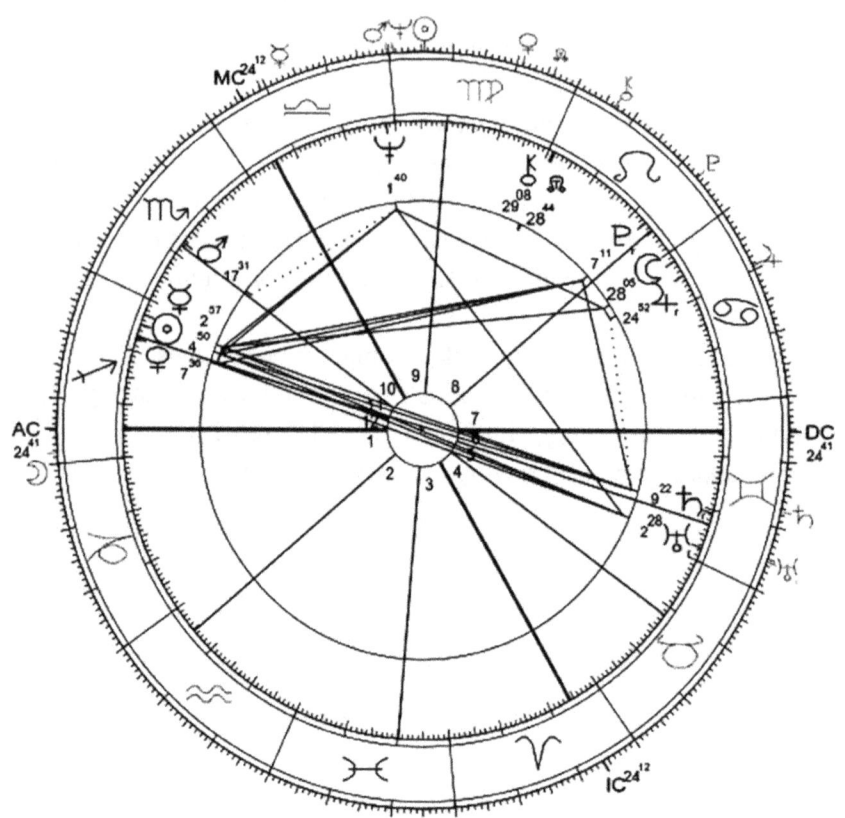

ASTROLOGY DETAILS

Janis Joplin natal and transits chart via www.astro.com (Astrodienst).
Co-ordinates of Janis Joplin's natal chart: 29n54, 93w56.
Rodden Rating: AA.

JANIS JOPLIN

Janis Joplin's Natal Chart and the Transits to it on the Day she Died on 4th October, 1970

Janis Lyn Joplin was born on Tuesday, 19th January 1943, at 09:45am, in Port Arthur, Jefferson, Texas, USA. At the time of her birth, the Sun was in Capricorn, the Moon in Cancer, and the ascendant in Aquarius. This all suggests that Janis was ambitious, sensitive, intellectual, and original.

Ambition is associated with Capricorn in terms of business, career, and executive status. However, after she found fame, Janis wrote to her parents declaring that, for her, ambition was not to do with "positions and money." Through experience, she identified it as "needing to be proud of yourself" and "how much you really need to be loved." In addition, she wrote that "being a star is losing its meaning" – suggesting that the fantasy and reality of being famous were two very different things (*Janis: Little Girl Blue*, Berg, 2016).

At the peak of her fame, and according to a former road manager, Dave Richards, Janis told him about a serious ambition she had, which was to open a bar. "When I get old, I can sit around and get drunk and play the piano and sing" (Amburn, 1994, 170). Richards continued that at the time of the conversation they were in a health-food shop, and he saw pearl barley. He joked with her about the foodstuff, and apparently that is where the idea for the name of *Pearl* came from for the name of Janis' highly successful album – and her caricature.

Sam Andrew commented that before she became super famous, she "dreamt of having a fancy car and home and being on the front of a magazine" (*Janis: Little Girl Blue*, Berg, 2016). She worked hard and was able to invest in a car and a home, showing her diligent Capricorn nature in making her dream a reality. She also achieved front cover status of magazines – e.g., *Rolling Stone* magazine in 1969.

Ambition, Drive & Energy

The theme of ambition is strong in Janis' natal chart, which is indicated by Mars being positioned in the tenth house, which is the area in the natural zodiac associated with Janis' Sun sign, Capricorn, and its ruler, Saturn. Mars is also unaspected in her natal chart and shows a wealth of cardinal (*see glossary*) energy.

It also indicates that Janis had a burning desire to succeed, coupled with the determination and strength to fight her way to the top. Nothing more than a demanding, exciting, and fulfilling career which impacted on the world would have satisfied her. Although she achieved this, it came with battles of addiction and confrontations with the right-wing suburbia where she grew up in the Deep South and occasionally revisited as an adult.

Mars in the tenth house shows that Janis may have found fame and notoriety for her sexual prowess and that her career needed to fill her with energy and vigour. Mars is also synonymous with action, sexuality, and anger. Mars' energy is direct, instant and visible – given that Mars is in Sagittarius (like Mars, it is associated with the fire element), it adds extra strength to her force and vigour.

Her publicist Maria Friedman wrote that when Janis performed, "her body throbbed with astounding energy" (Friedman, 1974, 250). Janis was indeed endowed with an inordinate power which at times may have affected the aggressive and quick-tempered side of Mars. Her colleague and friend described her as being "considerate, and she had a hot temper" (*Janis: Little Girl Blue*, Berg, 2016).

Mars in Sagittarius also suggests a need for sex to be fun and (for some) having a limitless supply of sexual partners with plenty of sexual adventures thrown in, and this was certainly the case for Janis, as ex-lovers have confirmed on film and in biographies. Janis had plenty of energy and was a capable fighter, both physically and in life generally. Mars positioned in Sagittarius also makes for a restless energy, which would have been advantageous to her when she was touring in different countries.

Another interpretation of the Mars in Sagittarius placement includes fighting and speaking out about one's beliefs. The aforementioned illustration (in Part 1), which shows her speaking up about her political beliefs, which included being in favour of integration, is one example. This was when she was still at school and shows the courage of her convictions, particularly as she paid the price for speaking truthfully, which will be discussed in detail further on.

Points of Interest in the Natal Chart

Her natal chart shows vigour in areas such as communication, idealism, and socialising. This is indicated by the preponderance of planets in air signs, which comprise Mercury and Venus in Aquarius, Saturn and

Uranus in Gemini, and Neptune in Libra. In addition, there are planets present in the third and seventh houses, which in the natural zodiac are ruled by the air element by their association with Gemini and Libra, respectively.

There are also signs in the natal chart that she had an assertive, extroverted, and instinctive nature. This is indicated by the positions of Mercury and Venus in Aquarius, Mars in Sagittarius, Saturn and Uranus in Gemini, Libra in Neptune, and Pluto in Leo. All of this will be discussed in detail further on.

Also present in her natal chart are two Grand Trines (*see glossary*), which are made up of the Sun, Neptune and Saturn, and the Sun, Neptune and Uranus. There are two planets in mutual reception (Mercury in Aquarius, and Uranus in Gemini). When she was born, six planets were retrograde (*see glossary*): Venus, Jupiter, Saturn, Uranus, Neptune, and Pluto.

There are also indications in her chart that ill-health and sickness were likely to be an issue in her life. This is shown by the preponderance of planets in the twelfth house, coupled with Pluto in the sixth house, and the Mercury opposite Pluto aspect in her natal chart.

Impressions Count

Aquarius, her ascendant (*see glossary*) sign, tells us that Janis was individualistic and original in her appearance, and that she also had a unique approach to life which made her edgy and different from the other people around her. The energy associated with the Aquarius ascendant is electrical in quality – potentially, it can be difficult to channel or control.

Through performance and style-setting, Janis found an outlet for her innovative expression. She had a genial quality, was both liberating and influential to other women, was iconic, and blazed new creative trails. She was quoted as having said, "Don't compromise yourself. You are all you've got". (https://legacyprojectchicago.org), which reveals her free and indomitable spirit.

Her dynamic and unique stage performance and her distinctive look of loose and thick, long hair, coupled with gritty, bluesy and gutsy vocals show her to have been experimental, as well as spontaneous, hitting the spotlight and bringing an original shared experience to her audience. Singer Odetta saw her perform and commented that Janis "... almost disappeared and became this musical thing ... She was so naked" (Echols, 2001, 261). After she sang *Piece of My Heart* at Woodstock, she dropped to her knees with tears in her eyes; one reporter later wrote, "She wasn't singing. She was bleeding" (www.facebook.com/), which shows just how emotionally honest and raw she was when she performed.

The Aquarian ascendant also shows that she was independent and wanted to bring different experiences into her life. Her brother, Michael, commented on his older sister, "She demanded to be different." He elaborated that, whilst his parents granted permission for their children to be different, they were unaware of what would happen if they did (*Janis: Little Girl Blue*, Berg, 2016).

This is borne out by the following example. There was an active Ku Klux Klan (KKK) chapter in her hometown, and when Janis was still in high school, she declared, "I think integration is the right thing to do" (ibid.). This angered many of her classmates and led to her being called a 'nigger lover'.

She was harassed by several classmates who bullied and intimidated her for three years. Janis was subjected to having rocks thrown at her and being spat at, and she was regularly called a whore. The perpetrators also threw pennies at her, saying that she needed the money more than they did (Amburn, 1994, 27/28). Reflecting upon that time during an interview with *Playboy* magazine at the peak of her fame, Janis commented that she was being punished for asserting her freedom and refusing to conform (Amburn, 1994, 28).

Her Truth & Nothing but the Truth

Janis' comment about integration was a good indication of Mercury in Aquarius in action, by way of her being independent and a radical-thinking person. Coupled with the Aquarius ascendant, it shows that it was imperative for Janis to speak her truth and be honest, irrespective of her going against the norm of what was considered acceptable in society and her environment.

Later in her life, and whilst being interviewed, she stated, "I would not bullshit myself" (*Janis: Little Girl Blue*, Berg, 2016), revealing her indomitable spirit and the need to be true to herself. Her sister, Laura Joplin, wrote, "The truth that she found was in her music ... She found a new reality for herself while she was singing" (Joplin, 2005, 391).

Not only does this show her independent thinking, but also her Capricorn/Saturn nature. She became isolated and long-suffering at school; Janis pushed the boundaries and found the stamina to endure the episode, albeit to her detriment in the long run. She never forgot the experience and had depression. Interestingly, in medical astrology, depression and melancholia are also associated with Saturn.

From the earlier part of the 1940s onwards, much of the southern US was dominated by the American far-right – white supremacy hate groups, such as the KKK. They were resistant to progressive change, and their followings increased significantly during the 1960s as a reaction to the rise of the Civil Rights Movement. Numerous groups used radical terror in the US as part of their white supremacist agenda, which included bombings, intimidation, and random violence (www.pbs.org).

Edgy & Distinguished

The potential for restlessness and nervous energy is also indicated in Janis' natal chart; through performance, she was able to find a positive outlet for these qualities. Uranus (the ruler of Aquarius) is positioned in the sign of Gemini and is found in the third house. In the natural zodiac, the third house is associated with Gemini and Mercury. Amongst other correlations, it also governs communication and mentality and in medical astrology is associated with breathing, the lungs, and the nervous system.

Author and journalist David Dalton, who spent a period of time with Janis on the road, observed that she was permanently restless, and he wrote, "All that static energy building up in her every day – like a 50 amp fuse about to blow" (Dalton, 2000, 151).

Interestingly, the third house cusp ruler in her natal chart is Venus, and in medical astrology this planet is associated with the neck, throat, and voice. Indeed, Janis had a distinctive singing voice and unique speaking voice. David Dalton described her voice: "Janis had the first electric larynx … It was filled with all the cackling, shrieking, fizzing, whining feedback of the electric guitar" (ibid.).

She was once advised that her hurtling style inevitably meant that her voice would not last long, to which she retorted that she "didn't want to be an inferior performer so that she could be inferior longer" (O'Brien, 2012, 90). Over time, "her voice took a beating from the booze and the cigarettes, and when she got really drunk, her voice wasn't just raspy, it would break as she tried to hold a note" (Echols, 2001, 285).

Janis recalled the time when she sang Odetta's *Careless Love* for her Beatnik friends. She was inspired by the singer, who excelled at singing blues, folk songs, ballads, and spiritual songs. After hearing Janis sing for the first time, she declared, "Far out, Janis, you're a singer," to which Janis replied, "No, I'm not, man. Fuck off, man." Janis added that when they told her she had a good voice, she thought, "Wow, that's far out" (Echols, 2001, 152).

When she laughed, Janis also had a notable loud cackle, as well as a quiet, husky, almost 'syrupy'-like tone when she spoke. Her friend Peggy Caserta commented, "I loved it when she smiled because it was generally followed by an infectious laugh" (Caserta & Falcon, 2018, 103).

Also positioned in the third house of her natal chart is Saturn, which indicates that she worked hard to achieve her ambition and eventually gained mastery over her voice and singing abilities. Saturn and Uranus positioned in the third house will be discussed further on in more detail. The potential and symbolism of the two planets in this house also suggest that in the community where she grew up, she found it repressive and alien to her way of thinking.

Pragmatism & Valuing Individuality

The Sun was at 28 degrees of Capricorn when Janis was born; the sign is ruled by Saturn, which is also known as the taskmaster and Lord of Karma. The sign is symbolised by the mountain goat, which is indicative of the sign's industrious nature: persistent to climb and achieve its goals – i.e., reaching the top. Capricorn is an earth sign, suggesting that Janis was practical, realistic, and purposeful.

Saturn is the ruling planet of the eleventh house in Janis' natal chart, the area which is associated with ideals and goals, as well as friends and groups. It suggests that she had a focus on practical and useful friendships and long-term goals related to groups, social circles, and achievements. It also suggests that her friends may have been more mature than her, be it through experience and wisdom and/ or their physical age.

It also suggests that she may have had an unconventional and unique approach to social situations and groups, as well as achieving success through effort and focus. Many of her friends were her colleagues, which is unsurprising given the amount of time that she had to spend with them. Naturally, she was closer to some than others.

Venus in Aquarius also indicates that she could mix with all kinds of people, irrespective of their age, class, income and race. She enjoyed being with forward-thinking partners and also enjoyed unconventional relationships. Venus in Aquarius also suggests that she had a marked affection for friends and commonly that friends became lovers; for example, her relationship with Peggy Caserta. It started principally as a friendship and then developed into a 'friends with benefits' partnership.

Convention & Radicalism

Capricorns are concerned with the backbone and structure of society and are at home with the establishment, recognising that class, rank, and a pecking order are realities of society. However, Janis' humanitarian and progressive nature led her to question the conservative and traditional community that she grew up in, as well as other areas of society.

She was acutely aware of the injustices, laws and rules, and political values of the generation and society into which she was born. She was aware of how her generation could potentially effect change – independence, truth, and breaking down barriers were important to her. Laura Joplin observed of her sister that "once she began challenging cultural values and standing for truth, she crossed an invisible line that could never be retraced" (Jolin, 205, 68).

Janis' friend, Linda Gravenites, commented that Janis was a member of the *Peace & Freedom Party* (Amburn, 1994, 193) – an American socialist political party which operates mainly in California. It was formed in 1967 and was born out of anti-Vietnam and pro-civil rights movements. When Senator Robert F. Kennedy visited San Francisco, campaigning for the Democratic Presidential nomination, he made street-corner speeches, and the two friends went to hear him speak (ibid.).

Observing the vast crowd at Woodstock in 1969, Janis commented to her friend, Peggy Caserta (who had joined her for the event), that in addition to those who were in attendance for the festival, there must be an enormous number of like-minded people who were not in attendance. She concluded that, "United we could quite possibly throw a vote. We could even put in our own president" (Caserta & Falcon, 2018, 103). This reveals her progressive thinking and values (Mercury and Venus in

Aquarius) and echoes the Neptune in Libra generation into which she was born, where many people yearned for peace after the Second World War and dreamt of a fairer society.

Interestingly, the Neptune in Libra (US) generation, also known as the 'baby boomers', saw the Democrat President Harry S. Truman introduce the 'Fair Deal' in 1949. This was comprised of a fair plan for full employment, public housing, and a number of other measures which became known as the Fair Deal.

Areas such as homelessness, racism, homophobia, sexism, war, and unemployment were areas that were on Janis' radar. At one point, she was out of work and claimed welfare for being unemployed, or, as her father termed it, living "on the dole" (Echols, 2001, 74); this was after she left home and lived in North Beach.

Shoplifting was part of their bohemian survival skill set. Chet Helms explained that on one occasion, Janis was arrested by the police on charges of stealing food from a supermarket in Berkeley. He revealed, "We all stole steaks from *Safeway* when we didn't have any money ... Janis had shoplifted in Austin too, but mostly for the thrill of getting away with it." He added that when they lived in San Francisco, stealing was done out of necessity (ibid.).

On the 16th of November in 1969, she was charged by Tampa, Florida police with using "vulgar and obscene language." The dispute between Janis and the police happened at a gig at *Curtis Hixon Hall*. Janis' fans were dancing on their seats, some pressing towards the stage, and others were swarming in the aisles.

The police arrived on stage as Janis began to perform *Summertime* and, with a loud-hailer, ordered the audience to sit down in their seats, and they insisted that Janis take control of her audience, to which she yelled to the officer, "I ain't telling them shit ... Don't fuck with those people ... What are you so uptight about ... Did you buy a $5 ticket?" Instead, she yelled at her fans, "If we don't hurt nothing, they can't do shit" (www.facebook.com).

More ranting proceeded, during which Janis apparently threatened to kick the officer's face in. She was allowed to finish her concert and was then arrested in her dressing room after the concert ended. She was released on bail soon after; the charges were subsequently dropped, but many venues refused to book her, including in her home state of Houston, on account of "her attitude in general" (www.independent.co.uk/).

Janis Joplin mug shot after being arrested in 1963. (Credit: Alamy).

There are several suggestions of her independent and radical nature in her natal chart, which can be seen through the following: the Sun trine Uranus; Mercury and Venus in Aquarius; and, as previously observed, Uranus in the third house; Sagittarius MC (*see glossary*); and the Aquarian ascendant, as noted earlier. These positions will be discussed in detail further on.

Paradoxically (or not), she did uphold society's convention and expectation for the tradition of the time. When she reached her mid- and later twenties, she had the desire to be married and wanted to raise a family – sadly, her dream never materialised.

Country Joe McDonald of *Country Joe & The Fish* commented that "there was a maternal feminine side to her that was never allowed to grow" (*Janis: Little Girl Blue*, Berg, 2016). He also observed that she was "always in search of love in some way … dealing with the reality of love was different from her fans' love – she needed a family but went right into the flame of fame." McDonald added that he loved her as a person, but not her image (www.youtube.com).

Detachment & Independence

The Sun trine Uranus indicates what an adventurer and free-spirited person she was, as well as being independent and original. It shows a determination and wilfulness to use creativity and inspiration differently. By feeling detached from and on the outside of others (which was certainly the case in her hometown), she was motivated by her feelings of being different.

One example of this can be seen by the comments that she made to presenter Dick Cavett during an episode of his television programme. He questioned Janis about her high school peers, and she answered, "I felt apart from them." In addition, she added that she was never invited by a guy to partner him at the high school proms (*Janis: Little Girl Blue*, Berg, 2016).

Channelling, Empathy & Sensitivity

The Sun is also trine Neptune and indicates that she was artistic, intuitive, emotional, receptive, psychic, and sensitive. All of these qualities would have helped Janis channel and express any creative work that she undertook, particularly in the fields of art, music, and writing. Then she could use her imagination in a constructive way, especially where the loss of ego is required and where she could lose herself and get inside a character.

One obvious example of this is through her singing and also identifying with her female idols, as well as the personalities in her songs where she could perform the part(s), conveying feelings that we all can recognise. The aforementioned characteristics add some warmth and softness to the cool and logical energy between the Sun and Uranus and provide a compassionate and sympathetic side to Janis' nature.

Although their artistic relationship was short-lived, Jorma Kaukonen commented that when he did play with Janis, he felt that "she channelled Bessie Smith without losing Janis" (*Janis Joplin & Jorma Kaukonen: The Legendary Typewriter Tape*, CD sleeve cover), which is in keeping with the previous interpretation of the Sun trine Neptune aspect and the ability to lose oneself, entering into a different zone.

The Sun positioned in the twelfth house suggests that there may have been an element of self-sacrifice in Janis' life; therefore, it could be argued that the sacrifice was in her personal life. She was solely focused on her music and singing career. Although raising a family was a desire for her later in her life, by that time she was hugely successful, and she decided the two would be incompatible. The sacrifice may also have been manifested by her not being able to sustain any real long-term relationships with either friends or lovers outside of the music industry.

This position also suggests that she was intuitive and sensitive and needed privacy for reflection, attuning herself to her feelings and thoughts. Indeed, she would have benefitted from periods of retreat and withdrawal to help shed what negative energies she may have picked up from other people. This would have helped Janis to regain a sense of her own boundaries again. By using her inner resources, such as intuition, and listening to her inner voice, she could be true to herself.

The Sun in the twelfth house can also indicate feelings of inferiority and poor self-esteem. Her sister commented on how Janis had questions about her desirability, particularly during her early teenage years when, like many teenagers, she gained weight and developed a skin affliction (*Janis: Little Girl Blue*, Berg, 2016).

One year whilst at university, Janis was voted 'the ugliest man' in an annual competition which gave students the opportunity to vote for the ugliest man in the university. On Monday the 5th of September in 1962, the *University News* journal published and headlined the result of the competition: *'Janis Wins Ugliest Man Competition'* – posters were hung all around the campus showing the win.

Janis was deeply affected by this, and her friend and musician, Powell St. John, recalled that "it crushed her – it was the saddest thing I ever saw – got her bad" – referring to how much it hurt Janis and made her cry (*Janis: Little Girl Blue*, Berg, 2016). Clearly, she was unable to shake off the malice; it knocked her confidence and exacerbated her already vulnerable self-esteem. It has been said of her that "Janis' feelings were always close to the surface. It was very easy to hurt her" (Echols, 2001, 65).

Her friend, Linda Gottfried, recalled that after Janis became famous, she (Janis) joked that during her years at North Beach she was so poor that "she even tried turning tricks but was too ugly to make it as a hooker" (Echols, 2001, 74), revealing a sardonic and annihilating view of herself.

Associate, Toby Ross, stated how amazed he was by her recurrent "expressions of doubt" and her "references to her appearance." She would say things like, "I'm so ugly ... You think I'm ugly, don't you?" He continued that "in school, they thought she was just an ugly girl of no significance – ugly and loud" (Friedman, 1974, 192). What a shame she didn't get to hear the thoughts of a fan who told Alice Echols, "Man, what a beautiful girl! She just looked so beautiful on stage ... it was like an aura came over her" – referring to her performance of *Ball And Chain* at the *Fillmore* (Echols, 2001, 182).

Compassion, humility, and sensitivity towards the disadvantaged, poor, and needy, as well as the underdog, are also associated characteristics with the Sun in the twelfth house position. Perhaps some of Janis' own experiences and observations were what motivated her to study social work, albeit for a short time. Her partner, David Niehaus, perceived that Janis "could feel others' pain – she couldn't block out others' pain" – showing her empathy and understanding (*Janis: Little Girl Blue*, Berg, 2016).

Both Sam Andrew and John Cooke observed how Janis sided with the underdog, taking a stand for what is right. Cooke wrote that she said, "It's not right to treat people badly because they are different." He continued, "This perception becomes a useful key to my understanding of what makes Janis tick" (Cooke, 2014, 85), which shows the placement of Venus in Aquarius in action by way of Janis valuing the differences and individuality of people.

Sam Andrew saw the depth of Janis' empathy and commented that if she saw an underdog being treated badly, she would always strongly react to that, especially if it was a woman. He said that "She would come to the defence of that person ... That was an enduring quality in her" (ibid.).

Astrologer and author Sue Tompkins observed that often Sun-Neptune people "know what it feels like to be lost and adrift and are exceptionally good at stepping in to heal any breach of this kind" (Tompkins, 1990, 120).

Janis' later publicist, Myra Friedman, was also aware of Janis' tolerant and sympathetic nature; she observed that her client's "judgement was independent of categories." She added, "Her tenderness toward runaways and street people was overwhelming, as was her gentleness toward the deserted, the rejected, and the ugly" (Friedman, 1974, 138).

Friedman was immediately humbled by Janis on one occasion when Friedman described how she walked into Janis' room at the *Chelsea Hotel* in New York City to find that sitting in a chair near to Janis' bed "was a pathetic-looking young man with terrible skin and thick-lensed glasses, through which he kept staring at Janis." After he left, Friedman questioned Janis in dismay, "Jesus! Where in the hell did *he* come from? What a mess!" Janis replied, "I know he isn't very pretty, but you shouldn't talk about people like that. He's a person too" (ibid.).

We already know from Part 1 that Janis helped raise funds for good causes and was generous to those in need of financial support. Such kindness, openness and sensitivity would have made Janis an effective healer, being able to respond to the needs of others.

Janis' beloved dog, George, was a shepherd-mix rescue puppy; she acquired him soon after she moved to Haight-Ashbury. She described George as her 'salvation' (George-Warren, 2020, page 9 of photos), and she even took him to the Monterey Festival with her. She was often accompanied by him in her car as she drove around town. Sadly, he was stolen from her Porsche, never to be found again (www.janisjoplin.com). She also had a cat (un-named) when she had George and lived at Lyon Street; she referred to them as her 'family' and said that "they helped stave off a gnawing loneliness" (George-Warren, 2020, page 12 of photos).

The aforementioned qualities of the Sun in the twelfth house also echo themes of the aspect previously discussed – the Sun trine Neptune. This is because in the natural zodiac the twelfth house is associated with Pisces, and Neptune is the ruler of that sign.

Yearning for Love & a Wounded Heart

There are Venus and Neptune associations in her natal chart: Neptune is in the seventh house and also in Libra, the areas which in the natural zodiac are ruled by Venus; also, Venus is in the twelfth house, which in the natural zodiac is ruled by Neptune. These positions indicate variations which indeed were borne out in Janis' short lifetime – escapism through art, music, reading and writing, as well as escaping through her relationship with alcohol and substances, dreaming of love and the ideal relationship, co-dependency, yearning for a spiritual soulmate, putting loved ones on a pedestal, and attraction to people who need saving in some way – particularly if they are alcohol or substance abusers.

The latter we know to be true of Seth Morgan, who was Janis' fiancée when she died. Janis may have found relationships bewildering and confusing and, in searching for love, may have sacrificed herself in some way. She attracted artistic and poetic souls – this was true of her Beatnik friends and musicians. Interestingly, Amy Winehouse also had Neptune in the seventh house in her natal chart.

In astrology, the asteroid Chiron in one's natal chart represents 'The Wounded Healer'. Symbolically, it is believed to help a person understand their deepest wounds and encourage them to try and heal the difficult aspects of their past, mainly from their childhood.

Janis' natal chart shows that Chiron is in Leo in the seventh house and is positioned on the descendant (*see glossary*). Janis' inner child wounds may have included the following: feelings of inadequacy, being unseen, and being unappreciated for who she truly was. This was certainly borne out during her high school days, when she was bullied and victimised for being an independent thinker and unique in her appearance. Any feelings of inadequacy she may have had resulted in a need for external affirmation in adulthood through creative expression – e.g., performance and singing.

Astrologer and author Melanie Reinhart wrote that both Jimi Hendrix and Janis Joplin "expressed themselves with almost superhuman intensity; they bared their souls on stage, expressing pain and joy ... Chiron in Leo ... can be raw, visceral and uninfluenced by concerns of what others may think" (Reinhart, 1989, 128).

The hurt in the seventh house is also in relationships – both with oneself and with others. There seems to be a split between the needs of the self as well as another, which needs to be healed; an inner relationship needs to be found. The Sun quincunx (*see glossary*) Chiron in Janis' natal chart indicates that she may have experienced situations that left her feeling vulnerable (such as bullying), which opened her heart and raised her awareness of those who are ignored, the downtrodden, and those without a voice. This is certainly borne out by her compassion and empathy for the 'underdogs' that she met in her life. Essentially, the hardest lesson to be learnt when Chiron is in the seventh house is about relationships.

Janis Joplin, 1960s.
(Credit: Everett Collection/Bridgeman Images).

Astrologer and author Barbara Hand Clow observed that those with Chiron in the seventh house "have enormous potential to express the collective unconsciousness of their times" and that Chiron encourages these people to "crave the adoration and adulation of others. They need to understand how they are affecting people around them" (Hand Clow, 2007, 63). Interestingly, one of Janis' idols, Bob Dylan, also has Chiron in the seventh house of his natal chart.

Chiron conjunct the North Node *(see glossary)* in her natal chart indicates that there was potential for Janis to create a way of living her life where she could have been a healer, initiator, or spiritual teacher, and until that was found, she may have experienced frustration. Although her life was short-lived, she was a healer in the sense that she helped those in need and was an initiator for white women to sing the blues in the world of rock 'n' roll, as well as leading several bands. Had she had a longer life, she may have developed these areas further and may have become a spiritual teacher – certainly, there is other symbolism in her natal chart which shows this.

A Sweet-talker who Valued Learning, Reading & Writing

Returning to the twelfth house again, Mercury is conjunct Venus. It suggests that Janis valued the beauty of language and gained pleasure from reading, speaking and writing. This would have been useful to her through her poetry and her letters and postcards home. The latter greatly contributed to the film *Janis: Little Girl Blue* and provides tremendous insight into Janis' feelings and thoughts – some of which indicate that although she had become successful in her music career, she was still seeking her parents' approval.

The Mercury and Venus contact also indicates that she could express herself with charm, ease, and wit, and that she attracted others with her voice. She loved conversation – something which was evident in television interviews and news reports, which she willingly engaged in.

One of Janis' favourite American television interviewers was the aforementioned Dick Cavett; she appeared on his television show, *The Dick Cavett Show*, on numerous occasions, and her appearances helped boost the show's ratings. Her final televised interview and performance was sadly just two months before her death. Cavett described her as having "... an unforgettable and captivating performance style, with a unique depth that resonated with audiences" (www.tpt.org/janis-joplin).

Mercury conjunct Venus also indicates that she valued literature and enjoyed reading books, comics, and magazines – *Mad* and *Time* being two of the latter. One of her favourite authors was F. Scott Fitzgerald; when she was young, she read and later re-read all of his books (his most famous book being *The Great Gatsby*).

She remarked to David Dalton, "I always did have a very heavy attachment for the whole Fitzgerald thing, that all-out, full-tilt, hell-bent way of living" (Dalton, 2000, 81). She added, "There was a time when I wanted to know everything. I read a lot. I guess you could say I was pretty intellectual" (Dalton, 2000, 151).

She also read some of the Beat generation's pioneering literary work, from poets and authors such as William S. Burroughs, Allen Ginsberg, and Jack Kerouac. The Beat Generation was a group of artists, poets, and writers who rebelled against the mainstream culture of the US that was left disenfranchised after World War II; their contributions helped define the counterculture generation.

In addition, Janis was also known to have read the then controversial book *The Sensuous Woman* by Terry Garrity (first published in 1969 in the US), *Rosemary's Baby* by Ira Levin, and also *Little Big Man* by Thomas Berger (Friedman, 1974, 307/308). The latter was made into a film and tells the story of a man who was raised and rescued by the Cheyenne Indigenous American people and who claimed to be the only white survivor of the infamous Battle of the Little Bighorn.

Apparently, another one of her favourite pieces of fiction was Thomas Hardy's *Jude the Obscure* (Amburn, 1994, 125). Janis also read the works of Gurdjieff, Nietzsche, and Wilfred Owen; no doubt she was versed in the works of many other poets and writers. According to Sam Andrew, Janis also wanted to write a book (Amburn, 1994, 147/148).

Mercury trine Saturn suggests that she had the ability to absorb information and focus her mind when she wanted to and would have liked to be taken seriously in what she had to talk about. It could be argued that she mastered the language of the blues and rock 'n' roll – it came naturally to her; she understood it and communicated it with maturity and stamina.

Rocking the Blues & Focusing the Mind

This in turn granted Janis respect from other artists, as well as from her audiences. One example being the observation noted in Part 1 of Mama Cass watching her perform *Ball and Chain*. Janis revealed to author David Dalton, "I've learnt how to make feeling work *for* me" (Dalton, 2000, 151).

Peggy Caserta described Janis' vocals after seeing her perform with *Big Brother & The Holding Company* for the first time: "What I experienced was a force of nature … the band she was singing with was a perfect match for Janis' electric, plugged-in, a-thousand-women-at-once voice … and oh, the delivery" (Caserta & Falcon, 2018, 49). The quote illustrates Janis' energetic and unique performance.

Uranus in Gemini indicates that not only was she able to grasp new ideas quickly but also that Janis was gifted, versatile, inquisitive, and nervous. She may have been able to manage changes in her life by talking things through and convincing herself that she could handle new situations – such is the adaptable and versatile nature of Gemini. Her free-thinking and independent style lifted her above the ordinary of suburbia, which from an early age she was desperate to escape from.

Lightbulb Moments & Intuitive Thinking

This placement is helpful for gravitating towards original ideas and revolutionary ways of communicating. This is borne out by her leading her bands with a volcanic and distinctive voice, which she became known for. Uranus in Gemini also lends itself to enlightening and intuitive communication and thoughts.

A poignant though accurate illustration of this is borne out when she revealed to Peggy Caserta, whilst they were on the beach in Marin County (one of her favourite places), *"When I die, I want my ashes spread here. Right here, so I can always be a part of this … I just get the feeling I'm gonna die young, sometimes"* (Caserta & Falcon, 2018, 115). Such ideas and thoughts must have added to her edgy disposition throughout her short life.

Janis sent a letter to her family at the end of January in 1968, thanking them for birthday and Christmas gifts they had sent her. Janis revealed to them, "… *25?! I never thought I'd even survive this long*" (Joplin, 2005,

256). After she learnt about the death of Jimi Hendrix, which was just seventeen days prior to her own death, she commented to some, "God damn it, he beat me to it" (Echols, 2001, 297). To others she said, "I wonder, if I died … what would happen? Would they talk about me as much as they talk about Jimi? No, that's a terrible trick for publicity." Ironically, she added, "Two rock stars can't die in the same year" (www.facebook.com).

Janis was part of the youth counterculture movement, which was revolutionary in San Francisco in 1967. It became celebrated and recognised as the *Summer of Love,* where breaking convention to help bring about personal and/or social change was pivotal in that generation's thinking.

From the get-go, it seemed inevitable that Janis was driven to break convention and that she felt a calling to pursue an unconventional path outside of conservative and mainstream Texas. She certainly found the hippie scene in 1966 at Haight-Ashbury – a community of kindred souls.

Uranus is positioned in the third house of her natal chart, which in the natural zodiac is associated with Gemini; given that Uranus is in Gemini in her natal chart, this adds a strengthened energy for originality, rebelliousness and doing things differently. Her brother commented with fondness about Janis that "she liked rocking the boat" (*Janis: Little Girl Blue,* Berg, 2016).

The third house is associated with early education; therefore, it is interesting to know the following. Janis' childhood friend from Woodrow Junior High School, Karleen Bennett, recalled that her friend "wouldn't follow directions in the choir, so they kicked her out." She added that "Janis couldn't figure out how to make herself like everyone else, thank goodness" (ibid.). This shows Bennett's appreciation for her friend's independence and originality. She, like Janis, didn't enjoy living in Port Arthur, Texas. After she became famous, Janis was asked about her hometown on American television; Janis replied, "Port Arthur is a bummer" (ibid.).

In addition to having a well-developed and informed intellect, the positions of Mercury in Aquarius and Saturn and Uranus in Gemini suggest that Janis was restless with nervous energy, which she would have benefited from channelling creatively, which, as we know, she certainly did! Caserta described Janis as having innocence: "a childlike excitability" (Caserta & Falcon, 2018, 52). David Dalton described there being "a Huck Finn innocence to her' (*Janis: Little Girl Blue*, Berg, 2016). Whatever her interests were, she would have needed to find something which was concrete and meaningful to her, which she did – through performance and singing.

Roots & Branching Out

In Janis' natal chart, the IC (*see glossary*) in Gemini (ruled by Mercury) points to her home being a place where conversation and books were integral. Certainly, in her home as a child, her parents encouraged this. Mrs Joplin recalled, "We included the children in all our conversations … and we wanted them to voice their opinions and ideas about everything" (Friedman, 1974, 12), which shows the IC Gemini in action.

Mrs Joplin read to Janis when she was a youngster; her daughter particularly warmed to magical tales. Before she started attending school, Janis could read and had a library card (Friedman, 1974, 10). Aged just six years old, Janis began writing plays so that she could stage them with her friends; her father built her a puppet theatre. Friedman commented that "Janis pressured herself towards achievement" – which illustrates her ambitious Capricorn nature (Friedman, 1974, 11).

When Janis was a teenager, she had a summer job at her local library; there she drew illustrations for the children's section bulletin boards. It generated a local newspaper story in the *Port Arthur News* and photograph and was headlined: '*Library Job Brings Out Teenager's Versatility*' (Joplin, 2005, page 10 of platelets, top right-hand photo).

Laura Joplin recalled that when her sister was in her junior year at high school, she hung around with a group of guys, and they all read good literature and discussed intellectual topics at length (Joplin, 2005, page 11 of platelets, bottom left photo).

Janis' road manager, John Cooke, perceived that "her intellect isn't disciplined or academically trained … it fires at will." He added, "She's got an opinion about everything and states it forcefully, astutely, originally" (Cooke, 2014, 87). He said, "She's very articulate and amenable to reason until she makes up her mind. Then her opinion is cast in stone" (Cooke, 2014, 85). This shows her determined, broad-minded and innovative thinking (Mercury in Aquarius in action!).

Caserta reminisced that Janis had an "endearing, enthusiastic, mile-a-minute chatter" (Caserta & Falcon, 2018, 113), especially when she was trying to be persuasive.

The MC (*see glossary*) in Sagittarius (ruled by Jupiter) suggests that for Janis, a career where independence and the opportunity to broaden her mental and physical horizons would have been satisfying to her. If her parents had had their way, their daughter would have become a teacher (*Janis Little Girl Blue,* Berg, 2016).

Jupiter is associated with abundance, excess, and believing that 'more is better' – Janis certainly enjoyed an overload of alcohol and drugs. Positioned in the fifth house, Jupiter indicates an immense capacity for enjoyment, a tremendous appetite for pleasure and vast romantic adventuring.

Various commentators have remarked on her promiscuity and tremendous sexual appetite. One of her lovers said that "Janis really knew her way around a mattress," and a roommate of another lover claimed, "I knew she was extremely sexual. I knew it from being on the other side of a small apartment" (Echols, 2001, 180).

It has also been said that "there was sometimes a theatrical quality to Janis' lovemaking," which she was more than aware of. During 1970, she told a reporter, "I used to ask guys I was balling, 'Do I ball like I sing? Is it really me, or am I putting on a show?" (ibid.).

Janis' record producer, Paul Rothschild, claimed, "Her male balance was as strong as my female balance. We both acknowledged that place, the other side of the sexual whole" (O'Brien, 2012, 87).

Further associations of Jupiter include enthusiasm, generosity, opportunity, joviality, luck, fame, and wanderlust. Pluto is trine the MC in Janis' natal chart, which indicates that she was determined to achieve her vision and took control in making that dream come true by any means necessary.

Pluto is positioned in the sixth house of her natal chart and indicates that her work needed to be meaningful and generate some kind of intensity and passion, as her desire for power was focused on her work. Unsurprisingly, she found no satisfaction in temporary work in positions such as a keypunch operator and a waitress in a bowling alley prior to her becoming a famous singer.

Meaningful, Uncompromising & Powerful Pluto

Janis may have had to learn about power at work (power being an association of Pluto). One obvious example of this can be seen by her subversive nature when she shook the rock 'n' roll industry in the 1960s. She fronted her bands as a white woman who dynamically sang and powerfully performed the blues, digging the rock 'n' roll lifestyle. Themes expressed in the blues genre often include betrayal, grief, pain, and sex, as well as political and social comment, which are pertinent to Pluto correspondences.

The aspect of Saturn sextile Pluto in her natal chart is an energy which would have strengthened her willpower and sense of control; when she was heavily addicted to alcohol and heroin, she was always punctual for rehearsals and gave her best during studio time (*Janis: The Way She Was*, Alk & Findlay, 2015).

This shows her determination and control and that she had the ability to achieve tangible results (e.g., an album) through diligence, perseverance and self-discipline. The aspect of Saturn trine Neptune also shows that she could make her dreams a reality if she applied herself correctly and that she could give she could give structure to any artistic or imaginative fields.

Author Lucy O'Brien wrote that Janis "cast herself in a role so anti-social, so anti-traditional femininity … adopting a straightforward male rock 'n' roll persona made it easier for her to strive for superiority among men" (O'Brien, 2012, 88).

Sam Andrew, guitarist in *Big Brother & The Holding Company*, generously commented that the aforementioned band were "not talented enough to get in her way." Adding that "she achieved a high level of fame leaving *Big Brother*." Janis and Sam Andrew formed *The Kozmic Blues Band* after leaving *Big Brother & The Holding Company*. He commented that she was "non-compromising" and they were "both quick-tempered" (*Janis: Little Girl Blue*, Berg, 2016). Myra Friedman, her publicist when she was managed by Albert Grossman, observed Janis' "snappy rashes of temper" (Friedman, 1974, 197).

During an interview on American TV, and post-*Big Brother & The Holding Company*, Janis reflected upon the move to her new band, and she commented, "You grow together and then outgrow each other and have to go your separate ways." She also said, "You are only as much as you settle for ... I only do what I want to do" (*Janis: Little Girl Blue*, Berg, 2016).

The opposition (*see glossary*) between Mercury and Pluto also suggests that she had an obsessive desire for knowledge. This aspect would also have been useful for any research work that Janis may have needed to undertake. It also indicates that she had a perceptive mind and may have taken an interest in the deeper causes and motives of things. Janis had astrological knowledge and possibly an interest in the afterlife and the occult, as these are subjects also associated with Pluto.

David Dalton travelled with Janis and wrote that she had "considerable intelligence" and, in addition, said, "These books ... that she lugs about with her on her journeys have a curious effect, almost approaching possession" (Dalton, 2000, 77). This shows her to be a deep thinker and, as noted earlier, at times she may have had obsessive thoughts which may have included attention and consideration about death. Certainly, we know Janis had thoughts that she would die young, as observed by the earlier examples, and from a young age she had internal struggles.

Pluto is also associated with psychiatry. This is because its energy delves deep into the psyche of the individual to transform what lies underneath by releasing any blockages and discovering the hidden treasures in the personality. Therefore, any concentrated work that required having to 'dig deep' may have interested Janis; perhaps this was why she was drawn to astrology. We know from Part 1 that she sought therapy from a counsellor and visited a psychotherapist for mental health issues.

Drama Queen

Mercury opposing Pluto shows that Janis could express herself with great power and venom, which is certainly seen in her gutsy performances. Pluto in Leo suggests a compulsion to express herself dramatically. It is also an excellent position for directorship, which was ideal for Janis as lead singer in her bands.

There were times when she just liked to 'perform' off-stage – showing off, playing the diva, and demanding attention – which is borne out by the following example. When she returned from Rio, Brazil, she barged around town, always dressed in her stage costume of plumes and bracelets. Myra Friedman wrote that Janis "hawked her importance and demanded special consideration. She became vexed if she was ignored," and at times she threw tantrums (Friedman, 1974, 192). Her mother commented that even as a child, Janis had to have more attention than her siblings and that "she was unhappy and unsatisfied without it" (Friedman, 1974, 11).

Peggy Caserta observed that occasionally Janis liked to play the diva card; she wrote that "Janis would whip out her fame and put it to good use." Caserta recalled the occasion when Janis was booked to play at the *Hollywood Bowl* and invited her and Sam Andrew along. The trio arrived late, and the security guard halted them and prevented them from going inside. Caserta continued, "Janis threw one of her famed fits, which by then she had gotten quite good at" (Caserta & Falcon, 2018, 108).

Bedecked in her stage wear and burgundy plumes with a purple feather boa in her hair, Janis shrieked at the security guard, "Do you know who I am, you motherfucker? Do you know who I am?" Unbelievingly, the steward replied, "I don't care if you're Janis Joplin herself" – the marquee headline above his head read, *'JANIS JOPLIN IN CONCERT'*. Eventually, the trio gained entry (ibid.).

The diva behaviour also lends itself to the energy of unaspected Jupiter in her natal chart, because Jupiter's qualities are also connected with being excessive, bombastic, and grandiose. Publicist Maria Friedman wrote, "Janis was swamped in her own pizzazz and amplification quite apart from a word of print or even her stage performances" (Friedman, 1974, 128). The Leo descendant suggests that she may have also created drama and spectacle in her relationships, as Leo is associated with performance and theatre. Biographer Alice Nichols commented that "Janis' audience did eat up her flamboyant exploits, but it was Janis herself who had made her life a spectacle" (Echols, 2001, 278).

It's a Capricorn Thing

As noted earlier, Janis had knowledge of Sun sign astrology, and her enthusiasm for the subject can be seen in the following examples. In the song *Cry Baby*, she references her Sun sign, Capricorn, and infers that she/the character is 'long-suffering'. She also commissioned the aforementioned Dave Richards to paint her Porsche (a 1965 Super-90 cabriolet convertible) with psychedelic designs.

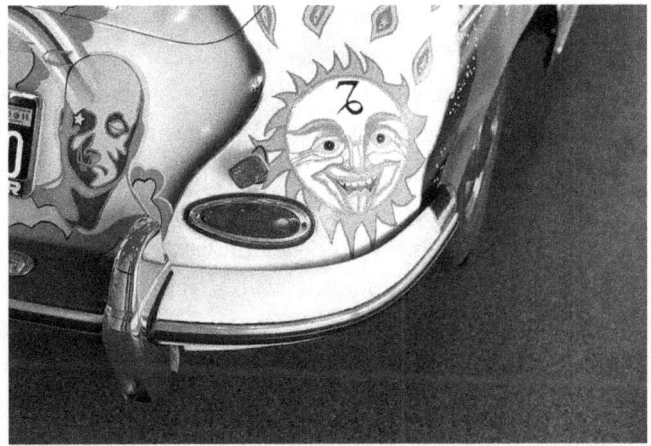

Janis Joplin's Porsche – Rock and Roll Hall of Fame – by Sam Howzit.

Janis Joplin's Porsche – Rock and Roll Hall of Fame – by Sam Howzit.

He granted her wish and included an image of a sun-face which had the glyph for Capricorn at the third eye position, which was on the offside rear of the car. Janis passed her driving test in 1958, aged sixteen (https://janisjoplin.com), and previously to the Porsche, she owned a second-hand Sunbeam which she bought when she went to San Francisco in 1966.

Her psychedelic Porsche became her distinctive trademark in San Francisco; she was frequently seen driving around town in it. After her death, and for a short while, the Porsche was a major attraction at the *Rock 'n' Roll Hall of Fame and Museum* in Cleveland.

In approximately 1967/68, Janis and Linda Gravenites were friends with two other women. All four of them were Capricorns and were known in the Haight-Ashbury neighbourhood as the *'Capricorn Ladies'* (Echols, 2001, 178).

She also wrote to her family when she was living with Country Joe McDonald, informing them (amongst other things) that he was also a Capricorn; years later, he commented about their relationship and reflected that "we were both control freaks" (*Janis: Little Girl Blue*, Berg, 2016).

Road manager, John Cooke, recalled that when he was being interviewed for the aforementioned job for *Big Brother & The Holding Company*, Janis asked him what sign he was. He answered "Libra", and she shrugged and said, "I don't care much about Libras one way or the other" (Byrne Cooke, 2014, 5/6). He got the job.

David Dalton observed and commented on Janis and astrology; he wrote, "... she did recognise in herself the afflictions of that sign – intense introspection and the tendency to go from the heights of ecstasy to the depths of depression" (Dalton, 2000, 142). Certainly, the 'intense introspection' that Dalton described is in keeping with the planetary energy and positions in the twelfth house of Janis' natal chart and the Mercury opposition to Pluto.

Laura Joplin recognised the practical and conventional Capricorn nature of her sister, as well as her unconventional side. She wrote, "There was a conventional part of Janis that always tagged along with her more noteworthy, eccentric bravura." Janis declared to her friend and lover, Powell St. John, "If there was a war, I'd go to work in a defence plant to free the guys to fight" (Joplin, 2005, 115).

Mercury in Aquarius also indicates that Janis thought 'outside the box' and was interested in unconventional subjects. The position also suggests that she was open-minded and arrived at her ideas and opinions independently. She had strong convictions, was not afraid of contradicting others, and was interested in the truth as she saw it – others may have viewed her ideas as shocking, unorthodox, and even quirky.

Humour & Wit

Saturn in Gemini indicates that she had a dry wit and could be prone to cynicism and sarcasm, as well as having a sharp and witty sense of humour. A small example of her wit can be seen in the following instance. During her final appearance on *The Dick Cavett Show*, after she and her band performed, Janis was interviewed by Cavett. He flirted with her and said, "Very nice to see you, my little songbird," to which she cackled and giggled.

Cavett then told her, "I wore my hip jacket for you," to which she replied in a dry and disbelieving tone, "You did? Are you sure?" To which Cavett grinned; the warmth and chemistry between them was obvious. The audience can be heard laughing heartily throughout the interview, which made for good viewing (www.youtube.com). Grace Slick of *Jefferson Airplane* said, "Janis would cackle; she'd laugh so hard and was fun to be with – very vocal, very outspoken, very funny" (George-Warren, 2020, page 15 of photos).

Connecting, Engaging & Feeling the Vibes

Those who were closest to Janis recognised what a feeling and sensitive person she was. Janis herself commented several times on the subject of emotions and reactions, particularly in the field of performance. Referencing how she and the audience instinctively connected with each other, she told Dalton, "I'm full of emotion and I want a release, and if you're on stage and if it's really working and you've got the audience with you, then it's a oneness you feel … I just want to feel as much as I can; it's what 'soul' is all about" (Dalton, 2000, 151).

She told Dick Cavett that when she was performing, she wasn't really thinking but trying to feel. She added that with a seated audience (like a television studio audience), "it's a weird trip" because performance is a shared experience, so when the audience dances, they are communicating with her and the band. Janis explained to Cavett about music and her performance that it "creates feelings as it's happening ... I get to experience a lot of different feelings; rock 'n' roll is rhythmic" (*Janis: Little Girl Blue*, Berg, 2016).

Home Alone, Isolation & Invasion of Boundaries

On a different occasion, Janis commented, 'Onstage, I make love to 25,000 people, then I go home alone" – the comment reveals a sobering glimpse into her world. She was at the height of her fame, but ultimately she was empty and desperately lonely. By using heroin, it may have fended off any post-performance depression and insecurities.

Her intense loneliness was described by her publicist Myra Friedman as "a tortured loneliness" (Friedman, 1974, 128), and singer Odetta commented, "Around her success, there was a terrible loneliness that was unbelievable" (Echols, 2001, 276). Capricorns can experience loneliness often due to a desire for a deep emotional connection and a fear of vulnerability. They may use work or other responsibilities as a way to avoid confronting their loneliness, which potentially could lead to further isolation for them.

Interestingly, one of her idols, Nina Simone, once said that "The saddest part of performing" was "that it didn't mean anything once you were offstage" – virtually mirroring Janis' aforementioned comment. Whilst Janis was performing to her audience, she was in command. It has been said that she abhorred the backstage situation afterwards.

Apparently, "it felt out of control to her, and she felt out of control." Dishevelled and exhausted from performing, drenched in sweat and smelly, her hair stringy and unkempt, she was expected to give more autographs, interviews, and photographs, as well as accept amorous advances of male groupies (Echols, 2001, 260/261). This was such a time when the twelfth house energy would come into play, with her need for seclusion and privacy.

Jupiter in Cancer suggests that she liked socialising, being around people, and having company; be that her family, friends, and/or her band – her soul-family, her tribe. Such was her caring and giving nature that at times this could be to her detriment. For example, after she became famous, she allowed hangers-on and users to invade her private space, often hanging out at her home for days at a time.

At her last home in Larkspur, California, it was observed that "it became a magnet for freeloaders, which began corroding her trust in everyone." Her roommate, Lyndall Erb, commented that even though "Janis disliked the parasitical quality of the scene, yet she felt she needed these people around her." She was exceptionally generous to them because she was exceptionally insecure, and, for her, "being exploited seemed preferable to being alone" (Echols, 2001, 276).

An Emotional and Nurturing Lunar

The Moon is in Cancer in her natal chart, and in the natural zodiac, the Moon is at home in this sign. It is also unaspected (*see glossary*) to any other planet, which means its energy is particularly strong and certainly, for Janis, was evident in her life. In addition to the Moon being unaspected, Jupiter is also in Cancer and is unaspected.

The Moon is in the fifth house of her natal chart and in this area suggests that Janis was emotional, dramatic, romantic (particularly in affairs of the heart), and took risks in the realms of love. She may have felt at home in love affairs with partners who were also talented, distinctive, and playful.

Creative expression was important to Janis; she nurtured her inspirational and original talents until she found the dynamic platform that showed her at her best. Planets positioned in the fifth and twelfth houses indicate how artistic, creative, and imaginative she was.

When Janis was a child, she had a serious interest in art, and her mother arranged for her to have some private art lessons. At one point, she had some of her paintings exhibited in a Beat coffeehouse called *Pasea's* in Port Arthur (Ambur, 1994, 29). When she studied art at college, Janis was especially taken with the angular portrait style of Italian artist Amadeo Modiagliani (Joplin, 2005, bottom-right platelet, opposite page 137). In addition, she also liked the work of Braque, Picasso, and van Gogh.

As an adult, Janis also enjoyed going to the theatre. For example, she saw the play *The Great White Hope* and the musical *Hair* – the latter twice (Friedman, 1974, 138). In 1967, she and a friend enjoyed going to see Japanese movies together (Amburn, 1994, 125). Clearly art, film, singing, and theatre were healthy escapes for her.

The aforementioned position of the Moon in Cancer and in the fifth house also suggests that she needed a partner who understood her needs and had a sensitive nature; whether she ever considered that herself, who knows. Certainly, David Niehaus saw those qualities in Janis, but when she returned to San Francisco after their trip to Brazil and started using heroin again, Niehaus couldn't endure to see her abusing herself and terminated their relationship.

The Moon in Cancer needs significant care and emotional security, to be loved and cared for, and craves a feeling of belonging in order to feel emotionally safe. Janis seemed to be at home and owned a sense of belonging when she moved to Haight-Aylesbury, where she was amongst like-minded people and kindred spirits.

Laura Joplin commented that Janis needed to make her life fit her values, and she found that in the music of 1960s. When she moved to San Francisco, Janis found acceptance there, and it propelled her forward (*Janis: Little Girl Blue*, Berg, 2016). She became a different person from the outcast that she was in Texas.

An example of the responsible (Capricorn) and nurturing (Cancer) side of her nature can be seen in her attitude towards the half a million strong crowd at Woodstock in the spring of 1969. Janis' appearance was significantly delayed due to many technical problems, rain, and also her state of mind, as she had been drinking and taking drugs.

When she finally appeared for her set on Sunday 17th August, at approximately 2:00/2:30am, she asked the masses who had been waiting in the mud and rain, "How are you out there? Are you OK, everybody? Staying stoned and you got enough water and you got a place to sleep and everything?" (genius.com/). This shows her sensitivity towards the crowd and their predicament.

The Moon in Cancer can also be indicative of a strong imagination, which would have helped with her artistic, musical, and literary pursuits; certainly, she had a feeling and affinity for some female singers of the past, including her idols, Bessie Smith and Billie Holiday. The position also suggests having a feeling for the past, especially with family heritage and legacy.

Sam Andrew recalled that Janis once proudly told him, "My people are pioneer stock; they came across the country and into Texas – they're tough. I've got those genes, and nothing's gonna happen to me." She told him this when they were in a hotel room; she was reflecting upon her friends who had died from substance abuse. Confidently and defensively she claimed to Andrew, "It's not gonna happen to me" (*Janis: Little Girl*

Blue, Berg, 2016). When a Moon in Cancer person is under stress, they can be self-justifying, moody, sulky, and touchy, and may withdraw into their shell to reflect.

The fifth house is also associated with children, and with the Moon in Cancer and positioned in this house, it suggests that Janis may have wanted to be a mother. Her sister confirmed this to be the case. Reflecting upon the termination that her sister had, Laura wrote that Janis' abortion "grieved her terribly. She really wanted children" (Joplin, 2005, 256). Janis must have been desperately upset when she had to make the choice between career or child. In fact, she was more than upset – according to Maria Friedman, "her reaction was one of moral horror," and Janis cried to her friend Linda Gravenites that "it was wrong, it was wrong." An inevitable depression followed Janis for several days after the abortion (Friedman, 1974, 94/95). Had Janis had a longer life, she may well have become a mother.

Mr & Mrs Joplin's Children

The third house is the area associated with (amongst other things) siblings, and in Janis' natal chart, Saturn and Uranus are positioned in the third house, as previously discussed. Janis was the older child, and she held a responsible attitude towards her siblings and encouraged their independence; they found her to be trustworthy and interesting, and she was a good friend to them, as well as a sister.

Michael Joplin recalled what a talented painter Janis was and said that as a child he was "always in awe of how well she was doing it." He also commented that when his sister moved to San Francisco, she used to send him underground papers, which he loved (www.newyorker.com). He commented that, "She was so articulate … our parents really urged us to be well read … I think she relished the rebel attitude."

He commented, "I remember sitting with Janis and her giving me lessons on how to draw," and that Janis "approached her visual art as she did her music – she just studied, studied, and studied" (www.mirror.co.uk). His latter comment shows Janis' compulsion to create art and music and how she easily zoned out whilst doing it, which is in keeping with some of the planetary activity in the third, fifth, and twelfth houses of her natal chart.

Laura recalled, "She read me bedtime stories and took me around the neighbourhood as a toddler." Some of her most significant memories include when Janis was still at home the year before she joined *Big Brother & The Holding Company*. At this time, Janis was attending college, and they shared a VW Bug car; they also shared clothes, as they were the same size.

They also "got into putting our hair up together and wearing jewellery. It was just intimate in a girly way." The last time Laura and Michael saw their sister was in 1970, when she returned to Port Arthur for her ten-year high school reunion, and Janis took Laura with her (ibid.). Just a few months later, their sister was dead.

Closing the Gig

On the 3rd of October, Janis was at the recording studios while the band were busy recording the instrumental track for Nick Gravenites' *Buried Alive In The Blues*; Janis was excited about the track and was eager to record the vocals the following day. After the band finished recording, some of them (including Janis) went on to a bar, *Barney's Beanery*.

There, she chatted about the forthcoming album with the organist Ken Pearson; they had drinks and talked about the future. They left the bar at approximately 12:30am, returning to the *Landmark Motor Hotel*, and each went to their rooms (Echols, 2001, 297/298). Peggy Caserta and Seth Morgan were supposed to stay that night with Janis in the *Landmark Motor Hotel* after she finished working in the recording studios; however, neither of them turned up.

Once she was in her room, Janis shot up heroin and then went to the hotel lobby to change a five-dollar bill. She bought some cigarettes and then chatted with the night clerk; she told him about her day and how excited she was about the recording. Janis returned to her room and sat on the bed. Still clutching her change, she put the packet of cigarettes on the bedside table and then fell forward. Alice Echols commented, "The heroin she shot up that night blasted her into unconsciousness" (ibid.).

The Los Angeles County coroner, Thomas Noguchi, issued his tentative findings, which revealed that Janis' accidental death was caused by an overdose of heroin and impacted by the heroin's purity. She had stopped using heroin for a while but started to use again just three weeks before her death; however, her body was ill-prepared for the shockwave of pure heroin. When she was found dead, there were hypodermic needle marks on her left arm, and, in addition, she was drunk.

It was eighteen hours before any of her band or crew realised that she had not been seen by anyone; unusually for her, she failed to attend the recording session in the evening, where she was scheduled to record vocals for the aforementioned track, *Buried Alive In The Blues*. Their road manager went to the *Landmark Motor Hotel* to see if Janis was there; he took the desk key and entered her motel room. There, he found her, lying on the floor; as he reached down and touched her, it was obvious that she was dead, as rigor mortis had set in.

On the 4th of October 1970, at 1:40am (www.astro.com), the date and time when Janis died, some relevant transits (*see glossary*) were making aspects to her natal chart, which is pertinent to what we know about the last part of Janis' life:

Transits

- Transiting Jupiter in the 8th house square natal Pluto.
- Transiting Uranus in the 8th house square natal Moon.
- Transiting Uranus in the 8th house sextile natal MC.
- Transiting Neptune in the 9th house sextile natal Sun.
- Transiting Saturn quincunx natal Mars.

The eighth and ninth houses are significant, as they are respectively associated with death and transformation, as well as abundance, expansion of the mind, adventure, exploration, and fame. The latter is from its association with Sagittarius and its ruler, Jupiter. It could be argued that Janis became more well-known around the world after her death, especially as her posthumously released albums were highly successful.

Uranus is associated with accidents, shocks, unpredictability, suddenness, and events that come out of the blue. Transiting Uranus in the eighth house (of death) and square the natal Moon can be interpreted as a sudden death at home. The *Landmark Motor Hotel* in Hollywood was Janis' temporary home, in room 105, while she and her band were staying in Los Angeles to record an album at the nearby *Sunset Recording Studios*.

Transiting Uranus sextile the natal MC suggests that Janis was excited about her career and that it was a good time to improve her professional life through experimentation and originality. She had the freedom to make that happen, where she could take a new direction and take advantage of any exciting opportunities.

It was also a period in her life when her reputation or social status may have received a boost with the possibility of greater fame and widespread attention. Sadly, that considerable prominence largely manifested through her sudden death. Transiting Jupiter in the eighth house, square the natal Pluto in the sixth house (the area of health/ill-health), adds leverage to the aforementioned notion of receiving greater fame and widespread attention.

Transiting Neptune in the ninth house sextile natal Sun is relevant because Neptune is associated with alcohol, escape, addiction, and drugs. Natal Sun is in the twelfth house, which is ruled by Neptune through it being the ruling planet of Pisces, which makes the energy stronger, and, therefore, Janis was susceptible. The heroin found in her body and her being drunk when she died are both indications of the aforementioned Neptune associations. The transit also points to widespread gossip and scandal; the latter subjects are also connected with Neptune.

Transiting Saturn in the third house quincunx natal Mars suggests that Janis needed to look after herself physically, as during this transit there was an increased likelihood of accidents and injuries; taking a slower pace and being more mindful of her actions would have been helpful to her. Emotionally, during this period of time, Janis may have experienced deep-seated fears and insecurities.

Certainly, the absence of Peggy Caserta and Seth Morgan on the evening that they were meant to stay with Janis at the *Landmark Motor Hotel* must have added to the deep loneliness that Janis ordinarily felt – let down by not one but two people. Interestingly, Saturn is associated with beginnings and endings, and Mars with needles.

As we already know, before Janis' death, Jimi Hendrix had died in September of 1970, and in July of 1969, his *Rolling Stone* friend, Brian Jones, died. It is largely believed that the death of the three icons gave rise to the term '*the 27 Club*' in pop mythology, as they all died aged 27. Her former lover, Country Joe McDonald, commented of Janis that "Sexism killed her … She was a strong, groovy woman. Smart, you know? But she got fucked around" (O'Brien, 2012, 87).

Appendices

APPENDIX 1. SATURN'S RETURN

Fans, researchers, and conspiracy theorists alike are fascinated by the phenomenon of the '27 Club'. This term refers to the group of famous actors, celebrities, musicians, and other artists who all died at the untimely age of 27. Amy Winehouse, Jimi Hendrix, and Janis Joplin are three of the more famous members of the club, and all three struggled with alcohol and substance abuse.

The pressures of fame, easy access to drugs, and the hedonistic culture of the entertainment and music industries can lead to destructive behaviours, which, sadly for some, result in premature death. In trying to understand the reasons behind their untimely demise, many have turned to astrology and numerology for answers and insight.

The age/number 27 is considered by some to hold magical potency, inasmuch as it is associated with completion and transformation, and others have looked to the astrological period of a Saturn return for explanation, but what exactly is a Saturn return?

In astrology, a Saturn return transit happens when Saturn returns to the same astrological sign and degree in the sky that it occupied at the time of a person's birth. Saturn's orbit around the Sun takes approximately 29.5 years – therefore, a Saturn return occurs roughly every 29.5 years. The first Saturn return occurs between the ages of 28 and 31 years old, the second Saturn return between the ages of 58 and 61 years old, and, if they are still alive, the individual experiences a third return in their late eighties.

The astrological significance is associated with discipline, maturity, and structure; during the time of the Saturn return, these areas may become more emphatic and evident in a person's life, where challenges and opportunities related to career, personal growth, and relationships become more important.

Given that Amy, Jimi and Janis did not live to experience their first Saturn return, it could be argued astrologically that they never reached maturity and/or achieved their full potential, continuing to live their lives unconventionally with the expectation of constant excitement and irresponsibility. Had the trio lived through their first and second Saturn returns, they would have occurred on the following dates:

APPENDIX 1. NOT THEIR SATURN RETURN

Amy: Her first Saturn return to 1 degree and 56 minutes of Scorpio would have been on 22nd October 2012, and she would have been 29 years old.

Her second Saturn return to 1 degree and 56 minutes of Scorpio would have been on 28th November 2041, and she would have been 58 years old.

Jimi: His first Saturn return to 9 degrees and 22 minutes of Gemini would have been on the 27th May 1972, and he would have been 29 years old.

His second Saturn return would have been on the 4th July 2001, and he would have been 58 years old.

Janis: Her first Saturn return to 5 degrees and 52 minutes of Gemini would have been on 23rd August 1971, and she would have been 28 years old.

Her second Saturn return to 5 degrees and 52 minutes of Gemini would have been on the 6th June 2001, and she would have been 58 years old.

South Saturn Delta was a posthumously-released song on the album of the same name by Jimi Hendrix. His playing at the Woodstock Music & Arts Festival of *The Star-Spangled Banner* (which is the national anthem of the US, symbolising its democracy and dedication to freedom) is significant to the date of Hendrix's second Saturn return, the 4th July, which is America's Independence Day.

APPENDIX 2. GLOSSARY OF TERMS

Astrology: is the study of the influence that the planets have on human lives.

Ascendant (AC): the sign of the zodiac ascending at the time of one's birth on the eastern horizon. It is also known as the Rising Sign.

Aspect: is an angle that the planets make to each other in the horoscope, as well as with the Ascendant, Midheaven, Descendant, and Lower Heaven (IC).

Axis: the areas on a natal chart where the Ascendant, MC, Descendant, and IC are situated. They are also known as the 'angles'.

Chart shapings: indicate the shape that the planets make in the chart; they comprise Bowl, Bucket, Bundle, Locomotive, See-Saw, Sling, Splash, and Splay.

Chiron: is an asteroid and in astrology symbolises 'The Wounded Healer'. It represents our deepest wounds and endeavours to heal them. Chiron orbits the Sun between Saturn and Uranus.

Clairvoyance: means 'clear-seeing' and is a type of psychic gift which allows the psychic to see the hidden.

Conjunction: can be a hard or soft aspect, depending on the energies of the planets involved.

Correspondences: associations, links.

Descendant (DC): the Descendant is the cusp of the 7th house.

Element: the four elements are earth, air, fire, and water – elemental balance is needed to sustain life. The twelve zodiac signs are each ruled by one of the elements. The fire signs are Aries, Leo & Sagittarius; the earth signs are Taurus, Virgo & Capricorn; the air signs are Gemini, Libra & Aquarius; and the water signs are Cancer, Scorpio & Pisces.

Grand Trine: consists of three planets that occupy different signs of the same element at 120 degree angles. In Joplin's natal charts, there are two grand trines: one is the Sun, Neptune & Uranus, and the other is the Sun, Neptune, Saturn & Uranus.

Hard aspect: refers to major angles created between planets, which comprise the conjunction, opposition and square angles (n.b. the conjunction is variable depending on the energies of the two planets involved).

Houses: a house in the natal chart reveals 'where' planetary energies express themselves. Each of the twelve houses in a chart rule certain areas of life: types of people and relationships, ideas, and circumstance.

APPENDIX 2. GLOSSARY OF TERMS

Imum Coeli/IC: *'Imum Coeli'* is Latin for 'bottom of the sky'. It is the 'nadir' or low point in the Sun's path and, if you could see the Sun, where it would be seen at midnight; it is also the cusp of the 4th house.

Major aspects: comprise conjunction, opposition, sextile, square, and trine angles.

Medical astrology: links the Sun, Moon, planets, and the Zodiac signs to human health. It associates them with body parts, diseases, and treatments.

Midheaven/MC Coeli: *Medium Coeli* is the Midheaven – where the Sun would be at noon at the top of the chart; it is also the 10th house cusp.

Modes: there are three modes in astrology, which are represented by cardinal, fixed, and mutable energies. They all represent the way in which a sign operates. **Cardinal** signs are initiators of action and are the signs of Aries, Cancer, Libra, and Capricorn. **Fixed** signs have staying power and are the signs of Taurus, Leo, Scorpio, and Aquarius. **Mutable** signs have a versatile attitude and are the signs of Gemini, Virgo, Sagittarius, and Pisces.

Moon's Nodes: the Moon's North and South Nodes theorise that one is born with overdeveloped and underdeveloped traits of our character. The North Node indicates traits which we need to develop in order to find inner happiness, and the South Node indicates the overdeveloped traits which we are comfortable with and retain for security purposes. The North Node is also known as the Dragon's Head, and the South Node the Dragon's Tail, and they are polarised by sign and house at 180 degrees. The Moon's Nodes are also associated with reincarnation.

Mutual reception: this happens when two planets are positioned in each other's signs within a natal chart. It tends to create a unique and beneficial connection which enhances each other's energies and function. In Janis Joplin's natal chart, the mutual reception was Mercury in Aquarius and Uranus in Gemini.

Natal chart: a natal chart is a picture of the positions of the signs, planets, and angles at the time of one's birth. It contains data such as date, time and place of birth to generate an accurate astrological chart.

Natural zodiac: the natural zodiac, in astrology, refers to a system where each of the twelve zodiac signs is naturally associated with a specific house in a birth chart. This association is based on the order of the signs and houses, with Aries naturally corresponding to the 1st house, Taurus to the 2nd, and so on. Furthermore, the planets are also thought to have a natural association with certain houses, based on their rulership of the zodiac signs.

APPENDIX 2. GLOSSARY OF TERMS

North Node: see **Moon's Nodes** for description.

Outer planets: Jupiter, Saturn, Uranus, Neptune, and Pluto.

Personal planets: (the inner planets) the Sun, the Moon, Mercury, Venus, and Mars.

Polarity: There are six polarities in astrology which are natural oppositions. They comprise Aries/Libra, Taurus/Scorpio, Gemini/Sagittarius, Cancer/Capricorn, Leo/Aquarius, and Virgo/Pisces. The signs are also male and female – air and fire are masculine, and earth and water are feminine.

Quincunx: in astrology, a quincunx (also known as an inconjunct) is an aspect formed when two planets/asteroids/symbolic points are 150 degrees apart.

Rodden Rating System: is a system developed by astrologer Lois Rodden, which classifies astrological data by grade to reflect its accuracy for research purposes for astrologers. Classification starts at 'AA', then 'A', and finishes at 'XX' – for further details see: https://www.astro.com/astro-databank/Help:RR.

Séance: from the French word meaning 'sitting', used to describe a meeting of people who have gathered to receive messages from spirits.

Soft aspect: refers to major angles created between planets, which comprise the conjunction, sextile, and trine (n.b. the conjunction is variable depending on the energies of the two planets involved).

South Node: see **Moon's Nodes** for description.

Transits (transiting): transits are the current positions of the planets as they move through the zodiac signs and interact with the planets in the natal chart. When a transiting planet makes an aspect (angle) to a planet in the natal chart, it can trigger specific events or emotional shifts, depending on the planets involved and the nature of the aspect.

Unaspected planet: an unaspected planet does not form a major aspect – soft or hard – with another planet. Potentially, it can form an energy which needs to be developed or used.

APPENDIX 3. THE NATURAL ZODIAC WHEEL

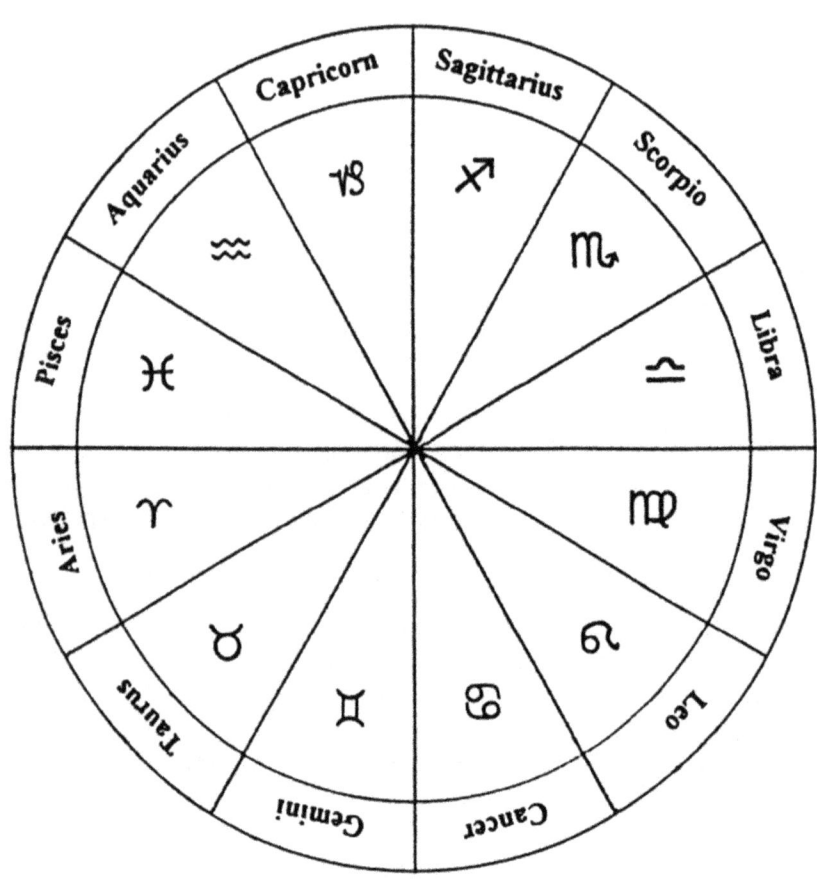

APPENDIX 4. THE MEANING OF THE HOUSES IN ASTROLOGY

When the time of birth is known for somebody, the natal chart is divided into twelve sections which are called 'houses'. This word is used to describe the sections of the natal chart which start from 1 through to 12. The first house always begins at the ascendant (also called the Rising Sign).

DEFINITION OF THE HOUSES

House Number	Meaning(s)
1	Appearance, first impression, persona.
2	Earnings, possessions, resources, values.
3	Communication, early education, mentality, cousins & siblings, neighbourhood.
4	Home, family, heritage & roots, parents.
5	Children, inner child, love affairs, pleasure, creativity.
6	Health, ill-health, work & co-workers.
7	Partnerships, spouse, significant relationships, one-to-one relationships.
8	Other people's money & resources, intimacy & sex, transformation, death – both physical and metaphysical.
9	Higher education, philosophy, religion, overseas travel, politics, publishing, in-laws.
10	Career, reputation, status, parents.
11	Clubs & societies, friends, kindred spirits, goals.
12	Hidden things, secrets, institutions, seclusion, imagination, retreat, spirituality, unconscious.

APPENDIX 5. IDENTICAL ASTROLOGICAL DATA IN AMY, JIMI AND JANIS'S NATAL CHARTS

	Amy	Jimi	Janis
The Sun in earth signs	✓		✓
The Moon in Cancer		✓	✓
The Moon in 7th house	✓	✓	
Mars in 10th house		✓	✓
Mars unaspected		✓	✓
Venus in 12th house		✓	✓
Planets in the sign they rule	✓	✓	✓
Saturn in 6th house	✓	✓	
Pluto in 6th house			✓
Neptune in 7th house	✓		✓
Jupiter in Cancer		✓	✓
Uranus in Gemini		✓	✓
Planets in the house they rule	✓	✓	
Planets at 0 degrees	✓		✓
Planets at 4 degrees	✓		✓
Planets at 28 degrees		✓	✓
Preponderance of mutable mode	✓	✓	
Bowl shaping of the planets	✓	✓	
Ascendant ruled by air element	✓		✓
Midheaven ruled by air element	✓	✓	
Descendant ruled by fire element	✓		✓
Imum Coeli ruled by fire element	✓	✓	
Sun conjunct Mercury	✓	✓	
Mercury conjunct Venus		✓	✓
Uranus trine Neptune		✓	✓
Saturn sextile Pluto		✓	✓
North Node conjunct Chiron		✓	✓

Acknowledgments & Sources

AMY WINEHOUSE

Astrology details

Amy Winehouse natal and transits chart via www.astro.com (Astrodienst).
Co-ordinates of Amy Winehouse's natal chart: 0w05, 51n40.
Rodden Rating: A.

Photo Credits:

Alamy:
Image ID 2P8PTJA , Credit Line 'Associated Press/Alamy'.
Title: British singer Amy Winehouse arrives at Westminster Magistrates Court in London. Tuesday, March 17th 2009 (AP – photo/Alaistair Grant).

Bridgeman Images:
Image ID DPA2132532: title Amy Winehouse
Image ID DPA2132533: title Amy Winehouse
Image ID DPA2132535: title Amy Winehouse
Image ID EVT5832061: title Amy Winehouse at The Tonight Show with Jay Leno, 2007 (photo) – byline Dave Bjerke.
Image ID IMO2070763: title Amy Winehouse
Image ID ZUM6438496: title Amy Winehouse, MTV Movie Awards, Gibson, Amphitheatre, Universal Hollywood CA., 3rd June 2007 (photo) – byline David Longendyke.
Image ID ZUM6438497: TITLE Amy Winehouse, Blake Fielder, TV Movie Awards, Gibson Amphitheatre, Universal Hollywood CA., 3rd June 2007 (photo) – byline David Longendyke.

Books

Barak, D. (2010) *Saving Amy* New Holland Publishers (UK) Ltd.
Hall, J. (2006) *Past Life Astrology, Use Your Birthchart To Understand Your Karma* Godsfield Press – a division of Octopus Publishing Group Ltd.
Newkey-Burden, C. (2008) *Amy Winehouse The Biography*, John Blake Publishing Limited.
O'Brien, L. (2012) *She Bop, The Definitive History of Women in Popular Music* Jawbone Press.
Parry, N. – curator (2021) *Amy Winehouse Beyond Black* Thames and Hudson Ltd.
Tompkins, S. (1989) *Aspects in Astrology A Comprehensive Guide To interpretation* Element Books Limited.
Winehouse, J. (2014) *Loving Amy, A Mother's Story* Transworld Publishers.

Winehouse, M. (2013) Amy *My Daughter,* HarperCollins Publishers.

The Amy Winehouse Estate (2023) Amy *Winehouse In Her Words* HarperCollins Publishers.

Ronnie Spector quote at beginning of Part One from (2021) *Amy Winehouse Beyond Black* Thames and Hudson Ltd. (page un-numbered).

DVDs

Taylor-Johnson, S (2024) *Back To Black* – scene of Amy in Ronnie Scott's nightclub tuning into her deceased grandmother's spirit.

Kapadia, A (2015) *Amy The Girl Behind The Name* Universal Music Group Company.

Marre, J. (2018) *Amy Winehouse, Back To Black a* BBC Studios Production in association with Eagle Rocks Film for Eagle Rock Entertainment.

Websites

https://www.amywinehouse.com/ – accessed on 24/05/2024 – 8th best album of all time applemusic

https://www.amywinehouse.fandom.com/wiki/Janis_Collins – accessed 29/05/2024 – Janis Seaton's birthday.

https://www.amywinehouse.fandom.com/wiki/Alex_Winehouse – accessed 30/05/2024 – Alex Winehouse birthday detail.

https://www.amywinehouseforum.co.uk/forum/topic/15211-origin-of-lioness-records/ – accessed on 16/06/2024 – Lioness Records inspiration for name.

https://amywinehousefoundation.org/ – accessed on 24/05/2024 – the role and mission of The Amy Winehouse Foundation.

https://www.ancestry.co.uk/genealogy/records/alec-winehouse-24-pqmtnv – accessed on 26/05/2024 – details of Alec Winehouse.

https://www.bbc.co.uk/news/uk-england-london-15453517 – accessed on 15/07/2024 – coroner's verdict of misadventure.

https://www.bbc.co.uk/news/uk-14266134 – accessed on 23/06/2024 – Tributes paid to Amy Winehouse after her death.

https://www.beateatingdisorders.org.uk/get-information-and-support/about-eating-disorders/types/bulimia/ – accessed on 02/10/2024 – bulimia nervosa

(https://www.daledavisbass.co.uk/) – accessed on 22/06/2024 – musical arranger and director for Amy Winehouse.

https://www.digitalspy.com/showbiz/a161949/emi-to-sell-winehouse-gift-cards/ accessed on 18/06/2024 – EMI collaboration successful.

https://www.express.co.uk/celebrity-news/1489574/amy-winehouse-back-to-black-final-words-frank-in-her-own-words-bbc-asif-kapadia-spt – accessed on 10/07/2024. – her death – last recorded words with Andrew Morris.

https://www.express.co.uk/celebrity-news/1946279/amy-winehouse-final-words-doctor-death – accessed on 31/10/2024 – Amy's admission to her doctor hours before she died *"I don't want to die"* – Reporter, Jennie Buzaglo – Showbiz reporter on 14/09/2024.

https://www.facebook.com/watch/?v=1004893287018407 – accessed on 14/10/2024 – quote about her pet canary called Ava and October Song.

https://faroutmagazine.co.uk/amy-winehouse-collaborations-best-prince-rolling-stones/ – accessed on 16/06/2024 – Collaboration examples and speaking about musicians she can learn from.

ACKNOWLEDGMENTS & SOURCES

https://www.findagrave.com/memorial/157100503/cynthia-levy – accessed on 26/05/2024 – Date of Cynthia Gordon Levy's death.

https://www.fredperry.com/community-our-values – accessed on 1806/2024 – The Amy Winehouse Collection & Fred Perry Label.

https://www.geni.com/people/Celia-Gordon/6000000003048543817 – accessed on 26/05/2024 – details of Celia Gordon's birth & death dates.

https://www.geni.com/people/Larry-Levy/6000000020879883992 – accessed on 26/05/2024 – details of Larry Levy's date of birth and death dates.

https://genius.com/Amy-winehouse-intro-stronger-than-me-lyrics – accessed on 24/10/2024 -controversy about *Stronger Than Me Lyrics*.

https://www.geni.com/people/Max-Gordon/6000000003048942200 – accessed on 26/05/2024 – details of Max Gordon's birth & death dates.

https://www.theguardian.com/science/2003/jun/11/sciencenews.medicineand health – accessed on 09/07/2024 – details of Seroxat being banned to under 18s.

https://www.theguardian.com/music/2017/mar/12/amy-winehouse-tattoos-memories-henry-hate-exhibition-family-portrait – accessed on 25/09/2024 – Henry Hate on tattooing Amy Winehouse.

https://www.theguardian.com/music/2007/jun/12/news.amywinehouse – accessed on 04/11/2024 – Amy Winehouse admits to punching her husband when she is drunk.

https://www.last.fm/music/Amy+Winehouse/_/Intro+%2F+Stronger+Than+Me/+wiki – accessed on 25/06/2024 – about the song STRONGER THAN ME and her on-off experience with Chris Taylor.

https://www.looktothestars.org/celebrity/amy-winehouse – accessed on 22/06/2024 – details of charities supported.

https://www.mind.org.uk/information-support/types-of-mental-health-problems/eating-problems/types-of-eating-disorders/#Bulimia – accessed 11/07/2024 – Bulimia.

https://www.mind.org.uk/information-support/legal-rights/sectioning/being-assessed/ – accessed on 19/07/2024 what happens when somebody is lawfully sectioned.

https://www.mojo4music.com/articles/stories/amy-winehouse-remembered/ – accessed on 25/06/2024 – Chris Taylor and Amy's perception of him perceiving emotional strength.

https://www.musicradar.com/news/watch-a-21-year-old-amy-winehouse-bring-the-house-down-with-a-red-stratocaster-and-talk-about-her-love-for-the-guitar – accessed on 14/06/2024 – details about when Amy's red Fender Stratocaster guitar +Jimi Hendrix influence.

https://nida.nih.gov/publications/research-reports/common-comorbidities-substance-use-disorders/part-1-connection-between-substance-use-disorders-mental-illness – accessed on 13/07/2024. – SUD and co-occurring with mental disorders.

https://people.com/celebrity/divorce-drama-for-amy-winehouse/ – accessed on 19/06/2024 – Fielder-Civil tells newspaper he introduced Amy to crack and heroin.

https://www.reuters.com/article/business/finance/amy-winehouse-was-phone-hacked-reporter-claims-idUS2233027352/ – accessed on 18/10/2024 – report by Brent Lang on 2607/2011 – 'Amy Winehouse Was Phone Hacked, Reporter Claims'.

http://www.sfgate.com/cgi-bin/blogs/dailydish/detail?entry_id=67347 – accessed on 09/07/2024 – details about Blake Fielder-Civil receiving no money in his divorce settlement.

https://www.standard.co.uk/lifestyle/amy-winehouse-ex-husband-blake-fielder-civil-b1055469.html – accessed on 04/11/2024 – tempestuous and often violent relationship.

https://www.sylviayoungtheatreschool.co.uk/page/?title=Alumni&pid=74 – accessed on 13/06/2024 – full time student.

https://www.thejc.com/life-and-culture/amy-winehouses-ex-alex-clare-hits-the-big-time-m824igko – accessed on 19/06/2024 – Alex Clare and fame.

https://www.thejc.com/news/community/winehouse-mum-thanks-norwood-kgpjlwwq -accessed on 27/05/2024 – Norwood orphanage.

https://thewalrus.ca/we-failed-amy-winehouse/ – accessed on 31/10/2024 – comments about fame.

https://uk.linkedin.com/in/janis-winehouse-58838930 – accessed on 30/05/2024 – details of Janis Winehouse's' education.

https://web.archive.org/web/20111027211038/http://www.guardian.co.uk/music/2011/oct/26/amy-winehouse-verdict-misadventure – accessed on 10/07/2023 – inquest and misadventure.

https://web.archive.org/web/20170522213952/http://www.huffingtonpost.com/entry/amy-winehouse-jewish_us_55b1319ae4b08f57d5d3f5df – accessed on 1206/2024 – detail about Winehouse attending a Jewish Sunday School.

https://web.archive.org/web/20121024192708/http://www.contactmusic.com/news/generous-amy-winehouse-paid-for-pals-life-saving-operation_1239621 – accessed on 18/06/2024 – payment for friend's hernia surgery.

https://web.archive.org/web/20121118115829/http://www.looktothestars.org/news/5914-amy-winehouse-donates-clothes-to-charity-shop – accessed on 18/062024 – donation to charity shop of designer clothes.

https://web.archive.org/web/20081028204551/https://www.usatoday.com/life/people/2008-06-23-amy-winehouse_N.htm – accessed on 10/07/2024 – lung-health information.

https://en.wikipedia.org/wiki/Amy_Winehouse#Other_ventures – accessed on 19/06/2024 – detail about her fortune.

https://en.wikipedia.org/wiki/Amy_Winehouse#Death – accessed on 11/07/2024 – details of funeral.

https://en.wikipedia.org/wiki/Amy_Winehouse#cite_note-26 – accessed on 13/06/2024 – The Mount and Brit School.

https://en.wikipedia.org/wiki – accessed on 23/06/2024 – dates that Fielder-Civil was imprisoned.

https://en.wikipedia.org/wiki/Lioness_Records#:~:text=Lioness%20Records%20is%20a%20British,to%20create%20her%20own%20label. – accessed on 16/06/2024 – inspiration of Lioness Record label name.

https://en.wikipedia.org/wiki/Paroxetine – accessed on 09/07/2024 – details as to what conditions it is used to treat.

https://en.wikipedia.org/wiki/Amy_Winehouse#Posthumous_retrospectives – accessed on 11/07/2024 – details about the *Amy* exhibition at London & San Francisco.

https://en.wikipedia.org/wiki/Amy_Winehouse#Early_life – accessed 15/06/2024 – detail of where her paternal great-great grandfather came from.

ACKNOWLEDGMENTS & SOURCES

YouTube Films

https://www.youtube.com/watch?v=FgDPDu-D21A – accessed on 22/06/2024 – Amy Winehouse playing piano and singing Puppy Love to Josh Bowman.
https://www.youtube.com/watch?v=2JDapMUNmc4 – accessed on 19/06/2024 – Mitch Winehouse-No Regrets As A Father – Loose Women.

JIMI HENDRIX

Astrology details

Jimi Hendrix's natal and transits chart via www.astro.com (Astrodienst).
Co-ordinates of natal chart 122w20, 47n36.
Rodden Rating: AA

Portrait & Mural Credits:

Artists
Hetherington, M. *Jimi Hendrix portrait*
www.facebook.com/MarkHetheringtonArt and
    www.artpal.com/markhetherington#i6
www.markheth.wixsite.com/marksart
Zabou *Jimi Hendrix* mural
X zabouartist
https://www.zabou.me/
email contact@zabou.me

Books

Amburn, E. (1994) *The Obsessions and Passions of Janis Joplin* Warner Books
Bebergal, P (2015) *Season of The Witch, How The Occult Saved Rock and Roll* Jeremy P. Tarcher/Penguin.
Burdon, E. with Craig, Marshall, J. (2001) *Don't Let Me Be Misunderstood* Thunder's Mouth Press. /Quote from top of Part One of Jimi Hendrix from page 125.
Caserta, P & Falcon, M. (2018) *I Ran Into Some Trouble* Wyatt-MacKenzie Publishing.
Clifford, F.C. compiled by, (2018) *The Book Of Music Horoscopes* Flare Publications in conjunction with The London School of Astrology.
Cross, C.R. (2005) *Room Full Of Mirrors, A Biography of Jimi Hendrix* Sceptre, Hodder & Stoughton Ltd, A Division of Hodder Headline.
Dannemann, M. (1995) *The Inner World of Jimi Hendrix by his fiancée* Bloomsbury Publishing Plc.
Etchingham, K. (1999) *Through Gypsy Eyes, My Life, The 60s, And Jimi Hendrix* Orion Books Ltd.
Forrest, S. (2012) *Yesterday's Sky, Astrology & Reincarnation* Seven Paws Press Inc.
Hendrix, J.L. (2021) *Jimi Hendrix* Experience Hendrix & Authentic Hendrix, *Editions* White Star.
Hendrix, J. with Introduction by Peter Neal (2014) *Jimi Hendrix Starting At Zero* Bloomsbury Publishing Plc.
Hendrix, L. with Mitchell, A. (2012) *Jimi Hendrix A Brother's Story* Thomas Dunne Books.

Lawrence, S. (2006) *Jimi Hendrix, The Man, The Magic, The Myth* Pan Books an imprint of Pan Macmillan Ltd.
Mitchell, M. & Platt, J. (1993) *The Hendrix Experience* Reed Consumer Books Ltd.
Olliver, O. (2022) *Chasing the Dragons, An Introduction to Draconic Astrology* The Wessex Astrologer Ltd.
Redding, N. & Appleby, C. (1990) *Are You Experienced, The Inside Story of The Jimi Hendrix Experience* Fourth Estate Limited.
Roby, S. & Schreiber, B. (2010) *Becoming Jimi Hendrix, From Southern Crossroads To Psychedelic London, The Untold Story of A Musical Genius,* Da Capo Press.
Shapiro, H & Glebbeek, C. (1991) *Jimi Hendrix Electric Gypsy* William Heinemann Ltd.
Southall, B. (2012) *Jimi Hendrix Made In England* Ovolo Books Ltd.
Tompkins, S. (1990) *Aspects In Astrology, A Comprehensive Guide To Interpretation* Element Books Limited.

Acknowledgement is given to the work of Peter Neal and his colleague, the late Alan Douglas whose dedication, narrative, passion and time formulated the brilliant Jimi *Hendrix Starting At Zero His Own Story* publication (originally called *Room Full Of Mirrors*), which has been invaluable in helping to build a firsthand picture and understanding of the late great Jimi Hendrix.

Newspapers

The Times – Obituary – 'Jimi Hendrix: A Key Figure in the Development of Pop Music' – reporter unknown – Saturday, 19th September, 1970 page 14.
The Times – Coroner's Report, 'Jimi Hendrix – no sign of any drug addiction', by A.P. 29th September 1970 – page unknown.

Photo Credits

Alamy:
Image ID: 2GRGFOB, Pictorial Press Ltd./Alamy,
Title: JIMI HENDRIX (1942–1970), American rock musician during his enlistment with the US Army in 1961.
Image ID: 2Y6N2ND: Smith Archive/Alamy,
Title: Model Linda Keith wears this civet fur lumberjack cap at the showing of milliner Edward Mann winter collection. August 20th 1963.

Bridgeman Images:
Image ID: DPA2146294 title The Jimi Hendrix Experience 1967 (b/w photo).
Image ID: EVT1839000 title Jimi Hendrix, c. 1967 (photo).
Image ID: GCL3157582 title JIMI HENDRIX (1942–1970) American musician. Photographed during a concert at Berkeley, California in 1970.
Image ID: SZT718898 title Jimi Hendrix in the Star Club in Hamburg (b/w photo).
Image ID: XRE1874561 title Jimi Hendrix, USA c.1970 (b/w photo).
Image ID: XRH1706119 title Kathy Etchingham girlfriend of three years of Jimi Hendrix.

ACKNOWLEDGMENTS & SOURCES

Websites

https://americansongwriter.com/behind-the-death-of-jimi-hendrix/#:~:text=The %20musician%20died%20from%20an,asphyxia%20while%20intoxicated%20 with%20barbiturates.%E2%80%9D – accessed on 12/02/2025 – Behind the Death of Jimi Hendrix by Tina Benitez-Evans – updated 01/05/2024.

https://www.astro.com/ – accessed on 24/12/2024 – Date, place & time of birth for Jimi Hendrix.

https://www.bbc.co.uk/news/magazine-21292762 – accessed on 04/1/2024 – *Kathy Etchingham: Life as Jimi Hendrix's Foxy Lady* by Simon Watts – arguments over cooking-inspired *The Wind Cries Mary*.

https://en.wikipedia.org/wiki/Jimi_Hendrix_discography – accessed on 24/12/2024 – record labels.

https://en.wikipedia.org/wiki/Electric_Lady_Studios – accessed on 24/12/2024 – Electric Lady Studios.

https://en.wikipedia.org/wiki/Lansdowne_Crescent,_London – accessed on 24/12/2024. address of Monika Danneman's hotel suite.

https://www.findagrave.com/ – accessed on 24/12/2024 – Lucille Jeter Hendrix's death.

https:// www.fr.wikipedia.org/wiki – accessed 24/12/2024 – Hendrix felt smothered by her – Devon Wilson's childhood and death.

https://goldiesparade.co.uk/discography/prince-compilation-albums/power-of-soul/#:~:text=Jimi%20Hendrix%20has%20been%20long,black%20such%20 comparisons%2 – accessed on 26/12/2024 – quote from Prince learning from Jimi Hendrix.

https://www.guitarplayer.com/news/hear-jimi-hendrix-jam-with-eric-burdon-and-war-in-his-final-public-performance – accessed on 19/02/2025 – Jimi's last public appearance.

https://handelhendrix.org/ – accessed 24/12/2024 – Brook Street, English Heritage Blue Plaque.

https://www.historylink.org/File/3912 – accessed on 18/01/2025 – Al Hendrix and Ayako ('June') Fujita.

https://home.army.mil/campbell/101st#:~:text=The%20101st%20is%20 recognized%20for,on%20our%20Unit%20History%20page. – accessed on 24/12/2024 – The Screaming Eagles Unit.

https://www.theguardian.com/music/2013/sep/14/jimi-hendrix-linda-keith – accessed on 24/12/2024 – *"How I helped to make Jimi Hendrix a Rock 'n' Roll Star"* – Edward Helmore – 14/09/2013.

https://www.independent.co.uk/life-style/a-rock-legend-unto-herself-1345098.html accessed on 24/12/2024 – *A Rock legend unto herself* Mary Braid 01/05/1996.

https://www.jimihendrix.com/experience-hendrix-llc/ – accessed on 18/01/2025 – information about the company's mission.

https://www.jimihendrix.com/news/experience-hendrix-l-l-c-and-authentic-hendrix-llc-to-release-jimi-hendrixs-famed-star-spangled-banner-via-straxar-augmented-reali – accessed on 18/01/2025 – SraxARTM collaboration for Black Lives Matter movement.

https://www.jimihendrix.com/encyclopedia-item/january-16-1970-in-a-session-at-the-record-plant-overseen-by-engineer-bob-hughes-and-second-engineer-dave-ragno/ – accessed on 09/01/2025 – date of *Send My Love To Linda* being crafted.

https://www.linkedin.com/in/janie-hendrix-ab63a713 – accessed on 18/01/2025 – Janie L. Hendrix – President of JMH Productions.

https://www.musiclipse.com/2024/06/04/kathy-etchingham-a-love-story-as-jimi-hendrixs-most-important-girlfriend/ – accessed on 24/12/2024 – *"Kathy Etchingham A Love Story AS Jimi Hendrix's Most Important Girlfriend"* Alexandra G. – 04/06/2024 – *The Wind Cries Mary* – Devon Wilson inspiration behind *Dolly Dagger*. Herbie Worthington on Devon Wilson – string on a broom handle technique. Jimi's quote about the Brook Street flat being home.

https://www.musiclipse.com/2023/10/24/the-story-of-jimi-hendrixs-step-sister-janie-hendrix/ – accessed on 1801/2025 – quote about June and Jimi's relationship.

https://www.musicradar.com/news/watch-a-21-year-old-amy-winehouse-bring-the-house-down-with-a-red-stratocaster-and-talk-about-her-love-for-the-guitar – accessed on 14/06/2024 – Jimi Hendrix influence.

https://www.reddit.com/r/jimihendrix/comments/1fgr7la/i_worked_with_jimi_hendrix_the_last_3_years_of/?rdt=58316 – accessed on 24/12/2024 – Kramer on Hendrix changing his engineering life.

https://www.seattletimes.com/ – accessed on 24/12/2024 – Name of hospital where Jimi was born – Great Dixieland Spectacle – Al Hendrix's various jobs.

https://songmeanings.com/songs/view/3530822107858732015/ – accessed on 05/01/2025 – *The Ballad of Jimi* penned by Curtis Knight.

https://southseattleemerald.org/news/2020/09/19/bold-as-love-celebrating-jimi-hendrixs-life-50-years-after-his-death – accessed on 30/12/2024 – Jimi Hendrix Park & detail of statue.

https://study.com/academy/lesson/voodoo-religions-history-facts.html#:~:text=It%20is%20a%20spiritual%2C%20ancestor,%2C%22%20and%20%22voudou%22. – accessed on 06/02/2023 – Voodoo background.

YouTube Films

https://www.youtube.com/watch?v=-WHlz1p5KVo – accessed on 23/12/2024 – *Linda Keith Interview (1973)* – Foggy Melson Music.

Guitar Playing Techniques Glossary

Chording: Jimi played most of his chords using his thumb so that he was also able to ply a chord, as well as keep the rhythm going and play lead licks all at the same time so that to the listener it would seem like they were hearing two guitars instead of one.

Finger Tremelo (aka vibrato). This technique is applied by moving the string across the fret while slightly shaking one's wrist.

Harmonics: Jimi used every part of his guitar to obtain effects. He would tap the back of the headstock, different parts of the guitar neck and tap the body of the guitar to obtain various harmonic effects.

Octave Playing: Jimi played a tremendous amount in octaves; he would place a note on one string and play the same note on another string an octave higher.

Rhythm Guitar: Jimi was an skilful rhythm guitarist sometimes he would play the rhythm on dead strings. He would damp the strings with his fingers and produce a scratchy rhythm using his pick.

ACKNOWLEDGMENTS & SOURCES

Slide: It is believed that Jimi never used the conventional metal bottle-neck for slide-playing. What he did use was one of his rings, or for more dramatic effects he would use the edge of a speaker cabinet or the microphone stand.

String-Bending: Unconventionally, Jimi would bend the string upwards, as opposed to downwards which was the conventional technique which most guitarists used then.

Tremelo Arm: Jimi spent many hours bending his tremelo arm by hand. This was because by playing a right-handed guitar left-handed, the tremelo arm would be in line with the bass E string which would make it difficult to use the tremelo arm while playing. Jimi bent the arm down across the strings so that the tremelo arm was in line with the high E-string which is the normal position for a right-handed player.

JANIS JOPLIN

Astrology details:

Janis Joplin natal and transits chart via www.astro.com (Astrodienst).
Co-ordinates of Janis Joplin's natal chart: 29n54, 93w56.
Rodden Rating: AA

Books

Amburn, A. (1994) *Pearl, The Obsessions & Passions of Janis Joplin* Sphere Books an Imprint of Little, Brown Book Group.
Angel, A (2010) *Janis Joplin Rise Up Singing* Amulet Books an imprint of ABRAMS.
Bebergal, B. (2015) *Season of the Witch, How The Occult Saved Rock n Roll* Jeremy P. Tarcher/Penguin.
Byrne Cooke, J. (2014) *On The Road With Janis Joplin* Berkley – an imprint of Penguin Random House LLC.
Caserta, P. & Falcon, M. (2018) *I Ran Into Some Trouble* Wyatt-MacKenzie Publishing Inc.
Clow Hand, B. (2007) *Chiron, Rainbow Bridge Between the inner & outer planets* Llewellyn Publications.
Dalton, D. (2000) *piece of my heart: On the road with Janis Joplin* Marion Boyers Publishers
Echols, A. (2001) *Scars of Sweet Paradise, The Life And Times of Janis Joplin* Virago Press
Friedman, M. (1974) *The Intimate Biography of Janis Joplin Buried Alive* Plexus Publishing Limited.
George-Warren, H. (2020) *Janis Her Life And Music* Simon & Schuster UK Ltd.
Herman G. (1982) *Rock 'N' Roll Babylon* Plexus Publishing Limited.
Joplin, L (2005) *Love Janis* itbooks an imprint of HarperCollins Publishers.
O'Brien, L. (2012) *She Bop, The Definitive History Of Women In Popular Music* Jawbone Press.
Willett, E. (2008) *Janis Joplin, Take Another Little Piece Of My Heart* Enslow Publishers, Inc.

CD

Janis Joplin & Jorma Kaukonen, The Legendary Typewriter Tape 06/25/64 Omnivore Recordings 2022. Janis Joplin compositions copyright 1970, *Strong Arm Music*, administered by Wixen Music Publishing, Inc/ASCAP.

DVDs

Janis Joplin, Her final hours – final 24 a dramatization 2007, Cineflix Productions, director Paul Kilback, Recreation Director Chris Bould, Narrator Danny Wallace.

Janis, Little Girl Blue 2016, written and directed by Amy J. Berg, Copyright 2015 Janis Productions LLC & Thirteen Productions LLC. Packaging copyright 2016 Dogwoof Ltd.

Petulia 1996 (originally released in 1968), directed by Richard Lester, based on a novel by John Hasse. Warner Bros. Pictures – *Janis Joplin and Big Brother & The Holding Company* as themselves and starring Julie Christie & George C. Scott and co-starring Richard Chamberlain.

The way she was: Janis, 2015, directed and edited by Howard Alk & Seaton Findlay, executive producer F.R. Crawley, produced by Crawley Films Limited.

Newspaper

The Times

Obituary 06/10/1970, page 14 *'Foremost female blues singer of her generation'* – Melody Maker award/ and description of Janis Joplin.

Photo Credits:

Alamy:
Image ID: 2WKDD5K, Bill Waterson / Alamy

Bridgeman Images:
Image ID: EVT1823496
Image Title: Janis Joplin, 1960s (b/w photo).
Image ID EVT5802958
Image Title: JANIS JOPLIN, 1960s, from the documentary "Janis" released in 1975 (b/w photo).
Image ID: EVT1810820
Image Title Janis Joplin, 1960s (b/w photo).
Image ID: SS12206685
Image Title: Janis Joplin American Rock Singer (1943-1970). Creator: Unknown photographer, (20th century).
Image ID: SZT5932782
Image Title: Janis Joplin, c.1965-1970 (b/w photo).
Image ID: UIG5932772
Image Title: Janis Joplin, 1960s (b/w photo).
Image ID: XRF1656261
Image Title: Singer Janis Joplin With Big Brother and the Holding Company (Studio Brass Section) c. 1967 (b/w photo). Creator: unknown photographer, (20th Century).

ACKNOWLEDGMENTS & SOURCES

Websites

Stevie Nicks quote at top of *Part One* from: https://faroutmagazine.co.uk/how-one-singer-changed-stevie-nicks-life-forever-i-knew-that-a-little-bit-of-my-destiny-had-changed/ – accessed on 05/03/2025.

https://www.astro.com/astro-databank/Joplin,_Janis accessed on 19/07/2025 – date and time of death.

https://www.azquotes.com/quote/849221 – accessed on 11/04/2025 – Joan Jett on Janis Joplin.

https://americanahighways.org/2023/01/01/music-reviews-carter-family-zappa-joplin-kaukonen/ accessed on 15/03/2025 – THE LEGENDARY TYPEWRITER CASE with embryonic Janis Joplin & Jorma Kaukonen of Jefferson Airplane and the benefit evening rehearsal.

https://americansongwriter.com/revisit-janis-joplins-iconic-1969-woodstock-performance-with-full-setlist/ – accessed on 06/04/2025 – her addressing the audience at Woodstock and showing care.

https://www.bbc.co.uk/programmes/b0188f9t – accessed on 12/04/2025 – Suzi Quatro Radio 2 '*In Search Of Janis*'. Documentary.

https://www.britannica.com/place/Haight-Ashbury – accessed on 30/03/2025 – Haight-Ashbury – Janis's addresses.

https://www.choicemag.co.uk/category/features/suzi_quatro___i_ve_always_been_a_rocker_at_heart – accessed on 12/04/2025 – Suzi Quatro on being marketed as ' the new Janis Joplin'.

https://www.cookephoto.com/index.html – accessed on 16/03/2025 – Joplin familar with The Carter Family folk group music.

https://www.discogs.com/release/21045997-The-Waller-Creek-Boys-Featuring-Janis-Joplin-The-Waller-Creek-Boys-Featuring-Janis-Joplin?srsltid=AfmBOopZ7gLomMwE0rBpRmuk2uP7na – accessed on 15/03/2025 – detail of The Waller Creek Boys featuring Janis Joplin.

https://www.ellecanada.com/culture/music/florence-welch-inspired-by-janis-joplin – accessed on 11/04/2025 – Florence Welsh on Janis Joplin and what she learnt from her.

https://en.wikipedia.org/wiki/Janis_Joplin – accessed on 22/03/2024 – benefit performance for Mance Lipscomb.

https://en.wikipedia.org/wiki/Nick_Gravenites – accessed on 29/03/2025 – lead singer in the reformed *Big Brother & The Holding Company*.

https://en.wikipedia.org/wiki/James_Gurley – accessed on 27/03/2025 – Nancy Gurley's death & James Gurley charged with murder.

https://en.wikipedia.org/wiki/Seth_Morgan_(novelist) – accessed on 06/04/2025 – Birth, career & death.

https://www.facebook.com/photo.php?fbid=10159740889895845&id=12229005844&set=a.344561500844 – accessed on 29/03/2025 – Nick Gravenites song writing for Janis.

https://www.facebook.com/poprockuniverse1974/posts/in-1969-at-the-famous-woodstock-festival-janis-joplin-performed-late-at-night-sh/1247664120057779/ accessed on 05/07/2025 – Pop Rock Universe's Post – Janis dropped to her knees – quote about her not singing but bleeding.

https://www.facebook.com/poprockuniverse1974/photos/janis-joplin-upon-learning-of-jimi-hendrixs-death-said-the-followingi-wonder-if-/1143916780

432514/?_rdr – accessed on 20/06/2025 – quote about Janis asking 'I wonder if I died what would happen' / 'two rock stars can't die in the same year'.

https://www.facebook.com/TheSoundFM/photos/1969-janis-joplin-calls-out-a-policeman-at-her-concert-in-tampa-florida-when-he-/1155118549954820/?_rdr – accessed on 01/06/2025 – quotes on what Janis Joplin said to the police officer when she was arrested in Tampa.

https://faroutmagazine.co.uk/janis-joplin-song-inspired-by-jimi-hendrix/ Janis inspired by Jimi – Half Moon track on Pearl – numerological and astrological by nature – accessed on 10/03/2025

https://faroutmagazine.co.uk/how-janis-joplin-inspired-steven-tyler-to-become-a-singer/ – accessed on 11/04/2025 – Steve Tyler on how Janis Joplin influenced him to become a singer.

https://faroutmagazine.co.uk/how-one-singer-changed-stevie-nicks-life-forever-i-knew-that-a-little-bit-of-my-destiny-had-changed/ – accessed on 11/04/2025 – Stevie Nicks on Janis Joplin's influence.

https://www.famsf.org/artworks/handbag-made-for-janis-joplin – accessed on 20/03/2025 – details of handmade handbag by Linda Gravities.

https://fherehab.com/news/janis-joplin-addiction – accessed on 19/04/2025 – *Janis Joplin's Struggles With Addiction* 23/08/2024 – by Chris Foy.

https://genius.com/Janis-joplin-piece-of-my-heart-live-at-the-woodstock-music-and-art-fair-august-16-1969-lyhrics – accessed on 05/07/2025 – Janis addressing the crowd at Woodstock when she finally appeared for her set.

https://www.independent.co.uk/arts-entertainment/rock-pop-when-janis-and-jim-filled-the-air-with-profanity-1125946.html – accessed on 01/06/2025 – *Rock and Pop: When Janis and Jim filled the air with profanity'* by Maeve Walsh, Sunday 14th November 1999. Janis Joplin arrested by police after her concert in Tamba for using vulgar language.

https://janisjoplin.com/biography/– accessed on 30/03/2025 – moving to California and returning home and then back to California.

https://janisjoplin.com/biography/ – accessed on 04/03/2025 – enrolled as sociology student – unfinished studies.

https://janisjoplin.com/porsche/ – accessed on 03/06/2025 – when Janis passed her driving test.

https://www.janisjoplin.net/life/friends/nancy-gurley/ – accessed on 26/03/2025 – influenced by Nancy Gurley's Earth Mother fashions/ payment towards Gurley's legal expenses.

https://jazzhistoryonline.com/ – accessed on 29/03/2025 – Billie Holiday's recording of *Summertime*.

https://www.last.fm/music/Kozmic+Blues+Band/+wiki#:~:text=After%20splitting%20from%20Big%20Brother,Andrew%20and%20future%20Full%20Tilt – accessed on 05/04/2025 – members of the Kozmic Blue Band.

https://www.last.fm/music/Full+Tilt+Boogie+Band/+wiki – accessed on 05/03/2025 – members of the Full Tilt Boogie Band.

https://legacyprojectchicago.org/person/janis-joplin – accessed on 01/06/2025 – quote from Janis Joplin on not compromising yourself.

https://www.mirror.co.uk/3am/celebrity-news/janis-joplins-brother-bursts-tears-33106983 – accessed on 16/03/2025 – Dorothy Joplin wanted to be a Broadway singer.

ACKNOWLEDGMENTS & SOURCES

https://www.mirror.co.uk/3am/celebrity-news/janis-joplins-brother-bursts-tears-33106983 – accessed on 06/07/2025 – 25th June 2024 – Tom Bryant Associate Editor – *Janis Joplin's Brother Bursts Into Tears* – articulate, painting – art lessons.

https://myfloridahistory.org/date-in-history/november-15-1969/janis-joplin-arrested-tampa-fl – accessed on 01/06/2025 – information as to why Janis Joplin was arrested by Florida police in 1969.

https://www.newyorker.com/culture/culture-desk/my-big-sister-janis-joplin – accessed on 16/03/2025 – Joplin family brought up on show tunes – The Threepenny Opera + Laura & Michael's memories of their sister.

https://overdressedforlife.com/2017/04/10/fashionable-quote-of-the-week-by-janis-joplin/ – accessed on 20/03/2025 – quote from Joplin about Linda Graveties work and photo of the handbag.

https://www.pbs.org/wgbh/americanexperience/features/klansville-faq/ – accessed on 25/05/2025 – dates of Klu Klux Klan, right wing groups' radical violence.

https://www.plannedparenthoodaction.org/issues/abortion/abortion-central-history-reproductive-health-care-america/historical-abortion-law-timeline-1850-today – accessed on 27/06/2025 – year when US terminations became legal.

http://www.powellstjohn.com/biography.html – accessed on 15/03/2023 – details about band's formation.

https://www.royalalberthall.com/about-the-hall/building-and-history/our-history/janis-joplins-only-solo-british-performance#:~:text=On%2021%20April%201969%2C%20American,at%2 – accessed on 30/03/2025 – details of her appearance at The Royal Albert Hall.

https://samandrew.com/big-brother-and-the-holding-company-part-one-1965-1966/ -accessed on 31/03/2025 – Janis supportive to the band.

https://stories/nobody-knows-you-when-youre-down-and-out/#:~:text='Nobody%20Knows%20You%20When%20You,released%20sometime%20around%20Jun – accessed on 29/03/2025 – artist & date for original recording of *Nobody Knows You When You're Down & Out.*

https://www.theguardian.com/music/2010/jan/11/james-gurley-obituary – accessed on 27/03/2025 – James Gurley obituary.

https://time.com/archive/6877253/music-blues-for-janis/ – accessed on 06/04/2025 – *Music: Blues for Janis* obituary incl. Seth Morgan.

https://www.tpt.org/janis-joplin-american-masters/video/american-masters-dick-cavett-janis-joplins-influence-him-and-his-show/#:~:text=Dick%20Cavett%2C%20a%20for – accessed on 27/05/2025 – Dick Cavett's quote about Janis Joplin's influence on his TV show.

https://www.udiscovermusic.com/stories/janis-joplin-bessie-smith-headstone/ – accessed on 17/03/2025 – Janis Joplin & Bessie Smith's former housekeeper paid for Bessie Smith's headstone.

https://vinepair.com/articles/how-janis-joplin-earned-a-fur-coat-by-drinking-southern-comfort/ – accessed on 30/03/2025 – Barefoot, wearing Levis, carrying autoharp, Janis's antique cigarette holders.

https://web.archive.org/web/20141214223015/http://stthomassource.com/content/community/people/2002/07/01/internet-maven-peter-j-de-blanc-dies – accessed 22/03/2025 – Peter de Blanc – obituary – worked with computers and technology.

https://www.wikitree.com – all accessed on 06/03/2025 for details of the East & Joplin family, birth, marriages, deaths.

https://www.wikitree.com/wiki/Bowman-5343 – details of Anna Belle (Bowman) East.

https://www.wikitree.com/wiki/East-960 – details of Cecil Walter East.

https://www.wikitree.com/wiki/East-959 – details of Dorothy Bonita (East)

https://www.wikitree.com/wiki/Hanson-2843 – details of Laura Mildred (Hanson) East.

https://www.wikitree.com/wiki/East-1082 – details of Ulysees Simpson Grant East.

https://www.wikitree.com/wiki/Joplin-108 – details of Seeb Winston Joplin.

https://www.wikitree.com/wiki/Joplin-121 – details of Charles Alexander Joplin.

https://www.wikitree.com/wiki/White-24520 – details of Margaret Elminor (White) Joplin.

https://www.wikitree.com/wiki/Porter-7534 – details of Florence Elizabeth (Porter) Joplin

https://www.wikitree.com/wiki/Joplin-108 – details of Seth Ward Joplin.

YouTube Films

https://www.youtube.com/watch?v=-Lh9aaRpo2Y – accessed on 06/04/2025 – Q & A Amy Berg, Dick Cavett, & David Niehaus on remembering Janis Joplin. – she inspired a lot of women

https://www.youtube.com/watch?v=Y8eYKVmkYx0 – accessed on 31/03/2025 – *Janis Joplin's Ex-Boyfriend Country Joe McDonald Discusses Dating/Living with Janis Joplin.*

https://www.youtube.com/watch?v=irJ4QsacyyY – accessed on 15/06/2025 – Dick Cavett interviewing Janis Joplin – humour /his hip jacket.

www.ingramcontent.com/pod-product-compliance
Lightning Source LLC
Chambersburg PA
CBHW061258110426
42742CB00012BA/1961